The AS/400 Owner's Manual

The AS/400 Owner's Manual

Mike Dawson

First Edition

First Printing, March 1997

© 1997 Midrange Computing

ISBN: 1-883884-40-3

Midrange Computing
5650 El Camino Real, Suite 225
Carlsbad, CA 92008

V3R6

To my daughter Jerilyn Sommer, her husband Sean,
and their children Patrick and Brandon.

Contents

Introduction

Welcome to the wonderful world of the AS/400!

If you're new to the machine, I'm jealous because you're starting on a road that I know will be marked by wonderful discoveries.

If you're an AS/400 veteran, read on. I think I've put together the last manual you'll ever need.

I've been working on the AS/400 since its birthday. Before that, I worked on the System/38, since 1982, the S/34, and the S/36. I consider myself somewhat comfortable with the AS/400.

It wasn't all sweetness and light, however. Learning the System/38 (the AS/400's pappy) was a gruesome experience for me. Maybe I am just a slow learner, but I veered all around the learning curve. If I can master this computer, anyone can.

The thing is—the AS/400 is such a rich machine—that AS/400 folks are always learning. Several years ago when IBM literally turned the AS/400 inside out, from proprietary to open, they left all the old, proprietary stuff in place. The open functions were added on! IBM has added instead of replaced functions since day one. The result is a computer that, when you dig down into it, never stops yielding a high-grade ore of surprises.

Anyone new to the AS/400 can't help but feel overwhelmed with it. I see new customers looking bewildered and asking things like, "Do I have to know all that stuff? What's important and what isn't?"

Take heart because that feeling never really goes away. Veterans are often asked to do things with the AS/400 that they have done once before, long ago, or that they recently have heard can be done, but don't really know how to accomplish. It happens all the time.

This book was born from that frustration. I still remember how, when I was just starting on the machine, I wished I could go out and buy just such a publication as this one. "Don't make me wander all over the manuals," I whined to IBM support more than once. "Just tell me what to do!"

Take journaling for an example. Journaling is something most AS/400 shops do to some degree. If you are new to the computer, you probably don't know where to start, and the journaling manual is a good 3 inches thick. If you're not new to the AS/400, your shop (maybe you) set up journaling on several files about four or five years ago. You automated the process to such a degree that, if you had to go to the journaled data today for recovery, it would be a struggle!

Why? The process is typical of the many AS/400 techniques that can be complex but easily automated. You don't even think about some issues until you have a data problem. Guess what? Because the AS/400 never hiccups, your problems are infrequent. So, the one time in five years you need to recover some data, journaling isn't exactly on the tip of your tongue.

That's the purpose of *The AS/400 Owner's Manual*. If you're new to the machine, you can quickly read this book and get a mixture of what to do, how to do it, what's the best way to do it, and a smattering of technical background. If you want to go beyond the basics, the topics include references to IBM manuals. If you just want to read more on the subject, each chapter contains a bibliography.

Rookies and veterans quickly can be productive in any of the major areas for getting an AS/400 up and running and keeping it running well.

In summary, I wrote the book I wanted to find in a bookstore.

Enjoy it.

More importantly, enjoy the AS/400.

1. Starting the AS/400

Booting up an AS/400 is referred to as IPLing the AS/400. The abbreviation comes from the term *initial program load* (IPL). This is similar to booting or rebooting a personal computer (PC) except that an IPL does many more tasks. Compared to a PC boot, an IPL takes a lot more time and it is done less frequently.

1.1 WHAT AN IPL DOES

An AS/400 IPL does more than just start the operating system. Additionally, it:

❖ Resets storage.

❖ Recognizes new licensed-program products.

❖ Optionally applies delayed PTFs.

❖ Recognizes some changes in system values.

1.2 WHEN TO IPL

You will IPL anytime:

❖ You power on the AS/400. After a power failure or any abnormal end, expect your IPL to take a very long time.

❖ After you've installed delayed PTFs. For additional information, see chapter 2, section 2.1.2).

❖ After you've installed a new licensed-program product (LPP) from IBM.

❖ You have a problem with the system (at IBM support's direction).

❖ Your ADDRESSES USED reaches 90 percent.

❖ Your SYSTEM AUXILIARY STORAGE reaches 95 percent.

Of the preceding items, the last two require some discussion. Check them both with the WORK SYSTEM STATUS (WRKSYSSTS) command.

Just type on the command line:

```
WRKSYSSTS
```

When you do, you'll get a screen similar to the one shown in Figure 1-1.

```
                          Work with System Status                  SYS02
                                                        01/20/97   11:00:04
% CPU used . . . . . . . :       75.0    System ASP . . . . . . . :    29.88 G
Elapsed time . . . . . . :   00:00:00    % system ASP used  . . . :   77.7963
Jobs in system . . . . . :       8974    Total aux stg  . . . . . :   180.3 G
% perm addresses . . . . :       .010    Current unprotect used . :    4545 M
% temp addresses . . . . :       .032    Maximum unprotect  . . . :    6574 M

Sys      Pool    Rsrv    Max   -----DB-----  ---Non-DB---  Act-   Wait-  Act-
Pool    Size K  Size K   Act   Fault  Pages  Fault  Pages  Wait    Inel  Inel
  1     900824  182200   +++     .0     .0     .0     .0     .0     .0     .0
  2     734904       0    40     .0     .0     .0     .0     .0     .0     .0
  3      10000       0     5     .0     .0     .0     .0     .0     .0     .0
  4     300000       0     5     .0     .0     .0     .0     .0     .0     .0
  5     200000       0    10     .0     .0     .0     .0     .0     .0     .0
  6     400000       0    20     .0     .0     .0     .0     .0     .0     .0
  7     600000       0    30     .0     .0     .0     .0     .0     .0     .0
```

Figure 1-1: Sample of WRKSYSSTS command.

Note that the permanent and temporary address percentages are shown as the fourth and fifth items in the upper left column. Together these should not exceed 90 percent.

The system auxiliary storage is shown as an absolute number and as a percentage on the top two fields of the right column. Don't let the percentage get above 95 percent or you'll start to experience serious system degradation.

An additional factor with the system auxiliary storage is that, although an IPL will return some storage to you, you might not regain enough storage. If this occurs, you will be forced to re-IPL soon. In this case, check the contents of the system auxiliary storage for libraries and files that aren't system related. I'm referring to objects in ASP 1 here. Your system should be set up with ASP 1 dedicated to system objects and at least one other, ASP 2, to hold all non-system objects. For more information on ASPs, see section 3.3, DASD--User Auxiliary Storage Pools.

On a heavily utilized AS/400, addresses will creep up to 90 percent fairly quickly. Of course, upgrading to a larger model will solve that problem. While you're waiting for upgrade money to be available, schedule an IPL frequently enough to keep the addresses under control. Many at-capacity shops do a daily IPL.

1.3 ATTENDED/UNATTENDED AND MANUAL/NORMAL

IPLs are designated as one of two broad categories: attended or unattended. An unattended IPL will, if it can, bring up sign-on displays on all attached terminals. In other words, it will attempt to get the whole system up. The attended IPL will bring up a sign-on display on the system console before it brings up the rest of the system. This is your chance to get in and make changes to the system before it gets all the way up.

Before I go any further, take note that the *control panel* is the flat panel physically on the front of every AS/400, old and new. The panel has a place to insert a key, some LCDs, and green lights. The *system console* is a workstation through which you access the AS/400. This workstation gets dubbed the "system console" because it is physically connected to the first address of the first input/output processor capable of supporting workstations. In addition, the system console is named DSP01, it runs at a higher priority than other workstations, and data entry (or programming) is not done on it.

You tell the AS/400 which IPL you'd like by changing the IPL *mode* on the AS/400 control panel. The control panel is located on the front of your AS/400.

To set the mode on an AS/400, you must have the key in the slot. On older, gray-colored AS/400s, there was an actual key. On the newer, black models the key is a black, rectangular piece of plastic with a chip inside called a *keystick*. On the older models, you would turn the key to the MANUAL position. On the new models, you insert the plastic key/chip and press the MODE switch until a light illuminates next to the word MANUAL.

An IPL done with the AS/400 in manual mode is an attended IPL. The sign-on display will come up only on the system console and you'll have to sign on to continue the IPL. Note that the console is a lot like a dedicated workstation.

Most AS/400 IPLs are done in *normal mode* (sometimes referred to as *auto* or *automatic mode*), which is another way of saying unattended IPL. If you ever have a need to do a manual IPL, return the system's mode setting to normal when you're through. And remove and store the key if that is part of your security procedures.

1.3.1 What You Can Change With a Manual IPL

When you sign on to the display console during a manual IPL, you are presented with a menu of options. If you take option 1, you'll have a chance to change several system options. Figure 1-2 shows the screen you'll see.

```
                           IPL Options

Type choices, press the Enter key.

      System date  . . . . . . . . . . . . . .   XX / XX / XX   MM / DD / YY
      System time  . . . . . . . . . . . . . .   XX : XX : XX   HH : MM : SS
      Clear job queues . . . . . . . . . . . .   N              Y=Yes,  N=No
      Clear output queues  . . . . . . . . . .   N              Y=Yes,  N=No
      Clear incomplete job logs  . . . . . . .   N              Y=Yes,  N=No
      Start print writers  . . . . . . . . . .   Y              Y=Yes,  N=No
      Start this device only . . . . . . . . .   N              Y=Yes,  N=No
      Run #STRTUP1 procedure . . . . . . . . .   Y              Y=Yes,  N=No
      Run #STRTUP2 procedure . . . . . . . . .   Y              Y=Yes,  N=No
      Set major system options . . . . . . . .   N              Y=Yes,  N=No
      Define or change system at IPL . . . . .   N              Y=Yes,  N=No
```

Figure 1-2: IPL options that can be changed.

To change an option, simply position the cursor over it and type the new value.

What you see next depends on what you entered for the last two parameters of the screen shown in Figure 1-2 (Set major system options and Define or change system at IPL). If you left them both No (N), you will see the menu/program/ procedure indicating that either you typed on the sign-on display or that it is a part of your user profile. For more information on user profiles, see section 5.2, Managing User Profiles.

If you put a Y on SET MAJOR SYSTEM OPTIONS, you'll see the menu discussed in section 1.3.2, Set Major System Options. If you put a Y on DEFINE OR CHANGE SYSTEM AT IPL, you'll get a menu with six options to change system configurations. Because option 3 allows you to change system values, it is the most useful of these options. For additional information, see section 1.4, System Values Important to IPLs.

1.3.2 Set Major System Options

If you indicated (with a Y on the SET MAJOR SYSTEM OPTIONS parameter that you wanted to set some system options, you'll get the screen shown in Figure 1-3.

```
                     Set Major System Options

Type choices, press the ENTER key.

    Enable automatic configuration . . . . . . .  Y        Y=Yes, N=No
    Device configuration naming  . . . . . . . .  *NORMAL  *NORMAL, *S36, *DEVAD
    Default special environment  . . . . . . . .  *NONE    *NONE, *S36
```

Figure 1-3: Set major system options menu.

ENABLE AUTOMATIC CONFIGURATION tells the AS/400 to automatically configure any devices that start communicating with it that it doesn't know already. Most AS/400 shops leave this at the default value Y (Yes). If automatic configuration is selected, the AS/400 will want to know how you would like it to name the devices it creates. You can specify one of three options on the DEVICE CONFIGURATION NAMING parameter:

❖ *NORMAL (most common in AS/400 shops) names devices with a three-character prefix and a rotating numeric suffix. For example, displays are named DSP01, DSP02, etc., while printers are named PRT01, PRT02, etc.

❖ *S36 names devices with System/36 naming conventions. For example, displays are W1, W2, etc., while printers are P1, P2, etc.

❖ *DEVADR names devices using the device resource name. Examples would be DSP010203, PRT010204, etc. For additional information on resource names, see chapter 11, Communications; LANs, Frame Relay, and TCP/IP.

The DEFAULT SPECIAL ENVIRONMENT sets up a System/36 environment for customers, migrating from a System/36, who need to run the SSP operating system on the AS/400.

1.4 SYSTEM VALUES IMPORTANT TO IPLs

There are several system values that pertain specifically to IPLs on the AS/400. Display the current values of these and change them if you want by using the WORK WITH SYSTEM VALUES (WRKSYSVAL) command. Chapter 6 provides an overview of system values.

❖ QIPLDATTIM—IPL date and time. This is the date and time when the system will IPL itself automatically. Default value: *NONE.

❖ QIPLSTS—IPL status. Displays the way the system did the last IPL. You cannot change this value; you can only display it. Here are the codes and what they mean:

✓ 0—an IPL from the control panel of the AS/400.

✓ 1—an unattended IPL after a power failure (refer to system value QPWRRSTIPL).

✓ 2—an unattended IPL after the PWRDWNSYS command with the RESTART(*YES) parameter.

✓ 3—an unattended scheduled IPL as a result of system value QIPLDATTIM being used.

✓ 4—an unattended remote IPL, with system value QRMTIPL being set to 1.

❖ QIPLTYPE—Defines the type of IPL the system will do from the control panel:

✓ 0—an unattended IPL. No one needs to be there. However, if the control panel is set to manual mode, the IPL will be attended, manual.

✓ 1—an attended IPL with dedicated service tools (DST). However, if the IPL is done via a remote AS/400, due to a value in QIPLDATTIM being reached, or after a power failure, an unattended, normal mode IPL will be done regardless of this system value.

✓ 2—an attended IPL in debug mode. Set this only if you are experiencing problems with your AS/400 and only at the direction of the IBM CE or Rochester support.

❖ QPWRRSTIPL—Will the system automatically restart itself after a power failure?

✓ 0—No automatic IPL after a power failure (most common setting).

✓ 1—Automatic IPL after a power failure.

❖ QRMTIPL—Can a remote system start the AS/400?

  ✓ 0—A remote system cannot start the AS/400.

  ✓ 1—A remote system can start the AS/400.

❖ QUPSDLYTIM—If the AS/400 is connected to a smart, uninterruptible power supply (UPS), there is a set amount of time it will wait before it starts saving main storage and entering a controlled shutdown.

  ✓ *BASIC or *CALC—*CALC is the default. Neither of these are very popular options. A numeric value is preferred.

  ✓ *NOMAX—Is used when a user-written program controls the shutdown or when a generator will take over for the UPS after a few seconds.

  ✓ 0—Automatic system shutdown starts as soon as the UPS kicks in.

  ✓ 1-99999—The delay time in seconds before the system starts to shut itself down. This is the preferable method in most shops that rely only on a UPS. Work with your UPS engineer about the power consumption of your AS/400 and the rating of the UPS for a good time-delay figure.

❖ QUPSMSGQ—The message queue that receives messages about a power interruption. You can specify this as library/message queue.

1.5 IS THE IPL PROGRESSING?

Most of the time, your IPLs are unattended routine events. Sometimes, however, IPLs are done as a result of a problem. In case there is a problem, it is important for you to be able to read the LCD lights on the AS/400 console. Here are the main items (italicized Xs represent any letter or number):

❖ C1*XX* B*XXX*—Input/Output processor testing (1-5 minutes).

❖ C1*XX* 1*XXX*—Input/Output processor loading (1-10 minutes).

❖ C3*XX* 3*XXX*—System processor testing (2-10 minutes).

❖ C1*XX* 2*XXX*—System processor loading (2-10 minutes).

❖ C1*XX* 202E—Testing system main storage (30 sec-10 minutes).

❖ C1*XX* D009 —System power hardware ready (10 seconds).

❖ C1*XX* 2034—IPL control passed to system processor (10 seconds).

❖ C6*XX* 4*XXX*—Testing system configuration (1-10 minutes).

If attended, the display will appear on the system console. Sign on and make any changes. After this point, the length of time of each step depends on the size of your system and its condition when it went down.

- ❖ C6*XX* 4*XXX*—IPLing the system.
- ❖ C6*XX* 4260—System disk data recovery.
- ❖ C9*XX* 2*XXX*—Operating system starting.
- ❖ C900 29C0—Operating system recovering.

1.6 IPL STORAGE AREAS

An IPL can be made from one of two system storage areas: the A side or the B side. For the most part, you'll always be on the B side. Storage areas come into play when working with PTFs. For additional information, see chapter 2. To change the IPL storage area on the AS/400 physical console:

- ❖ Put the machine in manual mode (with the key in the slot, press the Mode button).
- ❖ Select function 02 (with the Select button).
- ❖ Press the Enter button.
- ❖ Select storage area A or B (with the Select button).
- ❖ Press the Enter button.
- ❖ Return the machine to the normal mode (with the key in the slot, press the Mode button).

1.7 STARTING THE AS/400

If the AS/400 is not running:

- ❖ Decide on the mode IPL you want and set the MODE to it.
- ❖ Make sure all DASD devices and the system console are powered on.
- ❖ Push the AS/400's power button to ON.

If the AS/400 is running:

❖ Decide on the mode IPL you want and set the MODE to it.

❖ Type on a command line on any workstation: PWRDWNSYS *IMMED RESTART(*YES)

❖ Press the Enter key.

❖ If you are in manual mode:

    ✓ Sign onto the system console when you can and do what is required to complete the IPL.

    ✓ Return the mode to normal.

    ✓ Store the console key if necessary.

1.7.1 Start a Remote AS/400

On the remote system, make sure you have set system value QRMTIPL to a 1. This allows the system to be powered off, but be waiting for a remote power-on command. For additional information, see section 1.4, System Values Important to IPLs.

Using the ECS (Electronic Customer Support) modem, dial the remote system from your local system. Wait while you hear the dial tone, ringing, and modem tone. After the modem tone, there will be silence. At this point, it is acceptable to break the connection to the remote system. There are a few areas where problems occur with remote systems' startup.

❖ The remote modem is turned off. Therefore, you can't start it remotely.

❖ The remote modem is turned off and then on. The system might start to bring itself up.

❖ The local system operator hangs up the phone too soon. Be certain to wait while the connection is made.

1.8 POWERING THE AS/400 DOWN

Be careful when powering down your AS/400. If you don't do it properly, the system will be said to have ended abnormally and the IPL will take longer. Depending on the size of your system and the damage from the abnormal end, it can take many hours to recover.

Before powering down your AS/400, make sure all batch jobs are ended and all users are signed off. Use the WORK ACTIVE JOBS (WRKACTJOB) command to verify this. You might have to end some jobs yourself. When you do, use option 4 on the WRKACTJOB screen, but press F4 before you press the Enter key. Override the *CNTRLD value with *IMMED on the screen you get, and then press the Enter key.

1.9 AUTOMATICALLY POWERING YOUR SYSTEM ON AND OFF

While this isn't strictly an IPL issue, I will discuss it here. You can have your AS/400 power itself on and off using any schedule you like. This method isn't used very much in 24-hour AS/400 shops or even 16-hour shops. A problem can occur if the automatic power-off happens in the middle of a nightly process that, for some reason, goes beyond its scheduled end time. Automatic power on and off is better suited for weekend and holiday shutdowns and for 8-hour shops.

To set your own power on-and-off schedule, type GO POWER on any command line and take Option 2 (CHANGE POWER ON/OFF SCHEDULE). From that screen, immediately press the F10 (CHANGE POWER ON/OFF DEFAULTS). The screen you'll get is shown in Figure 1-4.

```
                    Change Power On/Off Defaults
                                            System:    SYS02
      Type choices below, then press Enter.

      First day of week . . . . . . . .    2      1=Sunday, 2=Monday, 3=Tuesday,
                                                  4=Wednesday, 5=Thursday, 6=Friday,
                                                  7=Saturday

      Minutes before power off to send
         message . . . . . . . . . . .     30     0-60

                            Default      Default
      Week                  Power        Power
      Day                   On           Off
      Monday                05:30:00      _____
      Tuesday               _____      _____
      Wednesday             _____      _____
      Thursday              _____      _____
      Friday                _____      20:00:00
      Saturday              _____      _____
      Sunday                _____      _____
```

Figure 1-4: Change automatic power on/off defaults.

The "schedule" is predicated on the same thing happening each day of the week. In the example, the system is set to power off at 8:00 P.M. Friday and to power itself back on at 5:30 A.M. Monday. Prior to going down on Friday evening, the system will send a message to all users 30 minutes prior to shutting down. Note the MINUTES BEFORE POWER OFF TO SEND MESSAGE parameter in the upper part of the figure. The value can be changed from no message (0 minutes) to 60 minutes.

When the message appears, a security administrator (SEC ADMIN) or security officer (SEC OFR) can delay shutdown for up to three hours. But that's the last opportunity to delay a shutdown before the system comes down. For additional information on the role of security administrators and security officers, see chapter 6.

Return to the CHANGE POWER ON/OFF SCHEDULE screen (the screen used earlier to set defaults) by pressing F12. Figure 1-5 shows what it looks like with defaults set up.

```
                       Change Power On/Off Schedule                    SYS02
                                                          01/19/97  16:00:02
  Start list at  . . . . . . .    _____      Date

  Change times and descriptions below, then press Enter.  To change defaults,
    press F10.

                    Power       Power
  Date      Day     On          Off         Description
  01/19/97  Sun     _____    _____    _____

  01/20/97  Mon     05:30:00    _____    _____
  01/21/97  Tue     _____    _____    _____
  01/22/97  Wed     _____    _____    _____
  01/23/97  Thu     _____    _____    _____
  01/24/97  Fri     _____    20:00:00    _____
  01/25/97  Sat     _____    _____    _____
  01/26/97  Sun     _____    _____    _____

  01/27/97  Mon     05:30:00    _____    _____
  01/28/97  Tue     _____    _____    _____
                                                                        More...
```

Figure 1-5: Automatic power on/off schedule.

You can make schedule changes on this screen. Also, you can document why you made changes. You could even do all your on/off schedules on this screen. For the most part, however, power schedules are meant to be driven by the defaults screen.

1.10 BIBLIOGRAPHY

AS/400 System Startup and Problem Handling V3R6

2. Operating Systems, Licensed Program Products, and PTFs

2.1 OVERVIEW

The software on your AS/400 consists of the IBM-supplied software and software from other vendors. This book focuses on only the IBM-supplied software, and that software consists of three main parts: the operating system, called OS/400; any number of optional Licensed Program Products (LPPs); and any number of optional Programming Request for Price Quotations (PRPQs).

The basic OS/400 has quite a lot in it. Therefore, you can run many applications without purchasing anything else. LPPs are other software items that you purchase in addition to OS/400. LPPs include things like compilers, Office Vision, Backup/Recovery Management System (BRMS), and many others. PRPQs are basically something that either IBM developed on its own or, more likely, a customer felt it was so necessary that the customer paid for IBM to develop it. In such a case, IBM then decided the product would be profitable to sell to other customers, but not profitable enough to support. So PRPQs are offered to everyone for a generally low price and are unsupported.

All three basic pieces of software are continually improved through periodic releases of the software and through ongoing Program Temporary Fixes (PTFs).

2.1.1 New Releases

Let's start with new releases of software. Generally, new releases of LPPs and PRPQs are combined within a new release of the operating system. When you decide its time to upgrade your OS/400 to a new release, you'll also get new releases of all your IBM-supplied software.

Releases of OS/400 are named by three levels: version, release, and modification levels. When AS/400 people speak of a new release, they often drop the modification level. They also refer to the version and release simply by the letters V and R. For example, Version 3, Release 6, Modification 00 is just called "V 3 R 6."

New releases are generally offered in roughly 18-month intervals. When they are available, they come with lots of fanfare from your local branch and every AS/400 news medium. It's almost impossible to miss a new release of OS/400.

Because they are available for years, you can decide when you would like to install a new operating system release. A good rule of thumb when dealing with anything from IBM is never be the first to get it and never be the last. Give all releases a while to settle in. Let other customers find out how stable the release is and, when you're comfortable, order and install it.

2.1.2 PTFs

PTFs are replacements for specific objects within OS/400 or LPPs. PTFs come out at any time in any frequency. They become available with little fanfare and you can go a long time without even being aware of them. They have weird codified names and you'll have to make an effort to know what problem each one fixes.

The two types of PTFs are normal and high-impact pervasive PTFs (better known as HIPER). HIPERs are PTFs that are quite serious. If you ever learn about a HIPER PTF that you haven't installed on your system, do so as soon as is humanly possible.

If you don't know when they're available or what they do, how do you keep on top of PTFs? IBM offers a service known as Preventive Service Planning (PSP) and it offers lots of help for keeping up with PTFs. PSP has general information about licensed program products, their cumulative PTF tapes, new releases of the operating system, and so on. The service tells you the HIPERs discovered on the operating system or LPPs and will tell you if any previous PTFs were found to be in error. Also, the service gives you tips and techniques about installing releases and PTFs. The tips and techniques should be reviewed prior to installing a cumulative PTF tape and from time to time just to review what Rochester is doing about the software on your system.

PSPs are available from IBM as a free service. Contact your marketer for information about signing up.

All that PTF jargon sounds intimidating, but keeping up with PTFs in reality can be a low-impact job. IBM always has a cumulative tape available that contains all the PTFs for a given release. Unless you're having a problem, just order the latest tape about every six months and install whatever is on it.

Sometimes, a new release of OS/400 or an LPP is a little "rough." In those cases, order and install the cumulative tape more frequently. If you do wait six months, problems can be unwieldy.

PRPQs generally don't have PTFs. But if they do, the PTFs are for something fairly serious. Make sure you get them. I'll discuss PTFs in more detail in section 2.5 Program Temporary Fixes.

2.2 ORDERING NEW RELEASES

When you order a new release of the operating system, you will get:

- ❖ OS/400 and licensed internal code (LIC).

- ❖ All current PTFs for new OS/400 and LIC.

- ❖ Licensed product program(s).

- ❖ All current PTFs for licensed product program(s).

- ❖ PRPQs and all current PTFs for them.

You place your order directly with your independent reseller (IR), value-added reseller (VAR), or direct from IBM. You usually will talk to someone over the phone and then follow up with a letter specifying the order in writing.

This sounds simpler than it is. When you originally purchased your AS/400, whomever you purchased it from is the holder of your customer profile. As far as IBM is concerned, this is the company that will handle all your future purchases. That's all right until your profile gets out of date. If you shop around for the best deals and add to your system from other dealers of AS/400 equipment and software, your profile could become out of date.

Consequently, when you order a new release of the operating system, the organization holding your profile might not know what equipment and software you currently own. It's your responsibility to ensure the release you are ordering will cover everything currently on your system. Hence, the initial discussion with the marketer prior to ordering new software. Always ask for a list of what the marketer thinks you have on your AS/400 and what is being ordered. Double check that against what you really do have on your machine.

I can't stress enough that you should make a double check of your configuration before making the order and to double-check the release again before starting its installation. This is especially true on the first order after you've initially installed the licensed program product. Frequently, your first OS release upgrade after a LPP has been installed will come minus the LPP.

When you order a new release of the operating system, PRPQs might not be automatically shipped with that release. Even if they are shipped with the release, they usually come with their own installation instructions. Ask specifically and triple-check for PRPQs and their PTFs when you order a new release.

2.3 OS/400 RELEASE INSTALLATION

Installing a new release isn't to be taken lightly. Plan to spend at least a weekend at it. If you have enough people, you can divide the weekend up so the installation process continues round the clock until it is finished.

First, do all your preparation. Then immediately prior to the installation weekend, contact IBM software support or your IR and ask them to double-check your planning just to see if you missed anything.

2.3.1 Planning

The planning part of installing a new release is as crucial as the actual installation. Release installation generally means spending weekend time and the process is quite lengthy. You don't want any surprises when you are doing a release installation. If the release fails to install, you'll have to reinstall the old system. It's your weekend. Do as much work as you can up front to ensure you encounter no surprises.

Probably the first thing you should determine is whether it is even possible to install the new release. This little matter will hinge on two things:

❖ The release level already on your system compared with the release level you want to install.

❖ The size of your system, how much of the system you have been using, and how much additional system space the new release will require.

First, check the release installation instructions for previous releases on your system so that you won't have a conflict when you load the new release. For example, when V2R3 came out, it could be installed only on AS/400s that already had V2R1M0, V2R2M1, V2R2M0, or V2R3M0. At that time, any Version 1 machines had to go to one of those V2Rx releases before it could go to V2R3. If you do not know what release level is currently on your machine, see section 2.3.1.4, Planning—What Release Level Am I on Now?

New releases come with sizing, timing. and performance information. Starting with release V3R6, releases will include a utility or two to help you with sizing and timing. Use whatever is available to ensure that you'll have enough memory and DASD to support the new release. Generally, the information and utilities will provide you with some idea of how long the actual installation should take.

2.3.1.1 Planning—Appropriate Directories

Enter DSPDIR (DISPLAY DIRECTORY) on the command line. This will display all the users on your system. Verify that QSECOFR and QLPINSTL are there. See Figure 2-1.

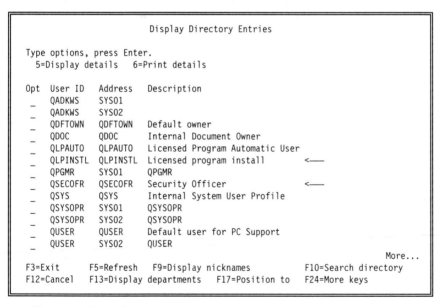

Figure 2-1: Output from DSPDIR command.

If either is not present, add the missing data with the following appropriate command:

```
ADDDIRE USRID(QSECOFR QSECOFR) USRD('Security Officer') +
        USER(QSECOFR)
ADDDIRE USRID(QLPINSTL QLPINSTL) USRD('Licensed Program +
        Install') USER(QLPINSTL)
```

2.3.1.2 Planning—Installation Hardware

Determine what tape drive you will use to install the release. If you have only one tape drive, use it. However, if you have multiple drives, select the one that is either in the system unit or attached to the system unit. The device you use will be any tape device that is designated online at IPL. To see if a drive is online at IPL, enter on the command line:

```
DSPDEVD <tape device description name>
```

You will get a screen similar to Figure 2-2.

```
                        Display Device Description                    SYS02
                                                           01/15/97  08:23:34
Device description . . . . . . . . :  TAP01
Option . . . . . . . . . . . . . . :  *BASIC
Category of device . . . . . . . . :  *TAP

Device type  . . . . . . . . . . . :  3490
Device model . . . . . . . . . . . :  D31
Resource name  . . . . . . . . . . :  TAP06
Online at IPL  . . . . . . . . . . :  *YES
Attached controller  . . . . . . . :  TAPCTL03
Assign device at vary on . . . . . :  *YES
Unload device at vary off  . . . . :  *NO
Shadowing message queue  . . . . . :  QSYSOPR
  Library  . . . . . . . . . . . . :    *LIBL
Text . . . . . . . . . . . . . . . :  CREATED BY AUTO-CONFIGURATION

                                                                     Bottom
```

Figure 2-2: Using DSPDEVD to determine if the tape device is online at IPL.

Once you have chosen the tape device you will use, check it thoroughly and clean the heads.

2.3.1.3 Planning—Multiple Systems

All systems must be on release levels that, although they may be different, must be compatible with each other. For additional information, see section 2.3.1.4, Planning—What Release Level Am I on Now? Follow those steps and note what release each of your systems are on currently.

Multiple systems must be what IBM terms *interoperable* for exchanging data and for making save tapes that can be restored on other systems. Typically, all the machines must support operating system release levels that are within 2 release levels for data exchange and within 1 release level for Save/Restore support. However, this could change with other releases. Always check the documentation that comes with the new release.

Check with the organization you are ordering your new release from to ensure the so-called interoperability of all your systems during the upgrade.

2.3.1.4 Planning—What Release Level Am I on Now?

Enter GO LICPGM (GO TO LICENSED PROGRAMS) on the command line.
See Figure 2-3.

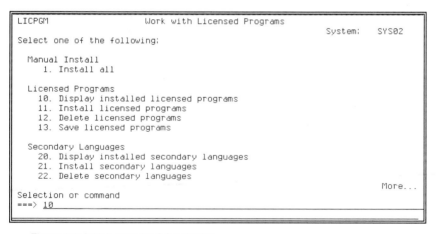

```
LICPGM                    Work with Licensed Programs
                                                   System:    SYS02
  Select one of the following:

    Manual Install
       1. Install all

    Licensed Programs
      10. Display installed licensed programs
      11. Install licensed programs
      12. Delete licensed programs
      13. Save licensed programs

    Secondary Languages
      20. Display installed secondary languages
      21. Install secondary languages
      22. Delete secondary languages
                                                            More...
  Selection or command
  ===> 10
```

Figure 2-3: Initial menu for GO LICPGM.

Take option 10 from the menu. This gives you the release level of OS/400 for that machine. See Figure 2-4.

```
                        Display Installed Licensed Programs
                                                    System:   SYS02
Licensed   Installed
Program    Release     Description
5716SS1    V3R6M0      OS/400 - Library QGPL
5716SS1    V3R6M0      OS/400 - Library QUSRSYS
5716SS1    V3R6M0      Operating System/400
5716SS1    V3R6M0      OS/400 - Extended Base Support
5716SS1    V3R6M0      OS/400 - Online Information
```

Figure 2-4: Detail of OS/400 and LICPGM installed.

The release level is in the column labeled Installed Release. There is one for each piece of OS/400. If you happen to scroll through and see different versions of the release level, determine if they are for support of previous versions of programming languages (described something like *PRV). If they are for different versions of the release level, don't worry about them. If they are not for different versions, check with your marketer. Note the release level listed for the bulk of your OS/400 modules.

2.3.1.5 Planning—Traps

If you've made changes to IBM-supplied objects in libraries other than QGPL and QUSRSYS, those changes will be lost. Some examples are:

❖ Changes to subsystem descriptions.

❖ Changes to IBM-supplied printers (like QPRINT) for things like rotation, lines per inch, and characters-per-inch.

❖ Some customers make duplicates of IBM commands. If you have duplicates and these are stored in Q-libraries other than the two mentioned above, those commands will be lost.

❖ If you've built your own logical files over IBM-supplied physical files (created on the fly when using commands that have OUTPUT(*OUTFILE) capability).

The preceding are just some of the examples. You will want to brainstorm with your staff for others. If you have any of these changes, either save the objects for separate restoration later or document the changes so you can redo them after the installation.

2.3.2 Saving the System

After you've done adequate planning, and immediately before you start install-ing a new release, always save your system with the SAVSYS command. If there is any problem with the installation, you will have to use this tape to restore your system. Of course, this step is not for customers installing OS/400 on new ma-chines.

To save your system, you must be user QSYSOPR, QSECOFR, or be a user with the specific SAVSYS authorities (see chapter 5). Select the tape drive that is online at IPL (see section 2.3.1.2, Planning—Installation Hardware), set aside a number of scratchable tapes, mount a scratchable tape on a tape device, and enter the command:

```
SAVSYS   <tape device name>
```

2.3.3 Installing the Release

You'll find that after all the preparation, actually installing the release can be boring.

2.3.3.1 Automatic/Manual Installation

There are two modes of release installation: AUTOMATIC and MANUAL. You will use AUTOMATIC (sometimes called NORMAL) most of the time. AUTOMATIC is the faster method. Like the name implies, AUTOMATIC will install the new release (plus optional licensed program products already installed on your system).

When you are using manual mode, do one or more of the following:

❖   Add DASD using mirroring or user ASP (auxiliary storage pool).

❖   Change the primary language (national, not programming) of the machine.

❖   Change the environment of the AS/400 (to S/36 for example) or change system default values or system configuration.

❖   Use tapes that were created with the SAVSYS (SAVE SYSTEM) command.

❖ Confirm that you have duplicated IBM libraries (the ones that start with a Q) on your system.

❖ Install for the first time one or more licensed program product on your machine.

Your new release package will contain release instructions in a document called the *Installation Guide*. Within that document are checklists for doing each step of the installation. Depending on which method you use, make sure you pull the checklist for AUTOMATIC or MANUAL installation. If you follow those steps, you shouldn't have a problem. Be careful! Sometimes waiting for the installation is so tedious that you forget a step from the checklist.

The *Installation Guide* even indicates which steps are fairly long. Therefore, you can allocate your installation activities efficiently. Most of the time, release loading is flawless but always be prepared for the worst. Make sure you've done your homework and that you have your system saved just in case.

2.3.3.2 Installation—Tips to Save Time When Installing a New Release

Use automatic mode if you can. Delete all QHST files to prevent them from being saved as system files. Enter on the command line:

```
WRKOBJ QSYS/QHST* *FILE
```

When the files are displayed, use a 4 and delete them all.

End all subsystems before starting. Enter on the command line:

```
ENDSBS(*ALL)
```

2.4 INSTALLING NEW LICENSED PRODUCTS

Sometimes you need to add new products to your AS/400. You install these initially on their own. Later, when you install a new operating system release, new product versions should be included on the release media. This section is about how to do the initial installation of these products.

Verify the system distribution directory, determine which tape drive you will use, and clean it. For additional information see section 2.3.1.1, Planning Appropriate Directories and section 2.3.1.2, Planning—Installation Hardware.

Sign on to the system as QSECOFR. Load the tape containing the new licensed program product on the tape drive. Change the message queue with the following command:

```
CHGMSGQ QSYSOPR *BREAK SEV(60)
```

End all subsystems with the command:

```
ENDSBS  *ALL  *IMMED
```

Change the message queue again with the command:

```
CHGMSGQ  QSYSOPR  *BREAK  SEV(95)
```

Enter the command:

```
GO  LICPGM
```

Take option 11, INSTALL LICENSED PROGRAMS. See Figure 2-5.

```
                        Install Licensed Programs
                                                      System:   SYS02
Type options, press Enter.
  1=Install

         Licensed  Installed
Option   Program   Status       Description
   _     5716SS1   *COMPATIBLE  OS/400 - Library QGPL
   _     5716SS1   *COMPATIBLE  OS/400 - Library QUSRSYS
   _     5716SS1   *COMPATIBLE  OS/400 - Extended Base Support
   _     5716SS1   *COMPATIBLE  OS/400 - Online Information
   _     5716SS1   *COMPATIBLE  OS/400 - S/36 and S/38 Migration
   _     5716SS1   *COMPATIBLE  OS/400 - System/36 Environment
   _     5716SS1   *COMPATIBLE  OS/400 - System/38 Environment
   _     5716SS1   *BACKLEVEL   OS/400 - Example Tools Library
   _     5716SS1   *COMPATIBLE  OS/400 - AFP Compatibility Fonts
   _     5716SS1   *COMPATIBLE  OS/400 - *PRV CL Compiler Support
   _     5716SS1   *COMPATIBLE  OS/400 - S/36 Migration Assistant
   _     5716SS1   *COMPATIBLE  OS/400 - Host Servers
   _     5716SS1   *COMPATIBLE  OS/400 - Openness Includes
                                                              More...
```

Figure 2-5: Detail of INSTALL LICENSED PROGRAM menu.

Install the new LPP by placing a 1 next to it. Next install any PTFs that came with the LPP.

The new product won't run until you re-IPL the AS/400. An IPL is required to run the initialize system (INZSYS) process. Without this step, the new product won't work.

Make a fresh save of your system after the IPL is complete (see section 2.3.2, Saving the System). Although you don't have to use manual installation if you have PRPQs, keep in mind that they generally require special installations and, therefore, are done manually. They come with their own instructions to do this.

2.5 PROGRAM TEMPORARY FIXES

As I mentioned at the beginning of this chapter, PTFs are fixes to bugs discovered in the operating system or in program products. Sometimes they are enhancements. They are a way of life on any computer software. PTFs are applied in two conditions:

❖ Temporary:

✓ Takes a little longer when they run.

✓ Can be removed in the future.

❖ Permanent:

  ✓ Becomes a permanent part of the program product.

  ✓ Runs fast.

  ✓ Cannot be removed.

Always follow the instructions that come with your PTFs. Learn how they are applied and how previous, temporary PTFs are to be treated. Temporary PTFs might have to be permanently applied or they might have to be removed before applying any new PTFs.

Most customers apply PTFs temporarily at least for a few weeks to see how they affect the system. Before any PTFs are applied permanently, make a system backup. In the unlikely event you have to back out the permanent PTF, the only way you can do it is to restore the system from a SAVSYS taken prior to making the PTF permanent. PTFs are further defined as two types:

❖ Immediate—Once applied, they take effect immediately.

❖ Delayed—Once applied, the don't take effect until after the next IPL.

Again, the instructions supplied with the PTFs will tell you how to install them.

2.5.1 Keeping Current With and Ordering PTFs

PTFs take more effort to keep up with than new OS releases. You can order PTFs through your marketing representative over the telephone. However, it can be more convenient just to order through the AS/400 ECS (Electronic Customer Support) modem. You still have the problem of keeping up to date with PTFs so you'll know what to order. Fortunately, you use the same command to keep updated as you do to order PTFs.

2.5.1.1 Keeping Current

There are four PTF codes designed to order general products for you. You order them through the command SNDPTFORD (SEND PTF ORDER). Here is its general form:

```
SNDPTFORD   SFyyvrm
```

Where *yy* is one of the following:

yy value to order

97	*PTF Summary List*
98	*PSP for Software*
99	*Cumulative PTF Package*

The values *v*, *r*, and *m* stand for the version, release, and modification level you will want to specify. For example, V3R0M5 would be 305 and V3R7 would be 370.

One other order code is used to order PSPs for hardware:

```
    SNDPTFORD MF98vrm
```

If you've ordered the cumulative tape (order option SF99vrm), when you press the Enter key, you'll have a chance to verify or change the mailing address and the contact name. Figure 2-6 shows the screen.

```
                       Verify Contact Information
                                                    System:    SYS02
  Type changes, press Enter.

       Company . . . . . . . . .    World Wide Widgets, Inc.
       Contact . . . . . . . . .    Mike Dawson
       Mailing address:
         Street address  . . . . .  999 N. Any Drive


         City/State  . . . . . . .  Scottsdale, AZ
         Country . . . . . . . . .  USA
         Zip code  . . . . . . . .  85999
       Telephone numbers:
         Primary . . . . . . . . .  602-555-1234
         Alternative . . . . . . .
       Fax telephone numbers:
         Primary . . . . . . . . .
         Alternative . . . . . . .
       National language version    2924    F4 for list
                                                            Bottom
    F3=Exit   F4=Prompt   F5=Refresh   F12=Cancel
```

Figure 2-6: Screen to change delivery information for the Cumulative PTF *tape.*

If you've ordered anything other than the cumulative tape, it can be delivered through the ECS into your computer. To display delivered PTFs, PTF summary lists, or general PSP documents, on the command line enter the command:

```
DSPPTF
```

Now press F4. You'll get a prompted screen that looks like Figure 2-7.

```
                  Display Program Temporary Fix (DSPPTF)

Type choices, press Enter.

Product  . . . . . . . . . . . .   *ALL        F4 for list
PTF numbers to select  . . . . .   *ALL        Character value, *ALL...
Release  . . . . . . . . . . . .   *ALL        *ALL, UxRxMx
Cover letter only  . . . . . . .   *NO         *NO, *YES
Output . . . . . . . . . . . . .   *           *, *PRINT, *OUTFILE
```

Figure 2-7: The prompted version of command DSPPTF.

Prompt (press F4) at the PRODUCT keyword because you'll never remember all the product codes. Figure 2-8 shows a product screen.

```
                  Specify Value for Parameter LICPGM

Type choice, press Enter.

Type . . . . . . . . . . . . . :   CHARACTER
Product  . . . . . . . . . . . .   *ALL

*ALL                               5716BR1 V3R6M0 Backup Recovery and
5716999 V3R6M0 AS/400 Licensed Int 5716CB1 V3R6M0 ILE COBOL/400
5716SS1 V3R6M0 Operating System/40 5716CX2 V3R6M0 ILE C/400
INFOAS4 V2R1M0 Information APARs    5716PT1 V3R6M0 Performance Tools/4
INFOAS4 V2R1M1 Information APARs    5716PW1 V3R6M0 Application Develop
INFOAS4 V2R2M0 Information APARs    5716QU1 V3R6M0 Query/400
INFOAS4 V2R3M0 Information APARs    5716RG1 V3R6M0 ILE RPG/400
INFOAS4 V3R0M5 Information APARs    5716TC1 V3R6M0 AS/400 TCP/IP Conne
INFOAS4 V3R1M0 Information APARs    5716XA1 V3R6M0 Client Access/400 F
INFOAS4 V3R6M0 Information APARs    5738FNT V2R2M0 Advanced Function P
INFODSL V0R0M1 Information APARs    5738PC1 V2R3M0 PC Support/400
1DEVEXR V2R2M0 AS/400 Device Exerc  5763XB1 V3R1M1 Client Access/400 f
5716AF1 V3R6M0 IBM AFP Utilities f  5763XC1 V3R1M1 Client Access/400 f   +
```

Figure 2-8: The prompted program information for the DSPPTF command.

Let's presume that you have ordered the cumulative PTF tape for the OS/400: V3R6M0. That product is the third on the list (or product code 5716SS1). Enter this number next to the PRODUCT parameter and press Enter to return to the first screen.

In the field PTF NUMBERS TO SELECT in Figure 2-7, enter the number you ordered when you did the SNDPTFORD command. For example, if you ordered the PTF summary list for V3R6M0 and now want to look at it, you would enter SF97360.

Enter the release number as V3R6M0 and *NO or *YES for COVER LETTER ONLY. Cover letters are a quick way to browse the highlights of the PTFs. You can ask for specific PTFs in their entirety later. Additionally, these summaries can be quite large. Therefore, I prefer to get a hard copy of them by entering *PRINT for the OUTPUT keyword.

Figure 2-9 shows a screen to determine if the summary PTF information you ordered has been delivered. From the report on this screen, you get a summary of all the PTFs by product that have been received on your AS/400 through the ECS modem.

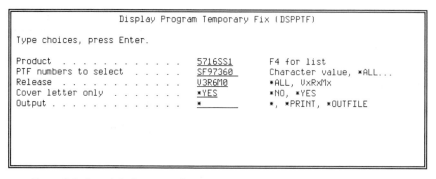

Figure 2-9: Completed command DSPPTF.

2.5.1.2 Ordering PTFs

After you've checked for available PTFs by reviewing their cover letters, you can order them through your marketing representative or through the Electronic Customer Support (ECS) modem on your AS/400. If you order through the branch or reseller, just telephone them. The ECS method is easier however. Enter the command:

```
SNDPTFORD <ptf number>
```

If you prompt the command, and ask for additional parameters, you will get the screen shown in Figure 2-10.

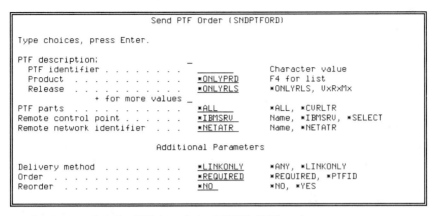

```
                       Send PTF Order (SNDPTFORD)

Type choices, press Enter.

PTF description:                        _
   PTF identifier . . . . . . . .  _____        Character value
   Product  . . . . . . . . . . .  *ONLYPRD        F4 for list
   Release  . . . . . . . . . . .  *ONLYRLS        *ONLYRLS, VxRxMx
           + for more values _
PTF parts  . . . . . . . . . . .    *ALL            *ALL, *CURLTR
Remote control point . . . . . .    *IBMSRV         Name, *IBMSRV, *SELECT
Remote network identifier  . . .    *NETATR         Name, *NETATR

                    Additional Parameters

Delivery method  . . . . . . . .    *LINKONLY       *ANY, *LINKONLY
Order  . . . . . . . . . . . . .    *REQUIRED       *REQUIRED, *PTFID
Reorder  . . . . . . . . . . . .    *NO             *NO, *YES
```

Figure 2-10: Ordering PTF through the AS/400's ECS modem.

As shown in Figure 2-10, you can order one PTF (by entering its number in PTF IDENTIFIER). By entering a plus sign (ON THE + FOR MORE VALUES parameter), you can order many PTFs. You can order complete PTFs (PTFs with cover letters) or only cover letters so you can review them and decide if you want the PTF.

If you order a PTF that requires prerequisite PTFs before it can be installed, you'll get them automatically. Don't be confused if you order one PTF and receive three or four.

IBM will attempt to send your PTF order via the ECS link. If you specified *ANY for DELIVERY METHOD and what you ordered is too large to ship by the link, IBM will make you a tape. If what you ordered is also too large for a single tape, you'll hear from your marketing representative.

If you specified *LINKONLY for DELIVERY METHOD and what you ordered is too large to ship via the link, you'll get a message right away at the bottom of the order screen. You then can break the order into several smaller orders.

Normally, you don't get PTFs that you've already received. This control can be nice. However, if you've lost the previous PTFs (as often happens), and you want those PTFs, specify *YES on the REORDER keyword.

2.5.2 Loading/Applying PTFs

There are two operations needed to install a PTF:

- ❖ Load PTF (LODPTF).
- ❖ Apply PTF (APYPTF).

2.5.2.1 Loading PTFs

When loading or applying PTFs from a cumulative tape, due to the varied relationships of the PTFs, you might be asked to perform different specific tasks. Always follow the instructions that come enclosed with the PTFs. Generally, you would first load the PTF from a source with the command:

```
LODPTF
```

Figure 2-11 shows a sample of that prompted command. You should know which PTFs are for what products. If you don't, check the documentation that comes with the PTF or press F4. You'll get a similar product display to what is shown in Figure 2-8.

```
                    Load Program Temporary Fix (LODPTF)

Type choices, press Enter.

Product  . . . . . . . . . . . .    _____     F4 for list
Device . . . . . . . . . . . . .    *SERVICE     Name, *SERVICE, *SAVF
PTF numbers to select  . . . . .    *ALL         Character value, *ALL
            + for more values       _____
PTF numbers to omit  . . . . . .    _____     Character value
            + for more values       _____
Superseded PTFs  . . . . . . . .    *APYPERM     *APYPERM, *NOAPY
Release  . . . . . . . . . . . .    *ONLY        *ONLY, VxRyMz
```

Figure 2-11:The prompted version of command LODPTF.

The DEVICE is where you tell the system where it can find the PTF to load. It can be in *SERVICE (delivered from the ECS), *SAVF (a save file, from another AS/400), or a device such as a tape drive. PTFs are on *SERVICE when they were received by the ECS modem. They can be in a *SAVF in a multiple-CPU system. In that case, they were loaded from a device, then saved, and physically moved to your system (or sent via SNDNETF). Another possibility is that the PTFs arrived on a tape. Just load the tape and specify the device on which it is loaded. This is the common way of loading cumulative PTFs, but not necessarily individual PTFs (which are usually on *SERVICE).

For the most part, customers take the defaults on the rest of the keywords when installing individual PTFs. When installing PTFs from a cumulative tape, you'll make more use of these fields. Here is a summary of what they do. With PTF NUMBERS TO SELECT, you to select only specific PTFs from a cumulative tape.

Note that PTFs are sent with their own Mandatory Special Instructions. If IBM really wants you to read those instructions, those PTFs won't be installed from the command when you USE PTF NUMBERS TO SELECT(*ALL).

With PTF NUMBERS TO OMIT, you to omit specific PTFs from a cumulative tape. You will do a lot of this for superseded PTFs. If its been a long time since you installed any PTFs and the cumulative tape contains earlier PTFs, you will have PTFs that have been superseded by newer PTFs. This is why the individual cumulative tape installation instructions are crucial.

Finally, the field SUPERSEDED PTFS refer to PTFs that have been applied to your system prior to this load. This field instructs the system to apply them permanently or to not apply them. Remember, PTFs that have been permanently applied cannot be removed. Follow any installation instructions to the letter.

2.5.2.2 Applying PTFs

After PTFs are loaded, they are applied with the command APYPTF. Figure 2-12 shows an example of its prompted screen.

```
                   Apply Program Temporary Fix (APYPTF)

Type choices, press Enter.

Product  . . . . . . . . . .   _____      F4 for list


```

Figure 2-12: Prompted command APYPTF.

Type the product name and press the Enter key. If you don't know the product, press the F4 key for a product list. After filling in the product code and pressing Enter, you'll get the screen shown in Figure 2-13.

```
                    Apply Program Temporary Fix (APYPTF)

Type choices, press Enter.

Product . . . . . . . . . . . . . > 5716SS1        F4 for list
Release . . . . . . . . . . . . .   *ONLY          *ONLY, UxRxMx
PTF numbers to select . . . . .     *ALL           Character value, *ALL
             + for more values      _____
PTF numbers to omit . . . . . .     _____       Character value
             + for more values      _____
Extent of change . . . . . . . .    *TEMP          *TEMP, *PERM
Delayed PTFs . . . . . . . . . .    *YES           *NO, *YES, *IMMDLY
```

Figure 2-13: Command APYPTF *after supplying the product code.*

In the example shown in Figure 2-13, the product is OS/400 itself. If you're applying an individual PTF, put that number in PTF NUMBERS TO SELECT. If you're
loading a cumulative tape, follow the instructions shipped with the tape. Generally, you'll only have one release of the operating system installed. Therefore,
*ONLY is sufficient for the RELEASE keyword. You'll want to select *ALL PTFS
and not OMIT any (next two keywords). However, specific cumulative tape
instructions could and probably will change this.

The EXTENT OF CHANGE keyword determines whether the PTF(s) applied will be
temporary or permanent.

This command will immediately apply any PTFs it can. If a PTF cannot be immediately applied because the operating system or licensed program product is
active, it will be marked as not applied and designated as a delayed PTF.

The DELAYED PTFS keyword concerns applying PTFs that have been previously
designated as delayed. These can be applied at the next IPL. In the case of licensed program products, delayed PTFs can be applied anytime that the particular product is inactive.

Most of the time you will have to re-IPL in order to make applied PTFs take
effect. NOTE: There is a power menu on the AS/400 that will power the system
down. Don't use this when you are IPL-ing to apply PTFs; it doesn't invoke the
APYPTF command. When you IPL to apply delayed PTFs, use the following
command after you have ended all subsystems:

```
PWRDWNSYS *IMMED RESTART(*YES) IPLSRC(x)
```

In the preceding command, *x* means the system storage area. As far as applying PTFs is concerned, see Table 2-1.

Table 2-1: Applying PTFs.

Storage Area	Description
A	Temporarily applies unapplied PTFs, or
	Removes specific previously temporarily applied PTFs.
B	Permanently applies previously temporarily applied PTFs.

If you have delayed PTFs that you want permanently applied, you will first have to IPL with storage area A. That will apply them temporarily. Then you will have to re-IPL to get them applied permanently.

After entering the command PWRDWNSYS and pressing the Enter key, you may see an INSTALL THE SYSTEM display. Enter option 1 for PERFORM AN IPL on that screen and press Enter.

You will get a WORK WITH PTFS display if you have any outstanding PTFs that have not been applied (they were delayed) or have been temporarily applied. From this screen, you can apply PTFs permanently or remove them temporarily or permanently.

PTF application might not work every time. There are many ways to start an IPL; the PWRDWNSYS is only one method. PTFs only get applied when the IPL is a result of a PWRDWNSYS command. Even then they will not apply if:

❖ The power-down part of the PWRDWNSYS command didn't complete normally (power was cut to the machine before it finished).

❖ Any abnormal condition existed in the AS/400 prior to issuing the PWRDWNSYS command. This can be due to:

✓ A job ending at any time using the END JOB ABNORMAL (ENDJOBABN) command.

✓ The system ending previously with any function check in the controlling subsystem.

✓ The system going down previous while rebuilding database files during another abnormal IPL.

For additional information on IPL, see section 1.7—Starting the AS/400.

2.5.3 Removing PTFs

Occasionally, you will have a problem with a PTF and you'll want to remove it. Or you'll be instructed to remove a previous PTF before you can load a new one.

PTFs can be removed temporarily or permanently. When a PTF is removed, the original object the PTF replaced is restored. When the PTF is removed temporarily, it reverts back to being loaded but non-applied. When the PTF is removed permanently, it disappears, non-loaded, non-applied.

There are a couple of rules about removing PTFs. You can't remove one that has another PTF that is dependent on it. You also can't remove a PTF that has its related operating system or licensed program product active. Finally, operating system PTFs can only be removed permanently. Table 2-2 summarizes these and other rules.

Table 2-2: PTF Apply/Load/Remove/Temporary/Permanent Rules Grid.

Condition/Type of PTF	Remove Description
Permanently applied	Cannot remove
Operating system PTF	Remove permanently only
Delayed PTF, applied temporarily	Remove temporarily only
Delayed PTF, applied temporarily, then removed temporarily	Remove permanently
Immediate PTF, applied temporarily	Remove temporarily or permanently
Immediate PTF, loaded but not applied	Remove permanently only

2.6 BIBLIOGRAPHY

All book titles are subject to change from release to release.

Licensed Programs and New Release Installation Guide

New Products Planning Information for Version 3, Release 6

Getting Started on the AS/400 System, Version 3

3. Configure Your System

3.1 OVERVIEW

Any AS/400 will run fine as soon as the operating system (see chapter 1) and applications are installed, and some user profiles are created (see chapter 5). You can sign on to a workstation right away, but don't really try to use the system this way. Sign on and do some configuring. The AS/400 comes with defaults that you can use to quickly bring up a basic, workable system.

If you are new to the AS/400 and going it alone, just make the basic configuration outlined in this chapter. Come back later, when you understand the system better, and make adjustments.

3.2 MEMORY: STORAGE POOLS AND ACTIVITY LEVELS

3.2.1 Storage Pools

Any *storage pool* is a pool of memory where one type of program/application runs. You ordered your AS/400 with a certain amount of memory. When you got your machine, that memory was divided into two special shared storage pools, *MACHINE and *BASE.

*MACHINE is the storage pool where the system tasks that you have no control over runs. *BASE can be where everything else runs until you build other pools and assign jobs to run in them.

Your AS/400 comes with the optimum memory assigned to *MACHINE. You can reset this, but you don't have to and probably shouldn't initially. Later, if you suspect problems with *MACHINE pool, you can adjust its memory within parameters. See chapter 9, Performance.

*MACHINE's memory can never be below 256Kb; the system will not allow it. Memory adjustments to *MACHINE can be made by changing the system value (see appendix A, AS/400 System Values) QMCHPOOL.

The amount of memory in *BASE cannot be adjusted directly because it is the total memory available on the system (less the memory used by *MACHINE and any other *private pools* or *shared pools*). You can, however, set system value QBASPOOL to a value below which the system will not allow *BASE to fall. QBASPOOL comes with an IBM-set value you shouldn't change until you're accustomed to using the AS/400. In addition to the minimum you can set, the system has a built-in minimum limit for *BASE memory (32 Kb) below which you cannot go.

*MACHINE and *BASE are sufficient to run your AS/400. Beyond them, however, you might want to consider using private or shared pools in your system for better performance.

Dividing memory into pools is like fencing the range. Although at first it might look like something is being lost, it isn't Actually, the control will make an AS/400 with a broad job mix run better. Fencing the range allows dissimilar animals to graze "together" within fences better than they would on the open range. Cattle could graze in their space, sheep in theirs, and goats in other places. Similarly, dividing memory into pools allows interactive jobs to run with batch jobs. The term *pool* is actually an amount of memory fenced in.

Here's how to use memory pools and enhance performance. You will have your interactive jobs running in an interactive *subsystem* (see section 3.5.6, Subsystems). You will also have your batch jobs running in a batch subsystem. If you do nothing with the configuration, both will use memory in *BASE.

There are two things that happen in the memory on any virtual machine—paging and faulting—that I have to define before we go any further. *Paging* is when memory pages for a relatively inactive program are written out to DASD so the system can load memory pages for the program (or its data) on which it is currently working. *Faulting* is when the AS/400 is working on a program (or its data) and attempts to go to a new memory page and doesn't find it. The system has to go look for the page and determine if it was either moved out to DASD to support another program or if it hasn't been loaded from DASD the first time, yet.

Now that you understand paging and faulting, let's return to performance and storage pools. Our example was interactive and batch jobs running in their own subsystems, but using *BASE as the memory. Interactive jobs typically run at a higher priority than batch jobs, and, therefore, get system attention much more often. The system might run through all interactive jobs—working on them two or three times—before it goes to any batch job.

With all jobs using the same storage pool, when the system needs memory for interactive job paging, it will probably take it from batch jobs. Because batch jobs run at a lower priority, they are "inactive" and their memory gets stolen. After several iterations of this, the system decides to work on a batch job. None of its previously loaded pages are around anymore. By the time the system finds them and returns them to memory, the time is up for working on the batch job and the system returns to the interactive jobs. This is called *thrashing*. It means a lot of work goes on and nothing gets done.

One way around this is to have interactive and batch jobs running in their own subsystems that have their own private pools of memory. In this scenario, paging for interactive jobs occurs only between interactive jobs. Meanwhile, paging for batch jobs occurs only between batch jobs.

The AS/400 goes one step further and offers shared pools of memory. The two pools that come with the AS/400, *MACHINE and *BASE, are *special shared pools,* and any others are *general shared pools.*

You can only have a total of 16 pools on your system. Because the system insists on using *MACHINE and *BASE, you can add only 14 to your system.

❖ Private pools are created and named on the subsystem description (see section 3.5.6, Subsystems). Their names are simple: 1 through 14. A private pool can only support one subsystem. A shared pool can support multiple subsystems and still maintain thrashing protection from other subsystems' jobs not using the pool.

❖ The AS/400 comes with predetermined names and, in two cases, predetermined uses, for these shared pools. Here's the list:
  ✓ *INTERACT —Supports interactive subsystems' jobs.
  ✓ *SPOOL—Supports spool writers (printing).
  ✓ *SHRPOOL1 through *SHRPOOL10— Names you can use for your own shared pools.

Whether you use private or shared pools, you can adjust their memory at any time you like. The more memory you assign to a pool the more work it can do. It is common to put more memory in the interactive subsystem's pool and take some away from the batch subsystem's pool during the day. By reversing the procedure in the evening, you take memory away from the interactive pool and give it to the batch pool.

Because it contains all the system's memory that isn't taken by all the other pools, *BASE plays a major part in moving memory around the AS/400. When you take from one pool and give to another, you do so by adjusting one pool down; the adjustment returns memory to *BASE, making it bigger. As you increase the other pool, the increased memory comes out of *BASE.

3.2.2 Activity Level

Before getting into activity levels, you need to know that AS/400 jobs have three states:

❖ Active—the job is running.

❖ Wait—the job is waiting for something to happen. For example, it is waiting for the system to retrieve a random record or it is waiting for the user go finish with a screen.

❖ Ineligible—

✓ The job is ready to run but the system is too busy for it.

✓ The system has spent its allocated time (measured in time slices) on the job and will work on some other jobs for a while.

Every storage pool has an activity level associated with it. In other words, there are limits to the number of jobs the computer will work on at one time within the pool. This is a confusing subject to most experienced AS/400 people because there is another value on subsystems that states the maximum number of jobs it can run at one time. These are not the same values.

The maximum active jobs on the subsystem refers to how many jobs are even allowed within the subsystem. For more discussion on maximum jobs and activity levels, see section 3.4.6, Subsystems. A storage pool activity level refers to how many of these jobs the system will work on at the same time. In the batch subsystem, you could easily have a maximum of six active jobs, but an activity level of 3. If you had six jobs in the subsystem, three would be active and three would be present but ineligible. When an active job goes into a wait or ineligible state, the system makes one of the ineligibles active. If the job that entered the wait state returned from that state and the system is working on three other jobs, it goes ineligible until one of the others goes to wait or ineligible.

This isn't as choppy as it sounds because jobs go into and out of states all the time. If you were monitoring the system I just described, you would mostly see six active jobs. You would see many waits and only occasionally catch ineligible statuses.

Overall throughput of any subsystem can be increased greatly by carefully setting the activity level. The exception to all this is the *MACHINE pool. It's the system's pool for its tasks and you can't change its activity level.

3.2.3 Using Memory and Activity Levels

3.2.3.1 Creating Private Pools/Assigning Shared Pools

Although you would think a private memory pool is closely associated with some kind of memory management command, it isn't. On the AS/400, it's associated closely with the subsystem and is created or changed by creating or changing the subsystem's description.

You create the subsystem description with the CRTSBSD command. Figure 3-1 shows the format for that. This command is discussed in more detail in section 3.4.6, Subsystems.

```
                 Create Subsystem Description (CRTSBSD)

Type choices, press Enter.

Subsystem description  . . . . .   _____    Name
  Library  . . . . . . . . . .     *CURLIB       Name, *CURLIB
Storage pools:
  Pool identifier  . . . . . .     _             1-10
  Storage size . . . . . . . .     _____      Number, *BASE, *NOSTG...
  Activity level . . . . . . .     _____        Number
              + for more values _
Maximum jobs . . . . . . . . . .   *NOMAX        0-1000, *NOMAX
Text 'description' . . . . . . .   *BLANK



                        Additional Parameters

Sign-on display file . . . . . .   *QDSIGNON     Name, *QDSIGNON
  Library  . . . . . . . . . .     _____    Name, *LIBL, *CURLIB
Subsystem library  . . . . . . .   *NONE         Name, *NONE
                                                              More...
F3=Exit   F4=Prompt   F5=Refresh   F12=Cancel   F13=How to use this display
F24=More keys
```

Figure 3-1: Prompted version of the CRTSBSD command.

For now, notice the area you use to specify the pools. You can define up to 10 pools for each subsystem description. These are referred to as the subsystem storage pools. There are three fields on this screen relevant to storage pools: pool identifier, storage size, and activity level.

❖ The *pool identifier* field is the subsystem pool number (1-10) within the subsystem; it is not the system name-number of the pool. Subsystems can have up to 10 pools assigned to them. Actually, you don't see many subsystems with more than three pools assigned to them, and most have two. For more information see section 3.4.6, Subsystems.

❖ The *storage size* field has two uses:

  ✓ If you want a private pool (no other subsystems can use it), specify the amount of memory to be in the pool. When you start the subsystem (STRSBS), you will have a private pool started for that subsystem with that amount of memory. The name of that private pool will be assigned by the system and it'll be the next available number between 1 and 14.

  ✓ If you want to use a shared storage pool, enter the name of the shared pool (e.g., *INTERACT or *SHRPOOL5). You don't specify the storage size; that is defined on the shared pool itself. You can adjust shared pools' memory with the WRKSYSSTS or CHGSHRPOOL commands.

❖ *Activity level* is the activity level for that pool. For additional information on activity levels, see section 3.2.2, Activity Levels.

❖ If you want more pools, put a plus sign (+) in the + FOR MORE VALUES parameter and the system will prompt you for up to 10 subsystem pools.

How do you know starting values if you've never configured a subsystem before? See section 13.5.2, Choosing Your Pool Configuration, in the IBM manual *OS/400 Work Management V3R6* for a table of these values.

3.2.3.2 Changing Pool Memory/Activity Levels

There are three commands that will change memory and activity level settings on pools. Each has its place. Table 3-1 shows the commands and where they are used.

Table 3-1: Memory Activity Level Commands.

Pool Name	Adjustments to Memory	Adjustments to Activity Level
*MACHINE	QMCHPOOL (sv) WRKSYSSTS	—— n/a ——
*BASE	—— n/a ——	QBASACTLVL (sv) WRKSYSSTS
ALL PRIVATE POOLS	WRKSYSSTS CHGSBSD	WRKSYSSTS CHGSBSD
ALL SHARED POOLS	WRKSYSSTS CHGSHRPOOL	WRKSYSSTS CHGSHRPOOL
sv) = System Value. Use CHGSYSVAL command to change these.		

Figure 3-2 shows an example of using the CHGSHRPOOL command to change attributes of a shared pool. Type the command (CHGSHRPOOL) on a command line and press Enter. The underlined values are changeable. Just put your cursor there and type in the new value.

```
┌─────────────────────────────────────────────────────────────────────┐
│              Change Shared Storage Pool (CHGSHRPOOL)                  │
│                                                                       │
│ Type choices, press Enter.                                            │
│                                                                       │
│ Pool identifier  . . . . . . . .  _____   *MACHINE, *BASE, *INTERACT... │
│ Storage size . . . . . . . . . .  *SAME        Number, *SAME, *NOSTG  │
│ Activity level . . . . . . . . .  *SAME        Number, *SAME          │
│ Paging option  . . . . . . . . .  *SAME        *SAME, *FIXED, *CALC   │
│ Text 'description' . . . . . . .  *SAME                               │
│                                                                       │
│ ┌────────┐                                                            │
│ │                                                                     │
│                                                                       │
│                                                                       │
│                                                                       │
│                                                                       │
│                                                                       │
│                                                                Bottom │
│ F3=Exit   F4=Prompt   F5=Refresh   F12=Cancel   F13=How to use this display │
│ F24=More keys                                                         │
└─────────────────────────────────────────────────────────────────────┘
```

Figure 3-2: CHGSHRPOOL *command.*

Just override the memory and activity levels to the new values you would like. If you don't want to change one or both, don't enter anything. The *SAME value means it won't make any change.

Private pools are changed within their subsystems. Figure 3-3 shows the prompted version of the CHGSBSD command.

```
┌─────────────────────────────────────────────────────────────────────┐
│              Change Subsystem Description (CHGSBSD)                    │
│                                                                       │
│ Type choices, press Enter.                                            │
│                                                                       │
│ Subsystem description  . . . . .  _____   Name                   │
│   Library  . . . . . . . . . . .  *LIBL        Name, *LIBL, *CURLIB   │
│ Storage pools:                        _                               │
│   Pool identifier  . . . . . . .  *SAME        1-10, *SAME            │
│   Storage size . . . . . . . . .  _____   Number, *BASE, *NOSTG...│
│   Activity level . . . . . . . .  _____       Number                 │
│              + for more values  _                                     │
│ Maximum jobs . . . . . . . . . .  *SAME        0-1000, *SAME, *NOMAX  │
│ Text 'description' . . . . . . .  *SAME                               │
│                                                                       │
│ ┌────────┐                                                            │
│ │                                                                     │
│                         Additional Parameters                         │
│                                                                       │
│ Sign-on display file . . . . . .  *SAME        Name, *SAME, *QDSIGNON │
│   Library  . . . . . . . . . . .  _____   Name, *LIBL, *CURLIB   │
│ Subsystem library  . . . . . . .  *SAME        Name, *SAME, *NONE     │
│                                                                Bottom │
│ F3=Exit   F4=Prompt   F5=Refresh   F12=Cancel   F13=How to use this display │
│ F24=More keys                                                         │
└─────────────────────────────────────────────────────────────────────┘
```

Figure 3-3: CHGSBSD *command.*

You can only make changes to private pools on this command. Specify the subsystem pool identifier (see section 3.2.4, Pool Names) and its new memory or activity level.

3.2.3.2 Deleting Pools

❖ You cannot delete or remove pools *MACHINE and *BASE.

❖ Delete private pools by ending the subsystem in which they run.

❖ Make shared pools inactive by ending the subsystems in which they run. They still will appear on the WRKSYSSTS command, but they will have zeros for memory and activity level, and you won't see a pool identification associated with them.

3.2.4 Pool Names

Nothing confuses AS/400 customers as much as storage pool names. First, the system names pools. Second, it's not very creative. Third, pools are sometimes referred to by their relative pool number within a subsystem and sometimes by their system-generated pool number-name, and, in the case of shared pools, by their shared pool names. Is that confusing? Let's walk through an example. Figure 3-4 shows the command WORK WITH SUBSYSTEMS (WRKSBS).

```
                       Work with Subsystems
                                            System:   SYS01
Type options, press Enter.
   4=End subsystem     5=Display subsystem description
   8=Work with subsystem jobs      Subsystem Pool 1
                                    ⇩   ⇗Subsystem Pool 2
                   Total        -----------Subsystem Pools-----------
Opt  Subsystem   Storage (K)    1   2   3   4   5   6   7   8   9  10
  _    QBATCH ⇦Subsystem   0    2   4
  _    QCMN01            0      2   6
  _    QCMN02            0      2   6
  _    QCMN03            0      2   5
  _    QCMN04            0      2   8⇦System Pool 8
  _    QCOMPILE          0      2  11
  _    QCTL              0      2    ⇘System Pool 11
                               ⇘                          More...
Parameters or command              System Pool 2
===>
F3=Exit    F5=Refresh   F11=Display system data    F12=Cancel
F14=Work with system status
```

Figure 3-4: WORK WITH SUBSYSTEMS command.

Here's a list of subsystems and their pools. The columns 1 through 10 refer to the subsystem pools. The numbers under those columns are the system pool names that occupy those subsystem pool slots. Let's look further at subsystem QCOMPILE. It has two subsystem pools: 1 and 2. It's number 1 pool contains system pool identification 2 (which is always *BASE) and its number 2 pool is system pool identification 11. If you put a 5 option on DISPLAY SUBSYSTEM DESCRIPTION, you can look at the subsystem's pool definitions: See Figure 3-5. command WRKSBS, with a display of QCOMPILE's pool definitions.

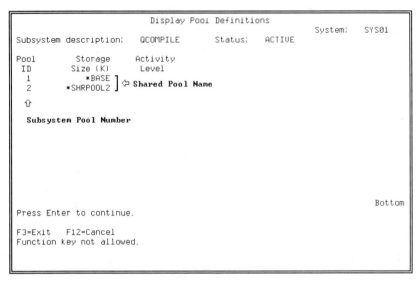

Figure 3-5: Command WRKSBS, displaying pool definitions.

Each row shows information about each of QCOMPILE's pools. Each row is a subsystem's pool number. Here you can verify that *BASE is the shared pool for QCOMPILE's subsystem pool 1. The shared pool name for QCOMPILE's subsystem pool 2 is *SHRPOOL2. Remember, from Figure 3-4, that the subsystem's pool 1 contains system pool number 2? Figure 3-5 shows that subsystem pool 1 is the shared pool. *BASE. By applying a little logic, you can infer that system pool 2 is shared pool *BASE.

Again, Figure 3-4 shows subsystem pool 2 containing system pool 11. Figure 3-5 shows subsystem pool 2 is really *SHRPOOL2. Apply the same logic and system pool 2 is a shared pool called *SHRPOOL2.

You can focus on memory pools—if you know the system pool number—with the WORK WITH SYSTEM STATUS (WRKSYSSTS) command. Figure 3-6 shows a sample of the WRKSYSSTS command.

```
                     Work with System Status                    SYS01
                                                  08/28/96   09:31:36
% CPU used . . . . . . . :       63.0    System ASP . . . . . . . :    22357 M
Elapsed time . . . . . . :   00:41:17    % system ASP used  . . . :   71.4165
Jobs in system . . . . . :       9789    Total aux stg  . . . . . :   187375 M
% perm addresses . . . . :     22.313    Current unprotect used . :     2854 M
% temp addresses . . . . :      4.707    Maximum unprotect  . . . :     3222 M

Sys    Pool    Rsrv    Max  -----DB-----  ---Non-DB---  Act-  Wait-  Act-
Pool   Size K  Size K  Act  Fault  Pages  Fault  Pages  Wait  Inel   Inel
 11    50000        0    4    .0     .3     .3    2.7    .0    .0     .0

 ⇧
 System Pool Number




                                                              Bottom
===> _____
F21=Select assistance level

```

Figure 3-6: Command WRKSYSSTS, information about system pools.

Here is the memory and activity level allocated to system pool name 11. It has 50,000Kb of memory and an activity level of 4. These lines are underscored to indicate that you can make changes to the pools from this screen.

If you weren't comfortable with the logic in connecting system pool numbers to shared pools, you could take the direct approach with the WORK WITH SHARED POOLS (WRKSHRPOOL) command. Figure 3-7 contains a sample of it.

```
                         Work with Shared Pools
                                                    System:   SYS01
     Main storage size (K)  . :       655360

     Type changes (if allowed), press Enter.

                    Defined    Max   Allocated   Pool  -Paging Option--
     Pool           Size (K)  Active  Size (K)    ID   Defined  Current
     *MACHINE         90000    +++      90000      1   *FIXED   *FIXED
     *BASE            88360     32      88360      2   *FIXED   *FIXED
     *INTERACT        10000      7      10000      8   *FIXED   *FIXED
     *SPOOL           12000      7      12000      3   *FIXED   *FIXED
     *SHRPOOL1       200000     10     200000      4   *CALC    *CALC
     *SHRPOOL2        50000      4      50000     11   *FIXED   *FIXED
     *SHRPOOL3        50000      4      50000     10   *CALC    *CALC
     *SHRPOOL4        40000     10      40000      5   *FIXED   *FIXED
     *SHRPOOL5        70000      7      70000      6   *FIXED   *FIXED
     *SHRPOOL6            0      0                 ⇧   *FIXED
               ↳                                                  More...
     Command    Shared Pool Name            System Pool Number
     ===>
     F3=Exit    F4=Prompt   F5=Refresh   F9=Retrieve   F11=Display text
     F12=Cancel
```

Figure 3-7: Command WRKSHRPOOL.

Here are the shared pool names and the system pool names (pool ID) to which they correspond. Notice three things about this screen.

❖   Like WRKSYSSTS, in Figure 3-6, the memory and activity levels are underscored (meaning you can make changes to them).

❖   *SHRPOOL6, at the bottom of the screen, has no memory or activity level assigned to it. Apparently, its subsystem was stopped at the time this was taken. Also, it has no system pool assigned to it. Therefore, it is totally dormant and it uses no memory.

❖   The system pool numbers 7 and 9 are missing. These must have been used as private pools for some subsystem(s). The command WRKSHRPOOL only shows shared pools (not private). Another thing you can get from the use of 7 and 9 and their omission here is how the AS/400 is really only going to allow a total of 16 pool IDs (including all private, specific shared pools, and general shared pools).

3.3 DASD—USER AUXILIARY STORAGE POOLS

The AS/400 stores data and programs on disk with a process called *data striping*. This is one of the benefits of the AS/400's single-level store architecture. With data striping, the customer doesn't allocate files to specific disk volumes. Actually, the customer isn't even aware of disk volumes. When the system writes to a file, it finds the least-used disk volume and writes it there. Therefore, pieces of any file are located all over the system. The benefits of striping are:

- ❖ All volumes are always balanced, with no effort from the customer.

- ❖ Read/write activities automatically make use of multiple arms, resulting in faster throughput.

The disadvantages of data striping are:

- ❖ If a disk drive is lost, the whole system could be lost. The customer must have adequate backup.

- ❖ The objects from some tasks, such as keeping a journal or saving, would perform better if they could be dedicated to specific disk volumes.

User auxiliary storage pools (ASP) ameliorate these disadvantages. An ASP is a set of specific drives that will limit the system to use for striping. Typically, specific objects are stored in specific ASPs.

You could have an ASP over several drives to hold a library and all its files. That would reduce the impact to the system due to a single drive failure. Only the data in the ASP the drive belonged to would have to be restored.

You could have an ASP hold save files (type *SAVF). Backups can be done faster to a *SAVF than to tape, and that would minimize the time a library was held up during backups. An ASP could be designated to hold only journals and receivers. In that way, performance would improve on a machine using journaling heavily.

If you're new to the AS/400 and this method of data storage, do not use ASPs to shoehorn your AS/400 into storing data like some other computer you're used to. Creating ASPs is a bigger deal than making the memory adjustments just described. You need to create or change ASPs only when you have the whole system to yourself. When you're done, you have to do another initial program load (re-IPL) for the AS/400. And, in the case of changes, you will have to do extensive save/restores. Don't enter the ASP business lightly. Typical AS/400 shops have four or fewer ASPs. This chapter gives you an overview of ASP, but if you really want to pursue it see section 4.2.2 of the *OS/400 Backup and Recovery—Advanced V3R6*.

3.3.1 Other ASP Considerations

❖ The ASPs you build will be considered user ASPs. Not every type of object can exist in a user ASP. The *OS/400Backup and Recovery—Advanced V3R6*, section 4, has a list of object types that are not allowed in a user ASP.

❖ Don't let a user ASP fill up.

  ✓ If it manages to overflow, the ASP is damaged and, until you remedy it, all objects in the ASP are considered damaged. The remedy involves taking down the AS/400.

  ✓ If a user ASP happens to overflow it does so into the system ASP. If the system ASP overflows, your system dies and you have a lot of work to do. Check the *OS/400 Backup and Recovery—Advanced V3R6*, section 4, for gory details.

  ✓ Be especially careful of ASPs used for making journals. They are most apt to overflow.

  ✓ If you incorporate user ASPs, establish thresholds, messaging (better yet, paging), and procedures to ensure that some action is taken quickly when an ASP becomes 90 percent or more full.

❖ User ASPs cause developers headaches in two areas.

  ✓ You cannot have dependent database files across ASPs. Therefore, all logical files that belong to a physical file must reside in the same ASP as the physical file.

  ✓ You cannot MOVOBJ or CRTDUPOBJ across ASPs.

❖ A disk drive on the AS/400 can actually have several storage devices within one physical unit. If you are creating an ASP to enhance recovery, include all the devices within each unit as part of the ASP.

3.4 THINGS THAT MAKE JOBS RUN

Once you have considered all the things you can do with memory and storage, there are still plenty of system settings that come together to make a functional AS/400 computer. It's helpful to know the default setting you can set for the AS/400. Also, it's nice to know what the AS/400 does to start a job.

3.4.1 Overview

The system is shipped with lots of defaults for all these pieces. Most of the defaults are unused, however, in the basic system configuration. Such a system only contains one subsystem (QBASE) and two memory pools (MACHINE and BASE). You can sign on to the AS/400 even with this minimum setup.

But you should at least configure the system beyond the base. Configuration can be done just using other default objects. For example, you have QINTER, QBATCH, and QCTL subsystems that you should set up. Within those subsystems, you should specify some memory pools to be shared.

While you're at it, though, be aware that for everything you have to build for the AS/400 comes with a default. Check the default objects as you go. Use them unless there is something horrible about them (in which case, you can just copy and change them). For example, for job descriptions every AS/400 comes with QDFTJOBD in library QGPL. Use it or copy, rename, and change it. To help you get a perspective of the pieces, the following section is an overview of the flow of batch and interactive jobs.

3.4.1.1 How the System Starts an Interactive Job

An interactive job is a real-time job performed at a workstation. The job's name is the same as the workstation name that the user signs onto. The interactive subsystem, through its workstation entries, does double duty.

* ❖ It projects the sign-on screen to the workstation.
* ❖ After the user signs on, it receives the sign-on screen and starts the job initiation.

When the user signs on, her or his authority is checked before the incoming screen gets to the subsystem. Assuming it passes authority, the job goes first to the subsystem's workstation entry. It already has a job name but not much else. The subsystem checks the workstation entry to see what job description to assign to the job. The workstation entry will specify one of three options for a job description:

❖ A job description—the system just goes out and gets it and assigns those job attributes to the job.

❖ *USRPRF—the system goes to the user profile that signed onto the terminal and gets its job description, and it assigns those job attributes to the job. For more information on user profiles, see chapter 5.

❖ *SBSD—the system goes to the subsystem it belongs to and gets its job description, and it assigns those job attributes to the job. See section 3.4.6, Subsystems.

The job description is important because one of the things it has is the routing data. The subsystem uses this to find a match in its set of routing entries. Generally, it will find a match because the last (or the only) routing entry contains an *ANY, which is the match for any unmatched jobs up to that point. The routing entry tells the subsystem what job class to use. The subsystem gets that class and retrieves run-time job attributes for the job. The routing entry also contains a program that should be started for the job. (NOTE: not the user, not the workstation, but the job is defined by the job description.) Usually the program is QSYS/QCMD. This brings up the AS/400 main menu. The user can start an application from there. When finished with the application, the user returns to the main menu to sign off. If there is a non-system program specified on the routing entry (which could be the main menu of an application) when the user finishes with that program or application, the user is automatically signed off.

Only when the user signs off does the job end. At that point, the workstation entry resumes displaying a sign-on screen on the display. To begin, you at least need:

❖ A workstation known to the system (probably courtesy of autoconfiguration).

❖ A valid user identification and password (see chapter 5).

Next, you need to build (or just use the defaults for) the following objects:

❖ A job description (default QGPL/QDFTJOBD will do).

❖ A job class (default classes have the same name as the default subsystems).

❖ A subsystem (probably called QINTER, another default).

After those objects are available, you need some "glue" to connect them:

❖ One or more workstation entries (WSE) in the subsystem. These connect the subsystem with a specific terminal and, when a user signs on, the job with a job description.

❖ One or more routing entries in the subsystem. When a match is found between the job description's routing data to one of these entries, the job is connected to a class and an initial program (usually QSYS/QCMP). A workstation entry with either the workstation's name or generic name will catch the workstation's name.

❖ A routing entry with *ANY for cmpval or a match of the data in the routing data in the job description. The routing entry should have:

✓ Reference to a job class or *SBSD.

✓ An initial program to call:

(Use QSYS/QCMP for a general AS/400 main menu.)

(Specify a program or application for users.)

Running commands or programs from your interactive display might make you feel like you are running many jobs. Nevertheless, you're only running programs within one job and that is your interactive job (or *session*).

3.4.1.2 *How the System Starts a Batch Job*

A batch job runs in the background; in other words, it doesn't tie up a workstation. Batch jobs are started in one of three ways:

❖ A user or program issues the SBMJOB (SUBMIT JOB) command.

❖ A subsystem is started and it starts one or more autostart jobs.

❖ A subsystem is started and it starts one or more preliminary or so-called prestart jobs.

Autostart and prestart jobs are jobs that have been added to the subsystem description with the ADD AUTOSTART JOB ENTRY (ADDAJE) or ADD PRESTARTED JOB ENTRY (ADDPJE) commands. Prestarted jobs basically start right away within the subsystem, but they take no resources until they are activated. For more information, see chapter 10 in the *AS/400 Work Management Guide*.

Autostart jobs and jobs submitted (with SBMJOB) go into a job queue before entering a subsystem to run. They might have to wait for other jobs to complete before they can enter the subsystem or they can fall right through, but they have to enter a job queue before they can enter a subsystem.

When a batch job enters the subsystem, it has a name (the name specified by the user or program within the SBMJOB command or the autostart job itself) and a job description. The job description can have routing data and that can be used to match on a routing entry to determine the job class and initial program that the subsystem will start.

This initial program can be confusing because most of the time it is simply QSYS/QCMD, and the SBMJOB contains the name of the program you want to start. QSYS/QCMD is a shell that executes AS/400 CL commands. Generally, programs are invoked with the CALL command, and QCMD just interprets the CALL <program name> and goes from there.

To run a batch job, you need:

❖ A valid user or executing program or autostart job.

❖ A SBMJOB command.

Presuming you have the preceding two items, you will need to build or use the defaulted objects for:

❖ A job description (or the default QDFTJOBD).

❖ A job queue (default job queues supplied with same names as default subsystems they serve).

❖ A subsystem (probably called QBATCH, another default).

After those objects are available, you need some "glue" to connect them.

❖ One or more routing entries in the subsystem. When a match is found between the job description's routing data to one of these entries, the job is connected to a class and an initial program (usually QSYS/QCMP).

❖ One or more uses of the ADDJOBQE (ADD JOB QUEUE ENTRY) command to connect one or more job queues to the subsystem.

❖ Aditionally, your subsystem should have enough memory to run an active subsystem with:

    ✓ One routing entry with a CMPVAL of:

        ➤ *any

        ➤ A match with the routing data from the job description.

        ➤ A match with the routing data from the sbmjob command.

        ➤ Enough memory to run the job.

3.4.1.3 All Together Now

It should be obvious that you have to have six things for any AS/400:

❖ Devices (done by autoconfiguration).

❖ Job descriptions.

❖ Job classes.

❖ Job queues.

❖ Subsystems with:

    ✓ Routing entry(s).

    ✓ Job queue entries. For batch subsystems only.

    ✓ Workstation entry(s). For interactive subsystems only.

    ✓ Storage pools.

❖ A valid user ID or password (see chapter 5).

After you read what each item is and what it does for you, you might want to refer to appendix C of the *OS/400 Work Management V3R6* for a list of these defaulted items and the IBM-supplied generic objects you can use.

3.4.2 Devices

All devices on an AS/400 need to be made known to it. This is done through *device configuration*. Here is a partial list:

- ❖ Workstations.

- ❖ Printers.

- ❖ Diskette.

- ❖ Controllers:

  - ✓ Drives.
  - ✓ Tapes.
  - ✓ Controllers.
  - ✓ Drives.

- ❖ Communications devices:

  - ✓ Lines.
  - ✓ Controllers.

3.4.2.1 Automatic Configuration

Let's get right to the nitty-gritty of AS/400 device configuration. You don't have to do anything if you switch on the automatic configuration when you first start up your AS/400. When your AS/400 comes up from the IPL the first time, you'll see a SET MAJOR OPTIONS display. The default for ENABLE AUTOMATIC CONFIGURATION is YES. Therefore, you don't have to do anything if you want it on. See section 1.3.2, Set Minor System Options.

With automatic configuration to add things like workstations, all you have to do is attach them and turn them on. The AS/400 configures a new device as soon as it senses its presence. If you don't use automatic configuration, you'll have to calculate a name for a device, describe it, then re-IPL before the system will recognize it.

When you enable automatic configuration, you'll be asked to choose among three naming schemes. Choose NORMAL NAMING because it's the most straightforward method. If you're coming from a System/36 shop and prefer its names, choose SYSTEM/36 STYLE.

3.4.3 Job Descriptions

Job descriptions define some of the non-run-time attributes of jobs. All jobs have a job description even if they use the default, QDFTJOBD. The primary elements of a job description are:

❖ Job description name.

❖ Starting information:

    ✓ Job queue in which the job will be placed (for batch jobs).

    ✓ Priority of the job while it is on the job queue (but not its run priority).

    ✓ Status on job queue (it can be on HOLD, in which case it won't run until it is released).

❖ Output information.

    ✓ Output queue.

    ✓ Print device.

    ✓ Output queue priority.

❖ Routing data.

❖ Accounting code.

❖ Message logging level. Whether to log lots of stuff to the job log or a little (see chapter 4).

The job description contains a few other similar things. Just keep in mind that you can make use of the system default values. Figure 3-8, Figure 3-9, and Figure 3-10 show how to create one of your own with the CREATE JOB DESCRIPTION (CRTJOBD) command.

```
                    Create Job Description (CRTJOBD)

  Type choices, press Enter.

  Job description  . . . . . . . .               Name
    Library  . . . . . . . . . .     *CURLIB     Name, *CURLIB
  Job queue  . . . . . . . . . .    QBATCH       Name
    Library  . . . . . . . . . .     *LIBL       Name, *LIBL, *CURLIB
  Job priority (on JOBQ) . . . . .   5           1-9
  Output priority (on OUTQ)  . . .   5           1-9
  Print device . . . . . . . . .    *USRPRF      Name, *USRPRF, *SYSVAL...
  Output queue . . . . . . . . .    *USRPRF      Name, *USRPRF, *DEV, *WRKSTN
    Library  . . . . . . . . . .               Name, *LIBL, *CURLIB
  Text 'description' . . . . . . .  *BLANK


                      Additional Parameters

  User . . . . . . . . . . . . .    *RQD         Name, *RQD
  Print text . . . . . . . . . .    *SYSVAL
                                                                   More...
  F3=Exit   F4=Prompt   F5=Refresh   F12=Cancel   F13=How to use this display
  F24=More keys
```

Figure 3-8: Screen 1 of the CRTJOBD command.

```
                    Create Job Description (CRTJOBD)

  Type choices, press Enter.

  Accounting code  . . . . . . .    *USRPRF
  Routing data . . . . . . . . .    QCMDI

  Request data or command  . . . .  *NONE


  CL syntax check  . . . . . . .    *NOCHK       0-99, *NOCHK
  Initial library list . . . . .    *SYSVAL      Name, *SYSVAL, *NONE
           + for more values
  End severity . . . . . . . . .    30           0-99
  Message logging:
    Level  . . . . . . . . . . .    4            0-4
    Severity . . . . . . . . . .    0            0-99
    Text . . . . . . . . . . . .    *NOLIST      *NOLIST, *MSG, *SECLVL
  Log CL program commands  . . . .  *NO          *NO, *YES
                                                                   More...
  F3=Exit   F4=Prompt   F5=Refresh   F12=Cancel   F13=How to use this display
  F24=More keys
```

Figure 3-9: Screen 2 of the CRTJOBD command.

```
┌─────────────────────────────────────────────────────────────────────┐
│                  Create Job Description (CRTJOBD)                     │
│                                                                       │
│ Type choices, press Enter.                                            │
│                                                                       │
│ Inquiry message reply  . . . . .    *RQD        *RQD, *DFT, *SYSRPYL  │
│ Hold on job queue  . . . . . . .    *NO         *NO, *YES             │
│ Job date . . . . . . . . . . . .    *SYSVAL     Date, *SYSVAL         │
│ Job switches . . . . . . . . . .    00000000    Character value      │
│ Device recovery action . . . . .    *SYSVAL                          │
│ Time slice end pool  . . . . . .    *SYSVAL     *SYSVAL, *NONE, *BASE │
│ Authority  . . . . . . . . . . .    *LIBCRTAUT  Name, *LIBCRTAUT, *CHANGE... │
│                                                                       │
│                                                                       │
│                                                                       │
│                                                                       │
│                                                              Bottom   │
│ F3=Exit    F4=Prompt    F5=Refresh    F12=Cancel   F13=How to use this display │
│ F24=More keys                                                         │
└─────────────────────────────────────────────────────────────────────┘
```

Figure 3-10: Screen 3 of the CRTJOBD *command.*

Sure there is a lot of stuff but all you really have to put in is the job name. You can change anything later with the WRKJOBD command. Figure 3-11 shows a sample of it.

```
┌─────────────────────────────────────────────────────────────────────┐
│                      Work with Job Descriptions                       │
│                                                                       │
│ Type options, press Enter.                                            │
│   1=Create   2=Change   3=Copy   4=Delete   5=Display                 │
│                                                                       │
│         Job                                                           │
│ Opt  Description  Library    Text                                     │
│                                                                       │
│  _   QICJOBQ      QGPL       Info Center Job Description               │
│  _   QINTER       QGPL       Interactive Subsystem Job Description     │
│  _   QMONTHLY     QGPL       Monthly JobD for Robot Jobs               │
│  _   QNFTP        QGPL       Transaction Program JOBD                  │
│  _   QNIGHT       QGPL       Batch Subsystem Job Description           │
│  _   QPFRCOL      QGPL       Performance Collection Job Description     │
│  _   QPFRMON      QGPL       Performance Monitor Job Description        │
│  _   QPGMR        QGPL       Programmer Job Description                 │
│  _   QPRIORITY    QGPL       Priority Job Description                   │
│  _   QPTY40       QGPL       Batch RUNPTY 40 - Backups                  │
│                                                              More...   │
│ Parameters for options 1, 2, 3 and 5 or command                      │
│ ===>                                                                  │
│ F3=Exit       F4=Prompt    F5=Refresh    F9=Retrieve   F11=Display names only │
│ F12=Cancel    F16=Repeat position to   F17=Position to   F24=More keys │
└─────────────────────────────────────────────────────────────────────┘
```

Figure 3-11: The WRKJOBD *command.*

The command displays one or more job descriptions. You pick the one you want to change and put a 2 to the left of it, press F4, and you can change any of its parameters.

The AS/400 comes with several job descriptions made for you. They are listed in appendix C of *OS/400 Work Management V3R6*.

3.4.4 Job Classes

A *job class* is another way (in addition to the job description) of giving jobs attributes. Where job descriptions supply jobs with non-run-time attributes, job classes give jobs their run-time attributes. A class contains three primary elements:

❖ Run-time priority is a third priority that is completely different from job queue and output queue priorities. This is the priority the job will have when it is active in the subsystem.

❖ Time slice in milliseconds is how long the CPU can work on this job before going onto another one.

❖ Eligible for purge. Always leave this at the default *YES. If the system needs to purge a job, it will regardless of this value. The difference is that if this parameters is *YES, the system will purge it and later restore it cleanly. When this parameter is *NO, the system will hack it to pieces when it purges it and have to work harder finding and reassembling those pieces.

The command to create a job class is CRTCLS. See Figure 3-12.

```
                          Create Class (CRTCLS)

 Type choices, press Enter.

 Class  . . . . . . . . . . . .   _____    Name
   Library  . . . . . . . . . .   *CURLIB       Name, *CURLIB
 Run priority . . . . . . . . .   50            1-99
 Time slice . . . . . . . . . .   2000          Milliseconds
 Eligible for purge . . . . . .   *YES          *YES, *NO
 Default wait time  . . . . . .   30            Seconds, *NOMAX
 Maximum CPU time . . . . . . .   *NOMAX        Milliseconds, *NOMAX
 Maximum temporary storage  . . . *NOMAX        Kilobytes, *NOMAX
 Text 'description' . . . . . . . *BLANK



                                                                   Bottom
 F3=Exit    F4=Prompt    F5=Refresh    F10=Additional parameters    F12=Cancel
 F13=How to use this display        F24=More keys
```

Figure 3-12: Prompted version of CRTCLS.

IBM has filled in some fairly decent default values (enough to make the class work). Before you start creating your own classes, however, you might want to try the IBM-supplied ones. They are listed in either *OS/400 Work Management V3R6* or the *AS/400 Programming Reference Summary*.

3.4.5 Job Queues (Batch Jobs Only)

Before a job becomes active in a batch subsystem, it must pass through a job queue. A *job queue* is simply a holding place for jobs entering the system. Sometimes a queue is empty and a job falls right through into the subsystem where it starts running. Other times a queue will be quite full of pending jobs and a new job entering will take its place in the queue.

Each job has a job queue priority assignment that comes from its job description. Jobs in the queue will be released to the subsystem in ascending order of these priorities. If all jobs have equal priority, they will be released in first-in-first-out order.

You can manipulate jobs on a queue. If you had five jobs on a queue and a sixth one entered, the sixth one won't start until the other five have started (and the subsystem is ready to accept another job). That is assuming all jobs on the queue have equal priority. If the sixth job is very important, you could change the sixth job's priority to a number lower than any of the other five jobs to get it to start sooner. Or you could hold all five jobs to ensure the sixth starts sooner.

To manipulate jobs on a queue, however, you must have special authority *JOBCTL (JOB CONTROL) on your user ID. For more on user IDs see chapter 5.

You create a job queue with the CREATE JOB QUEUE (CRTJOBQ) command. Figure 3-13 shows its format.

```
                  Create Subsystem Description (CRTSBSD)

 Type choices, press Enter.

 Subsystem description  . . . . .  _____   Name
   Library  . . . . . . . . . .    *CURLIB       Name, *CURLIB
 Storage pools:
   Pool identifier  . . . . . .    _____       1-10
   Storage size . . . . . . . .    _____       Number, *BASE, *NOSTG...
   Activity level . . . . . . .    _____       Number
              + for more values _
 Maximum jobs . . . . . . . . .    *NOMAX        0-1000, *NOMAX
 Text 'description' . . . . . .    *BLANK



                      Additional Parameters

 Sign-on display file . . . . .    *QDSIGNON     Name, *QDSIGNON
   Library  . . . . . . . . . .    _____    Name, *LIBL, *CURLIB
 Subsystem library  . . . . . .    *NONE         Name, *NONE
                                                                   More...
 F3=Exit   F4=Prompt   F5=Refresh   F12=Cancel   F13=How to use this display
 F24=More keys
```

Figure 3-13: Prompted version of the CRTJOBQ *command.*

All you really have to put in is the job queue name and its library; that is all most AS/400 customers actually do. There are some authority things at the bottom. You can read more about them in the *AS/400 CL Reference*. Their default values are adequate for most installations. Assign job queues to batch subsystems with the ADDJOBQE (ADD JOB QUEUE ENTRY) command. Its basic format is simple:

ADDJOBQE <library>/<batch subsystem><library>/<job queue name>

Prompt it by pressing the F4 key and you will get more parameters you can set.

As an aid to getting started, the AS/400 comes with several job queues for you to use or modify as you wish. They are listed in *OS/400 Data Management V3R6, OS/400 Work Management V3R6,* and *AS/400 Programming Reference Summary.*

3.4.6 Subsystems

I've been referring to subsystems, and it's time I explained something about them because they are essential to successful AS/400 installations. Subsystems are environments where jobs run. The best part is they are environments the customer defines. Therefore, you get to create the optimum environment in which to run your batch jobs and the optimum environment in which to run your interactive jobs. You can even have an optimum environment for one department's users and another subsystem for another department's.

AS/400 jobs only run in subsystems. You create a subsystem by creating its description. In other words, the command is CREATE SUBSYSTEM DESCRIPTION (CRTSBSD). See Figure 3-14.

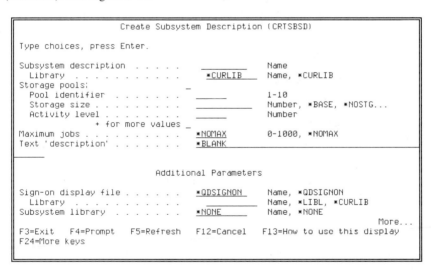

Figure 3-14: Prompted CRTSBSD command.

You don't have to do much more than just put in the subsystem name and library. Nevertheless, you should at least specify the memory storage pools. Section 3.2, Memory: Storage Pools and Activity Levels, introduces the topic, but there is more to it that I'll cover here.

I've already discussed how a subsystem can have up to 10 memory pools in which to run its jobs. What I didn't discuss is that the first pool, whatever it is, also has the subsystem driver running. You really don't want that activity in a private or general shared pool. You do want it in *BASE for any subsystem. So here is a rule: Any subsystem's number 1 pool is *BASE (referred to its system name, 2).

The next parameter, MAXIMUM JOBS, is the maximum number of jobs that the subsystem will allow to be active at any one time. Remember, jobs come into the subsystem from one or more job queues. It wouldn't be very efficient if you could just flood a subsystem. Therefore, this value sets a limit on the number of jobs that can be in the subsystem at any one time. This value is crucial. How many jobs you allow in also helps determine how much memory the subsystem should have assigned to it. Subsystem maximum jobs are discussed in section 3.2, Memory: Storage Pools and Activity Levels. Don't confuse it with storage-pool activity levels.

The MAXIMUM JOBS on the subsystem description specify how many jobs are in the subsystem at one time. The activity level specifies how many of those jobs the subsystem will actually be working on at one time. The big difference between the two is this:

- ❖ Maximum Jobs:
  - ✓ Set too low and job queues back up.
  - ✓ Set too high and throughput goes down.
- ❖ Activity Level:
  - ✓ Very little impact on the casual observer because jobs frequently change states.
  - ✓ High impact on overall throughput of the subsystem. Even if MAXIMUM JOBS are set too high, if activity levels are set correctly, throughput will be good.

You can use one of the defaulted subsystems that come with the system or you can create your own. Subsystem descriptions are created with the CRTSBSD command, and they are changed with the CHGSBSD command. But that is only the descriptions; subsystem do not become active until you start them. The command for that is STRSBS. See Figure 3-15.

```
                      Start Subsystem (STRSBS)

Type choices, press Enter.

Subsystem description  . . . . .                       Name
   Library  . . . . . . . . . . .     *LIBL            Name, *LIBL, *CURLIB




                                                                  Bottom
F3=Exit   F4=Prompt   F5=Refresh   F12=Cancel   F13=How to use this display
F24=More keys
```

Figure 3-15: Prompted STRSBS command.

The only parameter that you have to specify is the subsystem to start. When you bring up the AS/400 from an IPL, you need to have a program start all your subsystems or you need to start them yourself.

When you are done with a subsystem, you end it with the ENDSBS command. See Figure 3-16.

```
                       End Subsystem (ENDSBS)

Type choices, press Enter.

Subsystem  . . . . . . . . . . .                       Name, *ALL
How to end . . . . . . . . . . .     *CNTRLD           *CNTRLD, *IMMED
Delay time, if *CNTRLD . . . . .     *NOLIMIT          Seconds, *NOLIMIT





                                                                  Bottom
F3=Exit   F4=Prompt   F5=Refresh   F12=Cancel   F13=How to use this display
F24=More keys
```

Figure 3-16: Prompted ENDSBS command.

You need to specify either a subsystem or the general *ALL. The second parameter, HOW TO END, will accept either *CNTRLD or *IMMED. *CNTRLD is for a controlled shutdown. It will have the system properly close any active jobs before it ends. The *IMMED is for an immediate end to the subsystem. You might think *CNTRLD is the way to close a job, but in real life *CNTRLD can take a long time.

Most customers end a subsystem by checking it first for active jobs with the WRKACTJOB. If you find interactive jobs, you can call the users (or send a break message) and ask them to sign off. If you find batch jobs, you can terminate them if possible or call the users or programmers responsible and get them to terminate. Regardless, end all jobs in a subsystem manually, and then do an ENDSBS with the *IMMED option.

The AS/400 comes with several default subsystem descriptions that you can use. They are listed in the *OS/400 Work Management V3R6* or *AS/ Programming Reference Summary*.

3.4.6.1 Routing Entries

When a subsystem finally gets a job to start, it knows its name and some of its attributes (from the job description), but it doesn't know where to start. What job class (the run-time attributes) should the job have? What's the first program it needs to run? Determining these is called *routing the job*.

There are no routing objects on the system that you can directly create or change. You add routing entries to an already created subsystem description with the ADDRTGE command. You do further maintenance on them with the CHGRTGE and RMVRTGE commands.

You control a job's *routing* indirectly, through the these routing entries, and the routing-data parameter on the JOB DESCRIPTION (see section 3.4.3, Job Descriptions).

The system attempts to make a match between literals held in the routing data to those in the routing entries.. Theoretically, a job has a description that contains a code or statement or something in its routing data. The subsystem also has a list of routing entries. Each entry has a corresponding code or statement that the system uses to match to the job's routing data. When there is a match, the routing entry tells the system what class to make the job and what initial program to call for the job.

```
                        Display Job Description
                                            System:   SYS02
   Job description:   QINTER        Library:   QGPL

   Message logging:
     Level   . . . . . . . . . . . . . . . . . . . :   4
     Severity . . . . . . . . . . . . . . . . . . :   0
     Text . . . . . . . . . . . . . . . . . . . . :   *NOLIST
   Log CL program commands . . . . . . . . . . . :   *NO
   Accounting code  . . . . . . . . . . . . . . . :   *USRPRF
   Print text . . . . . . . . . . . . . . . . . . :   *SYSVAL

   Routing data . . . . . . . . . . . . . . . . . :   QCMDI
```

Figure 3-17: A sample of the routing data for a job description.

Figure 3-17 contains a sample of the routing data for a job description.
Figure 3-18 shows a sample of some routing entries from a subsystem.

```
                        Display Routing Entries
                                            System:   SYS01
   Subsystem description:   QINTER01      Status:   ACTIVE

   Type options, press Enter.
     5=Display details

                                                      Start
   Opt    Seq Nbr   Program     Library     Compare Value    Pos
             10     QCMD        QSYS        'QCMDI'           1
    _        20     QCMD        QSYS        'QS36MRT'         1
    _        22     QCMD        QSYS        'QRPTY25I'        1
    _        24     QCMD        QSYS        'QRPTY30I'        1
    _        26     QCMD        QSYS        'QRPTY35I'        1
    _        40     QARDRIVE    QSYS        '525XTEST'        1
    _       700     QCL         QSYS        'QCMD38'          1
    _      9999     QCMD        QSYS        *ANY

                                                      Bottom
   F3=Exit   F9=Display all detailed descriptions   F12=Cancel
```

Figure 3-18: Routing entries in the subsystem description.

Notice that the value to match is specified on the column under COMPARE VALUE
(CMPVAL). To the right of that is the compare position of 1. You can compare
different starting positions of the routing data. If a match is found, in most cases,
the initial program the subsystem will call will be QSYS/QCMD. This is an
AS/400 command processor program (CPP) that is able to execute commands.
Generally, it is named as a routing entry's initial program.

For more information about a routing entry, put a 5 on the option line and press
the Enter key. See Figure 3-19.

```
                       Display Routing Entry Detail
                                                     System:    SYS01
  Subsystem description:    QINTER01       Status:    ACTIVE

  Routing entry sequence number . . . . . . . :     26
  Program . . . . . . . . . . . . . . . . . :     QCMD
    Library . . . . . . . . . . . . . . . . :       QSYS
  Class . . . . . . . . . . . . . . . . . . :     QRPTY35I
    Library . . . . . . . . . . . . . . . . :       QGPL
  Maximum active routing steps  . . . . . . :     *NOMAX
  Pool identifier . . . . . . . . . . . . . :     2
  Compare value . . . . . . . . . . . . . . :     'QRPTY35I'

  Compare start position  . . . . . . . . . :     1




  Press Enter to continue.

  F3=Exit    F12=Cancel    F14=Display previous entry
```

Figure 3-19: Expanded routing entries in the subsystem description.

Note the use of this routing entry (a clue to which is provided on the routing data) QPTY35. Any job with this routing data would get run-time attributes from class QPTY35, which is a modified version of job class QINTER. The only difference is that the run-time priority is 35 (not 20). It is for low-priority interactive jobs.

Actually, using multiple routing entries and job classes like this is a fairly advanced procedure. If you're new to the AS/400, you can get by not specifying routing data information on any job description and by always specifying a single routing entry on subsystem descriptions with a compare value of *ANY. No check is made because the specification considers any job to be a match.

3.4.6.2 *Workstation Entries (Interactive Jobs Only)*

AS/400 workstations are devices. Workstations entries (WSE) are listed with the subsystem description and are similar to routing entries. They can contain the name of each display on the system and a job description to use when a user attempts to sign on from that display.

If you're using the system's autoconfiguration, it will have named your display station devices something like DSP01, DSP02, DSP03, and so on. You can identify every display station in your shop to the interactive subsystem by leaving those names and specifying one workstation entry with the generic name: D*.

Most AS/400 shops just use the generic name and have one line that serves as a WSE for every display on the system. The WSE can be used to associate a job description with each terminal. The WSE's main jobs are:

❖ Associate valid workstations that the interactive subsystem will support.

❖ Associate a job description with a user signing on. This is either done by specifying on the WSE:

✓ A job description.

✓ *USRPRF, which tells the subsystem to go to the user profile of the signing-on user and get the job description.

✓ *SBSD, which tells the subsystem to look at the job description specified on its description.

3.4.7 Output Queues

Any job on the AS/400 that produces printed output must put that output into an output queue. This printed output on the queue is called a *spooled output file*. A printer (called a *writer* on the AS/400) must be connected with an output queue before it can print anything.

Create an output queue with the CRTOUTQ command. See Figure 3-20.

```
                         Create Output Queue (CRTOUTQ)

 Type choices, press Enter.

 Output queue . . . . . . . . . .   _____   Name
   Library  . . . . . . . . . . .   *CURLIB      Name, *CURLIB
 Order of files on queue  . . . .   *FIFO        *FIFO, *JOBNBR
 Text 'description' . . . . . . .   *BLANK




                                                                     Bottom
 F3=Exit    F4=Prompt    F5=Refresh    F10=Additional parameters   F12=Cancel
 F13=How to use this display         F24=More keys
```

Figure 3-20: Prompted CRTOUTQ command.

This is one of those simple commands. Just supply the output queue name and the rest of the defaults are fine. Change any of those parameters with the CHGOUTQ command.

3.5 NEW SYSTEMS—WHERE TO NOW?

By now, you know the building blocks that make up job control and job environments on the AS/400. You also have a pretty good idea of interactive and batch-job flow.

The AS/400 comes with two subsystems up and running: QBASE and QCTL. As a minimum, you should also configure and start the following subsystems that are generic to the AS/400:

❖ QCMN to handle communication jobs. If your network is LAN-based, your terminals will come in through this subsystem before being handed off to QINTER.

❖ QINTER subsystem for interactive jobs.

❖ QBATCH subsystem for batch jobs.

❖ QSPL subsystem for printing jobs.

Review these subsystems. Also, review the generic job descriptions, classes, queues, and so on that came with your machine. Add some memory and routing information to the subsystems. Add a WSE entry to the QINTER subsystem. Then start the subsystems.

As you configure user profiles and allow your users online, the jobs they run will be pretty much where you want them. Later, as you get used to the AS/400, you'll make changes to most of this. You'll even be cloning new subsystems from the AS/400 supplied ones. For now, just build this basic configuration.

3.6 BIBLIOGRAPHY

OS/400 Backup and Recovery—Advanced V3R6

OS/400 Data Management V3R6

OS/400 System Operations for New Users

OS/400 Work Management V3R6

Getting Started with AS/400 V3R6

AS/400 System Startup and Problem Handling V3R6

AS/400 Programming Reference Summary

4. Logs, Messages, and Cleanup

4.1 OVERVIEW

The AS/400 keeps four types of logs for you. Some are automatic—they are just there for you to use—but with others you have to do something to start them. Logs record information about events as they happen. The four logs and a brief description of how automatic they are and where they are kept include:

- ❖ History (QHST):
  - ✓ Automatic.
  - ✓ Is kept in a physical file.
- ❖ Job:
  - ✓ Automatic, but you can change what is logged.
  - ✓ Is kept within active jobs or in spooled output files for completed jobs.
- ❖ Job accounting:
  - ✓ Not automatic; requires that you start it.
  - ✓ Is kept in a journal:
- ❖ Security audit:
  - ✓ Not automatic; requires that you start it.
  - ✓ Is kept in a journal.

Much of the data in logs are actually captured messages. The AS/400 uses messages quite extensively both internally and externally. Messages notify the user or the system operator that something is happening. But messages also start and stop tasks within the AS/400.

Logs and messages are nice but they quickly take up lots of DASD space. If you ask it to, the AS/400 automatically will organize messages with a utility called cleanup.

4.2 History Logs (QHST)

❖ Automatic.

❖ Are kept in a physical file.

Everything that the AS/400 does results in a message going somewhere around the system. In addition to their intended destinations, one place all high-level messages (system activities, job information, device status, operator messages, and more) go to is a history message queue (see section 4.6, Messages). A program receives those messages and writes them to a physical file called the history log. This history log is named QHSTyyjjjn where:

❖ *yy* is the year on which the physical file was created.

❖ *jjj* is the Julian date on which the physical file was created.

❖ *n* is a sequence number (0-9, A-Z).

The maximum number of records in this physical file is set in system value QHSTLOGSIZ. You can find out what history logs are currently on your system with the command:

```
WRKOBJ QSYS/QHST* *FILE
```

You can display current history log information with command DSPLOG. You can specify that you only want messages issued during a specific time period, by a specific job, or certain message IDs. Figures 4-1 and 4-2 show the prompted version of the command DSPLOG.

```
                        Display Log (DSPLOG)

 Type choices, press Enter.

 Log . . . . . . . . . . . . . . . > QHST          QHST
 Time period for log output:
   Start time and date:
   Beginning time . . . . . . . .   *AVAIL         Time, *AVAIL
   Beginning date . . . . . . . .   *CURRENT       Date, *CURRENT, *BEGIN
   End time and date:
   Ending time . . . . . . . . .    *AVAIL         Time, *AVAIL
   Ending date  . . . . . . . . .   *CURRENT       Date, *CURRENT, *END
 Output . . . . . . . . . . . . .   *              *, *PRINT




                                                                     More...
 F3=Exit   F4=Prompt   F5=Refresh   F12=Cancel   F13=How to use this display
 F24=More keys
```

Figure 4-1: Prompted version of command DSPLOG (Screen 1).

```
                        Display Log (DSPLOG)

 Type choices, press Enter.

                        Additional Parameters

 Jobs to display  . . . . . . . .   *NONE          Name, *NONE
   User . . . . . . . . . . . . .   _____     Name
   Number . . . . . . . . . . . .   _____         000000-999999
              + for more values     _____
                                    _____
 Message identifier . . . . . . .   *ALL           Name, *ALL
              + for more values     _____




                                                                     Bottom
 F3=Exit   F4=Prompt   F5=Refresh   F12=Cancel   F13=How to use this display
 F24=More keys
```

Figure 4-2: Prompted version of command DSPLOG (Screen 2).

```
                    Display History Log Contents

9 objects saved from library QUSRBRM.
Vary off completed for device TAP03.
Controller GE90S01 contacted on line TOKENRING2.
Job 195949/OPC/DAILYBKU ended on 09/13/96 at 01:08:17; 488 seconds used; end
Job 195984/QPGMR/QBRMSYNC started on 09/13/96 at 01:08:27 in subsystem Q1ABRM
Unit of work identifier APPN.SYS01-AD76201FFD90-0001 assigned to job 195984/Q
Job 195984/QPGMR/QBRMSYNC ended on 09/13/96 at 01:08:30; 1 seconds used; end
Job 195985/QUSER/XTRA0202 started on 09/13/96 at 01:08:43 in subsystem QCMN03
Unit of work identifier APPN.SYS02-AD76204AFB33-0001 assigned to job 195985/Q
Job 195985/QUSER/XTRA0202 ended on 09/13/96 at 01:08:44; 1 seconds used; end
Job 195983/QUSER/XTRA0202 ended on 09/13/96 at 01:09:48; 46 seconds used; end
Controller GE90S01 contacted on line TOKENRING2.
Bulk or convenience output stations are full in MLD MLD01.
MLD MLD01 requires operator intervention.
Controller GE90S01 contacted on line TOKENRING2.
Cleanup of job logs and other system output successfully completed.
Job 195977/QPGMR/QCLNSYSPRT ended on 09/13/96 at 01:14:57; 98 seconds used;
                                                                    More...
Press Enter to continue.

F3=Exit   F10=Display all   F12=Cancel
```

Figure 4-3: Results of command DSPLOG.

Figure 4-3 shows a sample of a screen of history log data. It might look like there isn't much there. However, if you put the cursor over any line and press the Help key, you'll get more information. Figure 4-4 shows an example of expanding one of the lines from Figure 4-3.

```
                    Additional Message Information

Message ID . . . . . . :   CPI9803      Severity . . . . . . . :   00
Message type . . . . . :   Information
Date sent  . . . . . . :   09/13/96     Time sent  . . . . . . :   01:08:28

Message . . . . :   Unit of work identifier APPN.SYS01-AD76201FFD90-0001
  assigned to job 195984/QPGMR/QBRMSYNC.
Cause . . . . . :   An advanced program-to-program communications (APPC) job
  has been started. The unit of work identifier may be used to associate the
  APPC job with the job on the remote system.
Technical description . . . . . . . . :   If this is a source program, the
  unit of work identifier was generated by the system. If this is a target
  program, the unit of work identifier was received on the program start
  request.



                                                                    Bottom
Press Enter to continue.

F3=Exit   F6=Print   F11=Display message details   F12=Cancel
F21=Select assistance level
```

Figure 4-4: Expansion of the line marked on Figure 4-3 with cursor.

You can programmatically read this log. *OS/400 Work Management V3R6* provides a sample of program and record layouts.

History logs can take up quite a bit of system space. You could opt to have the system automatically clean them up for you (see section 4.7, System Cleanup). That's probably the most convenient method. Also, any time you're going to do a SAVSYS, particularly prior to installing a new release of the operating system (OS), you could save yourself some time by deleting the history files before you start. For additional information on operating systems, see chapter 2.

4.3 JOB LOGS

❖ Automatic, but you can change what is logged.

❖ Are kept:

   ✓ Within active jobs.

   ✓ In spooled output files for completed jobs.

Every job that runs on the AS/400 collects messages in an internal log while it is running. AS/400 customers don't normally think of the job log as part of a running job. When the job finishes, the contents of the job log are written to a spooled-output file in queue QPJOBLOG or QEZJOBLOG.

You can limit the types of messages that any job logs. You can even turn off job logs if you want. However, when a job terminates abnormally, you get a job log anyway. It's somewhat risky turning off job logs altogether because it's the only audit of what happened within the job. Many jobs terminate normally, but—if you happen to encounter a problem—your only source for what went wrong could be the job log.

Job logs come down to this: Most of the time you don't need them and they take up valuable DASD space. The temptation is to not collect them. But the one time a crucial program fails, the only audit of what happened will probably be the job log. Job logs are a pain but when you need them, you really need them. Your task is to balance DASD space against the need for an audit trail.

4.3.1 Logging Level

You specify what messages you want collected for any job through the logging level. The parameter for this is LOG and it is on both the JOB DESCRIPTION and on the SBMJOB command. You can also change this parameter on an active job with the CHGJOB commands. Or you can change it on a job description with the CHGJOBD or WRKJOBD commands. There are three parts to the LOG parameter. Figure 4-5 shows a representation of it.

```
Message logging:
  Level  . . . . . . . . . . .    4        0-4, *JOBD
  Severity . . . . . . . . . .    0        0-99, *JOBD
  Text . . . . . . . . . . . .   *MSG      *JOBD, *MSG, *SECLUL, *NOLIST
```

Figure 4-5: Sample LOG parameter.

❖ Level accepts a numeric code from 0 to 4.

✓ 0 Nothing is logged.

✓ 1 Only messages sent to the job's external message queue and that have a severity greater than or equal to that specified under Severity (discussed below). Examples are job start/stop time and its completion status.

✓ 2 Level 1 messages plus.

Any requests/command from a CL program that have a severity greater than or equal to that specified under Severity (discussed below). All messages associated with those requests/commands as long as the messages have a severity greater than or equal to that specified under Severity (discussed below).

✓ 3 Level 1 messages plus.

Level 2 messages plus.
All requests/commands being from a CL program.
All messages associated with those requests/commands as long as the messages have a severity greater than or equal to that specified under Severity (discussed below).

✓ 4   Level 1 messages plus.

Level 2 messages plus.
Level 3 messages plus.
Any message that has a severity greater than or equal to that specified under Severity.

❖ Severity specifies the severity level of the requests/commands/ messages logged. On the AS/400, message have *severities* that range from 00 to 99. The 00 messages are informational only. The 99 messages tend to be the last message before a program abnormally terminates. Most serious job messages are level 30 or higher.

❖ *Text* is the amount of message text to be written to the job log. All messages on the AS/400 have two levels.

     ✓   Level 1 is the short, 80-bytes-or-less version.

     ✓   Level 2 is the long version for those new to the system or the particular message. This is sometimes referred to as the *second level message*.

The possible values for TEXT are:

❖ *MSG—Only the level 1 text of the message is written to the log.

❖ *SECLVL—Level 2 or Second Level messages are written to the log.

❖ *NOLIST—No messages are logged unless the program ends abnormally.

Most AS/400 shops specify a 4 for level and 0 for severity. After that, *NOLIST is fairly standard for stable, established shops and *MSG is used for others or for new applications. For AS/400-supplied job description objects, QCTL, QINTER, QBATCH, and QPGMR come with LOG(4 0 *NOLIST). You can create your own or change these with the CHGJOBD command.

There is one trap about message logging for interactive jobs. An interactive job ends only when the user signs off with the SIGNOFF command. A parameter on that command, LOG, can have a default of *NOLIST that allows no logging to occur no matter to what level your job-description logging level is set.

If you want logging to occur, you need to set the command's default to LOG(*LIST). Do so with the following command:

```
CHGCMDDFT SIGNOFF NEWDFT('LOG(*LIST)')
```

4.3.2 Displaying the Job Log

From time to time, you will want to look at the job log. The log can be a part of a running job or on the spool file for a completed job. To display the job log from:

❖ Current interactive job do any of the following:

✓ Type DSPJOBLOG on command line and press Enter, followed by F10.

✓ Type WRKJOB on command line and take option 10, press F10.

✓ Press F10.

✓ If a job is still active on the system, do either:

➤ WRKUSRJOB (you have to know who the user is) or,

➤ WRKACTJOB. Find the job and select option 5 (WORK WITH JOB), then select option 10 (DISPLAY JOB LOG).

✓ Press System Request key, option 3 (DISPLAY CURRENT JOB). Take option 10 (DISPLAY JOB LOG) and press F10.

✓ Sign off from your session, making sure LOG(*LIST) is set on the sign-off command. Then sign onto a new session and browse your job log from QEZJOBLOG.

❖ For any other job, do any of the following:

✓ If the job is no longer active in the system, do WRKUSRJOB, select option 8 (DISPLAY SPOOLED FILE) find last (which will be the latest) QPJOBLOG. Select option 5 (DISPLAY JOB LOG).

✓ WRKOUTQ QPJOBLOG (or QEZJOBLOG). The resulting list can be hundreds of screens long. Use F18 to quickly go to the bottom where the most current job logs are.

4.4 JOB ACCOUNTING

❖   Not automatic; requires that you start it.

❖   It is kept in a journal.

Job accounting captures information about jobs that you can use to do computer resource charge-back. A major feature of job accounting is the use of the accounting code. A job's accounting code can be fed to it through the job description or the user profile. Because its just a grouping device, you actually don't have to use it at all.

What's interesting about job accounting information is that it has basic information to monitor other things about the jobs on your system. It contains response time information, DASD IO information, user, and start/stop times so you can use it to monitor job performance. Job accounting is a useful tool. You can monitor performance by job without having to use performance monitor (see chapter 9). You can also capture things—such as the number of pages a job prints, the time a job entered the system, and the time it started (from which you can calculate the queue wait time)—performance monitor can't do.

With job accounting, you can uniquely identify groups of jobs, either through their job descriptions or the profiles of the users using them. For example, you could identify all the jobs accounting runs as ACC. You could further separate receivables from payables with the codes ACCAR and ACCAP. You have up to 15 characters to use for accounting codes.

4.4.1 Set Up Job Accounting

To get going on job accounting, start by creating the journal and a receiver to hold its output. These will be in a library. It is a good idea to create a special library and receiver unique for job accounting. Although you could set up job accounting into an existing database library, don't for performance reasons.

Create the library:

```
CRTLIB <library name of your choice>
```

Create a journal receiver. See chapter 8 for more information on the topic. Receiver names should be 10 characters long (6 alpha characters followed by 4 numeric, and generally start with 0001 as the numeric). This is an accounting journal; therefore, ACCJRN0001 would be a good name.

```
CRTJRNRCV JRNRCV(<your library name/receiver name of your choice>)
```

Create the journal. In this case, you have no choice about the library or journal name. Here's the command you use:

```
CRTJRN QSYS/QACGJRN
```

Set system value QACGLVL, which controls job accounting logging. Use the WRKSYSVAL command to reset its contents as needed to one of the following values:

❖ *NONE   Turns off job accounting.

❖ *JOB   Captures the performance portion of each job on a
               JB entry.

❖ *PRINT   Captures each job's printing information on a DB or
               SP entry.

❖ *JOB *PRINT   Combines *JOB and *PRINT entries.

4.4.2 Displaying Job Accounting Journal

Because job accounting information is in a journal, you have two ways of getting to the data:

❖ DSPJRN—if you're capturing a lot of from a journal.

❖ RCVJRNE—if you are looking for specific, real-time journal entries, RCVJRNE is usaually used within a CL program.

When you display journal entries, you might notice that you have two sets of fields:

1. Lots of fields that make up the journal header.

2. A big blank field for the original contents of the journaled data. In other words, it has no record definition.

If you do work with accounting journal entries, they appear in three formats: JB for job related records, DP for directly printed files, and SP for spooled files. You don't see many direct print jobs on an AS/400. Therefore, you don't see a lot of DP records. You'll be working mainly with JB and SP.

The AS/400 comes with two skeleton files and formats that contain the field layouts for these entries. They are known as the *field reference files* for the journal entries:

❖   QSYS/QAJBACG (format QWTJAJBE)

❖   QSYS/QAPTACG (format QSPJAPTE)

If you want to read those journal entries and you are a masochist, you could take the fields from those reference files and create a DDS for them. It's more realistic to just create duplicates of each (CRTDUPOBJ command) in your library. Name the duplicates whatever you like. Then, when you display the journal entries, use this command to extract job records:

```
DSPJRN JRN(QACGJRN) JRNCDE(A) ENTTYP(JB) +
    OUTPUT(*OUTFILE) +
    OUTFILE(<your library>/<your job file (the duplicate)>)
```

Use this to extract the printer records:

```
DSPJRN JRN(QACGJRN) JRNCDE(A) ENTTYP(DP SP) +
    OUTPUT(*OUTFILE) +
    OUTFILE(<your library>/<your printer file (the duplicate)>)
```

From there, you'll be able to build one or more logical files or a join logical over the physical files to process the data with a query or a program.

4.5 SECURITY AUDIT JOURNAL

❖ Not automatic; requires that you start it.

❖ It is kept in a journal.

While system history logs and job logs are always there, you must set up and activate the AS/400 Security Audit Journal if you want to use it. The Security Audit Journal audits security-related activities. You get to set what you want logged. It keeps the log in a journal (see chapter 8).

You can use security audit to focus on activities of an individual user, a specific object, or one individual's contact with a specific object. There are system-wide things you can monitor for and user-specific things. To set up security auditing on your system, perform the tasks in sections 4.5.1 and 4.5.2 in the order they are given.

4.5.1 Set Up the System for Security Auditing

❖ Create a library for the journal receiver with the CRTLIB command. Name it anything you like, but it should be a library just to hold this journal. Do not use this library for production files.

❖ Create a journal receiver in this library. Use 10 characters for its name (the first 6 of which are alpha characters and the last 4 are "0001." For example, SECAUD0001. Use this command:

```
CRTJRNRCV JRNRCV(<your library/your receiver name>) +
          AUT(*EXCLUDE) TEXT('Security Auditing + Journal Receiver')
```

❖ Create the journal with the CRTJRN command (use the library/file names as indicated:

```
CRTJRNJRN(QSYS/QAUDJRN) +
    JRNRCV(<your library/your receiver name>) + AUT(*EXCLUDE)
TEXT('Security Auditing + Journal')
```

4.5.2 Set the System Values

There are three system values that affect security auditing. Use the WRKSYSVAL command to display or change them:

❖ QAUDCTL (AUDIT CONTROL)—starts and stops security auditing. Change this to possible values other than *NONE and you will start capturing security audit information. Change it back to *NONE to stop capturing security audit information.

❖ QAUDFRCLVL (AUDIT FORCE LEVEL)—This is a performance thing; it blocks the audit records before they are written to the journal. There is a trade-off here. If you want absolute protection so that you won't lose any security journal records in the event of a system failure, set this value to 1. However, performance can be degraded. Rather than try to figure out optimum blocking, use the value *SYS and the system will calculate some optimum value for you. You won't lose any records if the AS/400 doesn't go down.

❖ QAUDENDACN (AUDIT END ACTION)—Tells the system what to do if it is unable to write an audit record to a journal. The default is *NOTIFY and the system just sends a message to the system operator. However, if your organization requires that the security audit be active in order for the AS/400 to even be up, you can specify *PWRDWNSYS. The instant the system is unable to write a record to the security audit journal, it does a PWRDWNSYS *IMMED. Because it can wreak havoc with your users, don't do this unless you absolutely must. Also, if you do select this, ensure you have good journal change/backup/ cleanup procedures in place. There are two reasons security audit may not be able to write to a journal:

  ✓ It is full and needs to be changed.
  ✓ It is damaged—in most cases an IPL is necessary to resume monitoring.

There are also two values, one on every object and one on every user profile, that affect what is audited.

❖ QAUDLVL (AUDIT LEVEL)—specifies what actions are audited on objects. See section 4.5.3, Set Security Auditing on Objects/Users. Because an audit level usually contains more than one value, see *OS/400 Security-Reference V3R6* for all possible actions.

❖ AUDLVL (AUDIT LEVEL)—a parameter on the user profile specifies what actions are audited for that user. See section 4.5.3, Set Security Auditing on Objects/Users. User profile AUDLVL is in addition to QAUDLVL settings. Because an audit level usually contains more than one value, see *OS/400 Security-Reference V3R6* for all possible actions.

4.5.3 Set Security Auditing on Objects/Users

Although security auditing has many possibilities, here are three common scenarios and how to set them up.

4.5.3.1 Specific File—Any User

❖ Change the specific file object's OBJECT AUDITING VALUE (OBJAUD) to *CHANGE or *ALL with the CHGOBJAUD command.

❖ Check the system value, QAUDCTL to make sure it includes *OBJAUD.

4.5.3.2 Many Files—One User

❖ Change the file object's OBJECT AUDITING VALUE (OBJAUD) to *USRPRF with the CHGOBJAUD command. (NOTE: the CHGOBJAUD command accepts generic library and file names; use these to save time. However, don't use *ALL/*ALL. Because it can take hours to implement. Also, carrying that much security auditing could degrade your system. It's better to specify any subset or *ALL files within a library.)

❖ Set the user profile's OBJAUD value to *CHANGE or *ALL using the CHGUSRAUD command.

❖ Check the system value, QAUDCTL, to make sure it includes *OBJAUD.

4.5.3.3 One File—One User

❖ Change the specific file object's OBJECT AUDITING VALUE (OBJAUD) to *USRPRF with the CHGOBJAUD command.

❖ Set user profile's OBJECT AUDITING VALUE (OBJAUD value to *CHANGE or *ALL using the CHGUSRAUD command.

❖ Check the system value, QAUDCTL, to make sure it includes *OBJAUD.

4.5.4 Managing System Audit Journal Receivers

The System Audit Journal is just a journal. For more information, see chapter 8. Because of the extra security on it (through the AUT(*EXCLUDE) parameter on the CRTJRNRCV and CRTJRN commands), only the security officer or owner can get to the information. Also, the system puts an exclusive lock on the journal while monitoring is taking place. Therefore, not everyone can get to the journal, and—even when the security officer can—many normal journal commands can't be done because of this system lock.

For these reasons, only use this journal and its receivers to journal security audit records. Do not use it to do any regular database file journaling.

If the value you specified in system value QAUDENDACN is *PWRDWNSYS, you really don't want this receiver to fill up. Create a special message queue for audit messages and associate that queue with the QAUDJRN journal. Then write a message-handling program that monitors this queue. If it gets a "threshold reached" message, it should change receivers and pass the message onto the system operator. For normal operation, you must periodically:

❖ Change receivers: CHGJRN JRN(QAUDJRN) JRNRCV(*GEN)

❖ Save the receiver with the SAVOBJ command, specifying object type *JRNRCV.

❖ Delete the old receiver after it is saved with the DLTJRNRCV command.

❖ If you want to look at the contents of a receiver, but don't know which one is current, WRKJRNA QAUDJRN will tell you which receiver is currently attached.

4.5.5 Viewing Security Audit Journal Receivers

You can view or use the contents of the security audit journal receivers by:

* ❖ Command DSPJRN QAUDJRN.

* ❖ Command DSPJRN QAUDJRN OUTPUT(*OUTFILE). Access the resulting outfile with query or a program.

4.5.6 Planning

Many AS/400 shops make the same set of mistakes when implementing security auditing. They ask for too much data so it becomes unusable. Or they set up elaborate auditing rules and never review the data.

Security auditing is nice and it gets rave reviews from auditors. But if you're not going to use it, don't bother. There is a performance cost to using it and it uses up DASD. Plan very carefully what it is about security you want to monitor. Ask yourself:

* ❖ Who am I concerned about?

* ❖ What objects am I concerned about?

* ❖ What types of security failures would I like to know about?

Then implement only these things and use the data. Unlike other logging, security audit journaling is sometimes activated for a short period of time just to monitor for a suspected problem. Then the monitor is turned off and the results are reviewed.

4.6 MESSAGES

The AS/400 lives and dies on messages. Messages are sent to everybody, including most of its internal functions (which rely on messages as triggers). History, job log, and security-audit journal entries all start life as mere messages.

4.6.1 Messages to You

At the simplest level, you can receive messages while you are on an AS/400 workstation. They will be in one of three forms: break, notify, or program.

4.6.1.1 Break Messages

You can't miss a break message because it interrupts you to display a full screen of just the message.

4.6.1.2 Notify Messages

You might miss a notify message because you'll only get a small icon on the lower left corner of your screen when you have received one. These icons vary in shape. Ask your system administrator what your icon should look like.

When you do get a notify message, you can look at it by entering the DSPMSG command on any command line. You will see what is known as your first-level message. If you would like more information about the message, use the arrow keys to move the cursor up to the message itself and press the Help key. You'll get the second-level message.

4.6.1.3 Program Messages

The third message you may receive is a program message. When it appears, it'll appear on the bottom line of your screen when you complete a command or program. Like notify messages, it is only the first-level message. If you want more information, put the cursor on it and press the Help key.

Also, look for a small plus sign on the far right side of the program messages. The plus sign indicates that there are more messages for you. You can look at the other messages by putting the cursor on the message and pressing the Page Down key. If you want to go back up the list, press the Page Up key. You can press the Help key on any of them to get the second-level message.

4.6.2 Message Constructions

Messages on the AS/400 are coded. The codes are keys to text and data stored in message files. The system comes with several message files, and you can create your own application. Many customers do that.

When you look at the contents of a job log (most of which is captured messages), you will see the message and its ID. Message texts contain variables. Variables are passed along with message texts in their own MSGDTA area.

To see what a message looks like, use the WRKMSGD command. It will give you a menu. In the menu, option 1 will give you the message text and option 2 has the MSGDTA.

If you're wondering what the AS/400 message texts and their IDs are, there is an alphabetical listing the *AS/400 Programming Reference Summary*.

All messages go first to a message queue before going anywhere else. When a user signs onto the AS/400, the user automatically is assigned a message queue (usually named after the user's profile). The workstation the user signs onto also has its own message queue, which is named after the device itself. When the user is running interactive jobs, messages will arrive on either queue. When an interactive user submits a job to batch, messages from that job will go to the system operator.

The device message queue is around as long as the device is known to the system. The user message queue goes away when the user signs off. Messages are directed at specific message queues. When an operator broadcasts a message telling everyone to sign off the system, a knowledgeable operator will send it to *ALL user messages queues. Only those currently signed on will get the sign-off notice. If the operator isn't so knowledgeable, the notice to sign off could be sent to *ALL device message queues. Users will see the notice to sign off when they sign on the next morning, and that tends to be confusing.

4.6.3 System Operator Message Queue: QSYSOPR

In special circumstances, you will want to create your own message queues with the CRTMSGQ command. In most AS/400 shops, the most important message queue comes with the AS/400 as a default and is called the system operator message queue: QSYSOPR. Here is where all the really important system stuff goes. All batch jobs and any problems on the system, unless otherwise handled, go to message queue QSYSOPR. There are two problems with this queue:

❖ Important things can get lost among many unimportant messages.

❖ Operators take lunch breaks and can miss time-crucial things.

The AS/400 has a way around these problems. You can create a special message queue just for really hot system messages. You can also write a program to intercept these and handle them. Create this special message queue with this command:

```
CRTMSGQ QSYS/QSYSMSG TEXT('System operator really important +
message queue')
```

Once this message queue is in existence, the AS/400 has a predetermined list of messages it will send to this queue instead of the QSYSOPR message queue. For a complete list of these messages and what they mean, see *OS/400 CL Programming V3R6*.

You can write a simple program to monitor and handle some of these messages. The messages it can't handle it forwards to the system operator. Messages it can handle are forwarded to the system operator and from there a copy is forwarded to the security officer for review. A sample of such a program can be found in of *OS/400 CL Programming V3R6*.

4.6.4 System Reply List

Some system messages really get to be a pain because they demand an answer from the user or operator, and its always the same answer. For example, a message to change forms on a laser printer that only ever contains blank white stock is a waste of time. However, a message to change forms on a line printer in the computer room won't be so predictable.

By using the System Reply List, you can have the system automatically respond to some messages. In that list, you can have the system parse out sections of a message to determine which ones to respond to and which ones to leave alone (and let the operator respond to).

Even with the System Reply List, not all jobs use it. A job has to have the parameter INQMSGRPY(*SYSRPYL) specified or it will ignore this list. Most jobs do not have this set.

The AS/400 comes with a basic System Reply List that looks like Table 4-1.

Table 4-1: System Reply List.

Sequence Number	Message Identifier	Compare Value	Reply	Dump
10	CPA0700	*NONE	D	*YES
20	RPG0000	*NONE	D	*YES
30	CBE0000	*NONE	D	*YES
40	PLI0000	*NONE	D	*YES

Table 4-1 is a little difficult to decipher. It means if any error starting with the error number's trailing zeros and going to the 9s in those spaces will receive a response. In other words, all messages CPA0700 through CPA0799 from any job with INQMSGRPY(*SYSRPYL) will be responded to automatically with a "D" (for a program dump).

You add reply list entries with the ADDRPYLE command. In the preceding printer example, if you want the system to automatically respond when an align-forms message (CPA4002) is received for any printer except the line printer in the computer room (designated QSYSPRT).

❖ If the align-forms message is not for QSYSPRT, it must be for a laser printer and the system will just reply with an "I" for ignore.

❖ If the align-forms message is for QSYSPRT, it is for the line printer and the message will be passed on through to the intended destination.

No problem. You just have to look inside the message identification, CPA4002, at its MSGDTA area. The command is WRKMSGD CPA4002. Figure 4-6 shows its first menu screen.

```
┌─────────────────────────────────────────────────────────────────────────┐
│                    Select Message Details to Display                      │
│                                             System:    SYS01              │
│  Message ID . . . . . . . . . :    CPA4002                                │
│  Message file . . . . . . . . :    QCPFMSG                                │
│    Library  . . . . . . . . . :      QSYS                                 │
│  Message text . . . . . . . . :    Verify alignment on printer &3. (I C G N R E)│
│                                                                           │
│                                                                           │
│  Select one of the following:                                             │
│                                                                           │
│       1. Display message text                                             │
│       2. Display field data                                               │
│       3. Display reply specifications                                     │
│       4. Display special reply values                                     │
│       5. Display message attributes                                       │
│                                                                           │
│      30. All of the above                                                 │
│                                                                           │
│                                                                           │
│  Selection                                                                │
│      __                                                                   │
│                                                                           │
│  F3=Exit    F12=Cancel                                                    │
└─────────────────────────────────────────────────────────────────────────┘
```

Figure 4-6: WRKMSGD menu.

Take option 1 to look at the full message text. See Figure 4-7.

```
┌─────────────────────────────────────────────────────────────────────────┐
│                    Display Formatted Message Text                         │
│                                             System:    SYS01              │
│  Message ID . . . . . . . . . :    CPA4002                                │
│  Message file . . . . . . . . :    QCPFMSG                                │
│    Library  . . . . . . . . . :      QSYS                                 │
│                                                                           │
│  Message . . . . :    Verify alignment on printer &3. (I C G N R E)       │
│  Cause . . . . . :    The forms may not be aligned correctly.  The first line│
│    for the file is &4.                                                    │
│  Recovery  . . . :    Do one of the following and try the request again.  │
│  Possible choices for replying to message . . . . . . . . . . . . . . . : │
│    I -- To continue printing aligned forms starting with the next line of the│
│       file, type an I.                                                    │
│    C -- To cancel processing, type a C.                                   │
│    G -- To continue printing aligned forms skipping to the next form and  │
│       printing the first line again, type a G.                            │
│    N -- To print the first line again on the next form and to verify the  │
│       alignment,                                                          │
│       1. Press Stop only if Start and Stop are two keys, or press Reset.  │
│                                                                More...     │
│  Press Enter to continue.                                                 │
│                                                                           │
│  F3=Exit    F11=Display unformatted message text    F12=Cancel            │
└─────────────────────────────────────────────────────────────────────────┘
```

Figure 4-7: Message text for message id CPA4002.

Go back to the WRKMSGD menu (see Figure 4-6) and take option 2 to see the MSGDTA layout. This is where the compare value will come from. See Figure 4-8.

```
                              Display Field Data

Message ID . . . . . . . . . :    CPA4002
Message file . . . . . . . . :    QCPFMSG
  Library  . . . . . . . . . :    QSYS


                                    Decimal      Vary
Field       Data Type     Length    Positions    Length    Dump
  &1        *CHAR           10                              *NO
  &2        *CHAR           10                              *NO
  &3        *CHAR           10                              *NO
  &4        *BIN             2                              *NO
  &5        *CHAR           10                              *NO
  &6        *CHAR           10                              *NO
  &7        *CHAR            0                              *NO
  &8        *CHAR            0                              *NO
  &9        *CHAR            0                              *NO
  &10       *CHAR            0                              *NO
                                                                More...
Press Enter to continue.

F3=Exit   F12=Cancel
```

Figure 4-8: Layout of MSGDTA FOR MESSAGE ID CPA4002.

Now add two reply message entries to the system reply list shown in Table 4-1. You can add CPA4002 immediately after CPA0700. Here's the command:

```
ADDRPYLE SEQNBR(12) MSGID(CPA4002) RPY(*RQD) + CMPDTA('QSYSPRT' 21)
```

Refer to Figure 4-7 and Figure 4-8. The message text on Figure 4-7 has a &3 as the variable that contained the printer name. On Figure 4-8, that variable is the third one in the list, and it starts on column 21. I used the column 21 to start comparing for value QSYSPRT on the example command as a result of that information.

This reply list entry will take care of a requirement that the system printer, QSYSPRT, align-form messages that will be forwarded to an operator who will have to respond to it (*RQD). Here's one without the compare message to catch CPA4002's for the other printers:

```
ADDRPYLE SEQNBR(14) MSGID(CPA4002) RPY(G)
```

I had to put the message for QSYSPRT first because the no-compare message would have passed anything (even QSYSPRT). Table 4-2 shows the system reply list after those changes.

Table 4-2: System Reply List After Changes.

Sequence Number	Message Identifier	Compare Value	Reply	Dump
10	CPA0700	*NONE	D	*YES
12	CPA4002	'QSYSPRT' 21	&RQD	*NO
14	CPA4002	*NONE	G	*NO
20	RPG0000	*NONE	D	*YES
30	CBE0000	*NONE	D	*YES
40	PLI0000	*NONE	D	*YES

That was easy. For other messages, be very careful about their placement. Remember that RPG0000, on sequence 20, implicitly includes all RPG messages (RPG0000 through RPG9999). The trailing zeros automatically create that range. Therefore, a message RPG0120 would include RPG0120 through RPG0129. In this case, any new RPG.... would have to be placed prior to the RPG0000 ahead of sequence 20. Once a message traps, the system quits looking any further.

4.7 SYSTEM CLEANUP

The AS/400 comes with an automatic system cleanup program that works fairly well for keeping the amount of old messages and logs down to a manageable size. To get into the cleanup screen, type GO CLEANUP on your command line and press the Enter key. You'll get the screen shown in Figure 4-9.

```
                          Change Cleanup Options                    SYS01
                                                        09/08/96  12:13:58
         Type choices below, then press Enter.

         Allow automatic cleanup . . . . . . . . . . . . .   Y            Y=Yes, N=No

         Time cleanup starts each day  . . . . . . . . .   01:00:00      00:00:00-
                                                                          23:59:59,
                                                                          *SCDPWROFF,
                                                                          *NONE

         Number of days to keep:
           User messages . . . . . . . . . . . . . . . .    2____        1-366, *KEEP
           System and workstation messages . . . . . . .    2____        1-366, *KEEP
           Job logs and other system output  . . . . . .    10___        1-366, *KEEP
           System journals and system logs . . . . . . .    7____        1-366, *KEEP
           OfficeVision/400 calendar items . . . . . . .    7____        1-366, *KEEP




         F1=Help   F3=Exit   F5=Refresh   F12=Cancel
```

Figure 4-9: Automatic cleanup screen.

The first parameter, ALLOW AUTOMATIC CLEANUP, accepts a Y or N and tells the system to do the clean up automatically. Put a Y here to allow the system to do automatic cleanup.

The TIME CLEANUP STARTS EACH DAY tells the system when to do the clean up. In the example, this customer wants the automatic cleanup to start at 1:00 A.M. every day. Because these times are in military time, that means 0100 (or 1:00 A.M.).

The parameters under NUMBER OF DAYS TO KEEP are the really interesting items. To the right of each is a number for the days.

❖   User messages. All old user messages are purged after the allowed time (in this case, after two days). This does not clean up the system-operator messages or security-officer messages.

❖ System and workstation messages. All old messages that belong to the system operator or to any device-message queue are erased after the allowed time.

❖ Job logs and other system output. All old job logs are purged after the allowed number of days.

❖ System journals and system logs. The system keeps its own journals to assist it in many tasks. This parameter says they will be purged after the allowed number of days. Included in system logs are the history logs (QHST) and problem logs generated by the AS/400 self-diagnostics. Also, included in this category are PTF cleanup.

❖ OfficeVision/400 calendar items. Such items are purged after the allowed number of days.

4.8 BIBLIOGRAPHY

OS/400 CL Programming V3R6

AS/400 System Operation V3R6

AS/400 Programming Reference Summary V3R6

OS/400 Security-Reference V3R6

OS/400 Work Management V3R6

5. People

5.1 OVERVIEW

The AS/400 can support as simple or as complex a set of users as the customer needs. A very small shop will have one or two people who have access to everything. Large shops will have many subsets of users, each with a unique set of rights and accesses.

In one sense, any person known to the AS/400 is a *user*. He or she becomes known to the AS/400 through something called the *user profile*. The user profile contains items specific to a person:

❖ Basic security information about the person.

❖ Special authorities granted to the person.

❖ Job processing information specific to the person, such as:

  ✓ Job queue.

  ✓ Output queue.

  ✓ Initial program or menu to call.

  ✓ Current library.

The security level of your AS/400 affects user profiles. An AS/400 with a security level of 10 will allow any user ID. If the AS/400 can't find a user profile for the ID, it'll build one automatically. AS/400s with security levels higher than 10 require users to sign on with a user ID that has a profile.

5.1.1 The New AS/400

A brand new AS/400 comes with several user profiles supplied in library QSYS. Here's a list of the external ones (external means you can use them to sign onto the system):

❖ QPGMR   Programmer and batch-user profile.

❖ QSECOFR   Security officer-user profile.

❖ QSRV   Services (all functions). This is the profile the person who services your AS/400 will use.

❖ QSRVBAS   Services (limited functions). This is the profile the person who services your AS/400 will use.

❖ QSYSOPR   System operator.

❖ QUSER   General user.

On a new AS/400, user profiles come with passwords equal to their names. For example, you can sign on as security officer on a new AS/400 by using QSECOFR user ID and QSECOFR password.

To secure your system, make sure you change these passwords as soon as you can. This is very important. For more information, see section 5.5, Changing Passwords to IBM-Supplied Profiles. Most AS/400 shops change the passwords but keep these generic profiles around because they make nice models for other user profiles.

In addition, there are several internal user profiles that attach to particular types of jobs. Internal means that you can't use them to sign-on; they are available to meet special needs. You don't have to do anything with the internal user profiles. Just recognize them when you see them from time to time.

❖ QDFTOWN   All objects on the AS/400 must be owned by a legitimate user. If a user no longer works for the company and the user's profile is deleted, the objects that user owned are then changed to being owned by QDFTOWN.

❖ QGATE   User profile to bridge into PROFS (VM/MVS on mainframes).

❖ QLPAUTO   Licensed program auto-installation user (see chapter 2).

❖ QLPINSTALL   Licensed program installation user (see chapter 2).

❖ QRJE   Remote job entry (RJE) user.

❖ QSNADS   SNADS user.

❖ QSPL   Spooling user.

❖ QSPLJOB   Spooling readers/writers job user profile.

❖ QSYS   Internal system user.

❖ QTCP   TCP/IP user.

These profiles are not used for signing onto the system. Do not attempt to change or delete these profiles. If you do, you might find internal functions suddenly not working.

5.2 MANAGING USER PROFILES

There are six user-profile commands:

- ❖ CRTUSRPRF   Create user profile.

- ❖ CHGUSRPRF   Change user profile.

- ❖ DLTUSRPRF   Delete user profile.

- ❖ DSPUSRPRF   Display user profile.

- ❖ RSTUSRPRF   Restore user profile.

- ❖ RTVUSRPRF   Retrieve user profile information (CL programs only).

A seventh user profile, the WRKUSRPRF command, gets you to any of these, except RTVUSRPRF, and it's handier to use.

The user profile information is pretty standard across all the commands. The CRTUSRPRF (with only the more common parameters shown) gives you an idea of what goes into a profile. See Figures 5-1 and 5-2.

```
                    Create User Profile (CRTUSRPRF)

 Type choices, press Enter.

 User profile . . . . . . . . . .   _____        Name
 User password  . . . . . . . . .   *USRPRF         Name, *USRPRF, *NONE
 Set password to expired  . . . .   *NO             *NO, *YES
 Status . . . . . . . . . . . . .   *ENABLED        *ENABLED, *DISABLED
 User class . . . . . . . . . . .   *USER           *USER, *SYSOPR, *PGMR...
 Assistance level . . . . . . . .   *SYSVAL         *SYSVAL, *BASIC, *INTERMED...
 Initial program to call  . . . .   *NONE           Name, *NONE
   Library  . . . . . . . . . . .   _____        Name, *LIBL, *CURLIB
 Initial menu . . . . . . . . . .   MAIN            Name, *SIGNOFF
   Library  . . . . . . . . . . .    *LIBL          Name, *LIBL, *CURLIB
 Limit capabilities . . . . . . .   *NO             *NO, *PARTIAL, *YES
 Text 'description' . . . . . . .   *BLANK
```

Figure 5-1: Partial prompted version of command CRTUSRPRF *(first screen).*

```
                          Additional Parameters

Special authority . . . . . . .    *USRCLS        *USRCLS, *NONE, *ALLOBJ...
            + for more values
Password expiration interval . .   *SYSVAL        1-366, *SYSVAL, *NOMAX
Maximum allowed storage . . . .    *NOMAX         Kilobytes, *NOMAX
Job description . . . . . . . .    QDFTJOBD       Name
    Library . . . . . . . . . .    *LIBL          Name, *LIBL, *CURLIB
Group profile . . . . . . . . .    *NONE          Name, *NONE
Owner . . . . . . . . . . . . .    *USRPRF        *USRPRF, *GRPPRF
Group authority . . . . . . . .    *NONE          *NONE, *ALL, *CHANGE, *USE...
Accounting code . . . . . . . .    *BLANK
Message queue . . . . . . . . .    *USRPRF        Name, *USRPRF
    Library . . . . . . . . . .                   Name, *LIBL, *CURLIB
Delivery . . . . . . . . . . . .   *NOTIFY        *NOTIFY, *BREAK, *HOLD, *DFT
Severity code filter . . . . . .   0              0-99
Print device . . . . . . . . . .   *WRKSTN        Name, *WRKSTN, *SYSVAL
Output queue . . . . . . . . . .   *WRKSTN        Name, *WRKSTN, *DEV
    Library . . . . . . . . . .                   Name, *LIBL, *CURLIB
```

Figure 5-2: Partial prompted version of command CRTUSRPRF (additional parameters).

There are 37 parameters on a user profile. I've just displayed the 24 common ones in Figure 5-1 and Figure 5-2. All of the parameters are fully described in *OS/400 Security-Reference V3R6.* Here's a short description of each parameter in Figure 5-1 and Figure 5-2:

❖ USER PROFILE NAME (USRPRF). Up to 10 characters in length, the user profile name can contain any letter, number, or #, $, _, or @. Although a user profile cannot start with a number, you can create one that contains all numbers but starts with the letter Q. The user then can sign on with just the numbers. Example: user profile Q12345 can be used as 12345. In real life, try not to exceed eight characters in length. Don't use special characters, and the user profile name doesn't have to be cryptic. Use a standard that means something (a user's initials and department code are popular choices).

❖ PASSWORD (PASSWORD). A password is only required when the system security level is greater than 10. Passwords can have up to 10 characters. There are many system values that affect password constructions. For more information, see chapter 6.

❖ SET PASSWORD TO EXPIRED (PWDEXP). The security officer or security administrator can use this (PWDEXP(*YES)) to force the user to change her or his password the next time she or he signs on.

❖ STATUS (STATUS). The profile may be allowed to sign on (STATUS(*ENABLED)) or not be allowed to sign on (STATUS(*DISABLED)). The system may disable a profile if the user exceeds the maximum number of unsuccessful sign-on attempts. Or the security officer or system administrator may make a profile disabled. Changing the STATUS from *DISABLED to *ENABLED can only be done by a security officer or system administrator and will allow the user to sign on again.

❖ CLASS (USRCLS). Controls the menu options the user sees on AS/400 menus. Possible values for this parameter are: *SECOFR, *SECADM, *PGMR, *SYSOPR, and *USER. *USER is the default value. Note the following:

✓ This value alone does not determine what commands the user has access to.

✓ This parameter can implicitly assign special authorities to a user.

❖ ASSISTANCE LEVEL (ASTLVL). Three possible values:

✓ *BASIC is best for new or occasional users. AS/400 Operational Assistant is used to provide messaging and help to users.

✓ *INTERMED is the default value. Provides complete information and capabilities to users. All options are available and displayed.

✓ *ADVANCED is only for very experienced users. All options are available, but possible options might not be displayed in order to make room for more information.

❖ INITIAL PROGRAM TO CALL (INLPGM). This is a two-variable, library/file parameter. It is used to automatically invoke a program when the user signs on. When it is used, it is almost always for users rather than for developers, operators, security officers, or system administrators.

❖ INITIAL MENU TO CALL (INLMNU). This is a two-variable, library/file parameter. If a INLPGM is not specified, this is almost always MAIN (meaning the AS/400 Main Menu is displayed when the user signs on). MAIN is the default.

❖ LIMIT CAPABILITIES (LMTCPB). Limit capabilities restricts the user's capacity to execute commands from a command line. Possible values are *NO (the default), *PARTIAL, and *YES. NOTE: limit capabilities has no affect on the commands within CL programs that the user executes.

❖ TEXT (TEXT). The text parameter contains up to 50 characters. Use this wisely. Spell out the user's name and perhaps his or her phone extension or LAN connection address. Decide early on whether to use "last-name-first" to facilitate alphabetic searching of user profiles.

❖ SPECIAL AUTHORITY (SPCAUT). This parameter has up to ten 10-character values. See section 5.2.2.1, Special Authorities, and chapter 5.

❖ PASSWORD EXPIRATION INTERVAL (PWDEXPITV). This parameter establishes how many days the password can be used before the system makes the user change it. Many shops leave this at the default, *SYSVAL, which relies on the number of days specified in the QPWDEXPITV system value. Don't use the *NOMAX value: the user will never have to change his or her password. Valid values are from 1 through 366 days.

❖ MAXIMUM STORAGE (MAXSTG). This parameter is numeric, up to 11 digits, and it specifies the amount of storage in kilobytes a user's owned objects can take in DASD. Also, this parameter is used in large shops and is placed on the profile of any user who can create and own objects. Typically, that is the development staff, but it can be power users as well. Maximum storage is nice for enabling a small staff to manage DASD utilization.

❖ JOB DESCRIPTION (JOBD). This parameter allows up to 10 characters for a job description. Many shops use the system default, QDFTJOBD. When the user signs onto the system, the subsystem's workstation entry contains the job description the system will use. If that value is *USRPRF, the system will get the job description specified on this parameter. For more information, see chapter 3 and especially section 3.4.1.1, How the System Starts an Interactive Job.

❖ USER GROUP (GRPPRF). This parameter has up to 10 characters, and it makes the user a member of a group. NOTE: A group user profile must already exist (see section 5.6, Group Profiles).

❖ OWNER (OWNER). This parameter has up to 10 characters. If the user is a member of a group, you can specify whether any object created by the user is owned by the user profile or the group user profile. Possible values are: *USRPRF (the default) and *GRPPRF. NOTE: If you are using group profiles, you probably want objects owned by that group.

❖ GROUP AUTHORITY (GRPAUT). If the user profile is a member of a group user profile and the ownership was set to *USRPRF, this parameters dictates what authority is granted to other members of the same group as the creator of an object. Possible values are:

   ✓ *NONE—The default. No specific authority is given to the group profile.

   ✓ *ALL—Group members have all rights to objects created by the user.

   ✓ *CHANGE—Group members can change the objects.

   ✓ *USE—Group members can use objects created by the user.

   ✓ *EXCLUDE—Group members are denied access to objects created by the user.

❖ ACCOUNTING CODE (ACGCDE). Up to 15 characters can be used to specify an accounting code for the user. This supports Job Accounting, which should be active (or plan to be active) for this to make sense. For more information, see chapter 4, and section 3.4, Job Accounting.

❖ MESSAGE QUEUE (MSGQ). Up to 10 characters can be qualified with a library name. Specify the message queue for a user profile. This is where any messages from other users or programs will be placed. Most of the time, just use the default, *USRPRF, which means the message queue should be the same name as the user profile. Otherwise, specify the message queue and library to which you want messages to go. If you do specify the message queue, you should specify a unique message queue for each user.

❖ DELIVERY (DLVRY). Specifies in what way messages on the queue are delivered to the user. Possible values are:

  ✓ *NOTIFY—The default. An alarm is sounded at the workstation and a message icon is displayed on the lower left corner of the screen. The user must use the DSPMSG (DISPLAY MESSAGE) command to see the message.

  ✓ *BREAK—The user's workstation is interrupted by the incoming message. It goes blank and displays the message.

  ✓ *HOLD—Messages are held in the message queue until the user requests them with the DSPMSG command.

  ✓ *DFT—Messages requiring replies are automatically responded to with their default reply value. Informational messages are ignored.

❖ SEVERITY (SEV). When DLVRY is set to *notify or *break only, this determines the lowest level message that is delivered to the user. The default is 00 (or all messages). You can set this to only receive more serious messages (like 30 for level 30 and above).

❖ PRINT DEVICE (PRTDEV). Use up to 10 characters to specify the name of the printer used to print this user's output. Possible values are:

  ✓ *WRKSTN—The default. All printed output is sent to a printer device with the same name as the workstation.

  ✓ *SYSVAL—All printed output is sent to the system printer (as defined in the system value QPRTDEV).

  ✓ Print Device name.

❖ OUTPUT QUEUE (OUTQ). Up to 10 characters can be qualified with a library name to define the output queue to which the printed output for the user will go. The possible values are the same as those for the PRTDEV parameter.

5.2.1 User Profile Parameter Considerations

When a password is assigned to a profile, there is no way to learn its value. Even security officers, who have all rights to everything on the system, can't learn the password.

For new users and for users who have forgotten their passwords, the procedure is as follows:

- ❖ For new users, create the user profile with any generic password.

- ❖ For forgetful users, change the user profile to any generic password.

- ❖ For both, set the parameter PWDEXP(*YES). Then tell the user the password. The next time he or she signs on, the system will force the user to change the password.

To really restrict users to one application, INLPGM and INLMNU can be used together. Name the application the user will access as the INLPGM and name *SIGNOFF as the INLMNU. When that user signs on, he or she will only see the application's menu (or main screen). When the user exits the application, he or she is automatically signed off.

The limit capabilities parameter (LMTCPB) has three possible values and will limit the user's access to the following commands, based on the following values:

- ❖ *NO. User can access all commands except where he or she is excluded by other security methods.

- ❖ *PARTIAL. User can only use these commands:
  - ✓ CHGPRF (change profile) to change INLMNU or to change current library.
  - ✓ Any commands that the fully limited user has.

- ❖ *YES. User is fully limited and can only use these commands:
  - ✓ SIGNOFF—Sign off the system.
  - ✓ SNDMSG—Send a message.
  - ✓ DSPMSG—Display a message.
  - ✓ DSPJOB—Display a job.
  - ✓ DSPJOBLOG—Display the job log.
  - ✓ STRPCO—Start PC organizer.

You can use the RTVUSRPRF (RETRIEVE USER PROFILE) command in a CL program to inquire about the user running the program. RTVUSRPRF can retrieve most of the user profile keywords into variables the program can use to make decisions about processing.

For PRTDEV and OUTQ parameters, most shops don't worry much about the PRTDEV, opting instead to send all printed output to one of two types of output queues. Developers and others who don't expect to print everything they generate can have a queue named the same as their user profile. When they want to print something, they move it—with the CHGSPLFA (CHANGE SPOOL FILE ATTRIBUTES) command—to a queue with an attached printer. Users who expect immediate output from their reports can get a designated output queue that normally has a printer attached.

5.2.2 Security

Two parts of the AS/400's built-in security are in the user profile: Special Authorities and Security Auditing. For more information on how special authorities fit the security picture, see chapter 6.

5.2.2.1 Special Authorities

Most of the AS/400 authorities are granted at the object level. That's nice for most things, but it ignores the need for something special in order to have both adequate security and still allow people to do their jobs. That something special is called the *special authorities*, and a user profile can have up to ten of them. While most AS/400 security is object-based, special authorities are user-based. Here is what they do:

❖ *ALLOBJ: The user can do anything to any object. This is reserved for SECOFR. (NOTE: when the system security level is set to 10 or 20, all users have *ALLOBJ special authority).

❖ *SAVSYS: Allows the user to perform backup/restore operations on all objects even if the user has no authority to an object. This authority is usually given to system operators.

❖ *JOBCTL: Allows a user to manage jobs running on the system. It allows a user to change jobs to other job queues and change output to different queues. For running jobs, the user can cancel or alter them or change their priorities. For the system, the user can start/stop the entire subsystems, load the operating system, and so on. This usually is granted to system operators.

❖ *SPLCTL: This allows a user to manage output queues. Users can display, move, print, release, cancel spooled output. This is commonly granted to all users who need to be able to browse their reports directly in output queues. The problem that can come up is one user browsing another user's output. The solution to that is to build "restricted" output queues. Then users with *SPLCTL can browse only those output queues where they are not restricted.

❖ *SECADM: Allows user to create and alter user profiles. Some AS/400 shops have a person dedicated to this function.

❖ *SERVICE: This allows service and dump functions. These are never given to someone who is not extremely knowledgeable about the system. This authorization is more often extended to the IBM service representatives than to anyone in house.

5.2.2.2 *Security Auditing*

Two conditions, associated with the user profile but not set with the CRTUSRPRF command, concern security auditing. The user-profile parameters for these are OBJAUD and AUDLVL, and they are only set with the CHGUSRAUD (CHANGE USER AUDIT) command. For additional information, see chapter 4 and section 4.5, Security Audit Journal.

5.3 MORE THAN ONE USER PROFILE

The procedures described in this chapter mean a lot of work for every user. In reality, users tend to bunch into just a few types of groups. Therefore, a lot of the data entry is repetitious. You can save time creating user profiles by copying existing profiles with option 3 (COPY) on the WRKUSRPRF command. Let's say you have a new user, Jennie A. Jones, who works in Accounts Receivable. You probably have a standard that says use the user's initials followed by a department code. Therefore, you create a user profile named JAJAR.

However, from there, you can use the WRKUSRPRF's option 3 to copy JAJAR and create another user profile for someone else in the same department. If you need to make any changes to the new profile (like the initial password), just take an option 2 (CHANGE) and make them. Such changes should be very minor.

One reason IBM loads the AS/400 with default user profiles is so that you have a basis in which to start. On a new AS/400, you can use WRKUSRPRF to copy QUSER into your first user profiles. However, QUSER (and the other supplied profiles) are in library QSYS. Copy them out to library QGPL and create all your user profiles in QGPL. That will save you a major headache the next time you load a new version of the operating system (which likes to replace library QSYS).

5.4 DELETING USER PROFILES

Use the DLTUSRPRF (DELETE USER PROFILE) or option 4 from the WRKUSRPRF commands to delete a user profile. This is easy, but you should know that behind the scenes the system removes the user profile as owner of any objects and from any authorization lists. Objects must be owned by someone. Therefore, the system changes the ownership to QDFTUSER (one of the IBM-supplied profiles). For additional information on security, see chapter 6.

5.5 CHANGING PASSWORDS TO IBM-SUPPLIED PROFILES

After signing on as QSECOFR, the first thing you should do on any new AS/400 is to change all the IBM-supplied passwords. You can use the list of user profiles from section 5.1.1, The New AS/400, or you can use the setup menu.

To get to the setup menu, type GO SETUP on the command line and press the Enter key. Take option 11, CHANGE PASSWORDS FOR IBM-SUPPLIED USERS, and change all the passwords from the same screen. This is the easier way. See Figure 5-3.

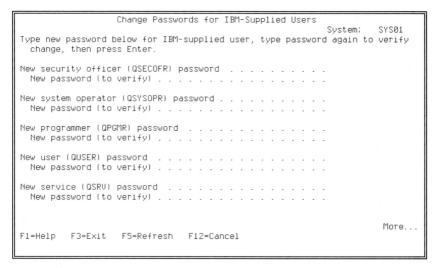

```
             Change Passwords for IBM-Supplied Users
                                            System:    SYS01
  Type new password below for IBM-supplied user, type password again to verify
    change, then press Enter.

  New security officer (QSECOFR) password . . . . . . . . . .
    New password (to verify) . . . . . . . . . . . . . . . .

  New system operator (QSYSOPR) password . . . . . . . . . .
    New password (to verify) . . . . . . . . . . . . . . . .

  New programmer (QPGMR) password . . . . . . . . . . . . .
    New password (to verify) . . . . . . . . . . . . . . . .

  New user (QUSER) password . . . . . . . . . . . . . . . .
    New password (to verify) . . . . . . . . . . . . . . . .

  New service (QSRV) password . . . . . . . . . . . . . . .
    New password (to verify) . . . . . . . . . . . . . . . .


                                                        More...
  F1=Help   F3=Exit   F5=Refresh   F12=Cancel
```

Figure 5-3: Screen from SETUP menu to change IBM-supplied passwords.

Change those values again whenever you have a key AS/400 person (who may know the passwords) terminate his or her association with the organization.

5.6 GROUP PROFILES

You can see how copying an existing user profile speeds things up when adding new users. Let's go on to how establishing group profiles can speed up granting similar object authorities.

Use group profiles when several users have the same security requirements. An example could be a group of developers, where each user can create his or her own programs and files. Without anything but user profile security, each developer would have to grant access rights to his or her objects to all other developers. Because it's just too error prone, this method wouldn't work for very long.

If all developers belonged to the same group-user profile (PGM, for example), and object ownership was assigned to the group user profile, instead of the user profiles, then any object created by one developer would be changeable by all other developers.

The same principle applies to groups of users. This is especially important where users access common database files. Make common-group users all part of a group profile (such as AR for accounts receivable). Then give them all common access to each database file by granting access to each file to profile AR. Plan the group profiles before you start doing the user profiles.

Create the group profiles as regular user profiles except specify PASS-WORD(*NONE). They don't become group profiles until you specify them on the GRPPRF parameter on a regular user profile.

In other words, create user profile PGM for developers. It will exist as just another user profile. Then create your first developer user profile and specify GRPPRF(PGM). As soon as you do, PGM has become a group profile on your system.

5.7 USER ROLES

Earlier, I said AS/400 users tend to clump together into like types. All the accounting users together is one type, but another way of labeling users on the AS/400 is through their role. Users have different roles within the organization or company and these roles will define how you set up user profiles and assign group profiles. Here is the typical mix of user roles on an AS/400:

❖ Security Officer. The system-supplied profile is QSECOFR. Sometimes referred to as "Sec-Offer," this user can do anything on the system except service functions. Service functions are better left to the IBM CE (customer engineer). The security officer has unlimited power to access objects on the system. Most AS/400 shops only have one or two security officers.

❖ System Administrator. No system-supplied profile is provided. The system administrator is an administrative position where someone usually is responsible for creating and maintaining user profiles.

❖ System Operator. The system-supplied profile is QSYSOPR. The system operator usually has authority to control jobs and do backup and restore functions.

❖ Programmers. The system-supplied profile is QPGMR. This user is any developer who can create programs and files and generally change records or delete files. What a programmer can do depends to a large extent on how a shop configures its AS/400 and on what libraries the programmers can access. This is a complex issue and many shops purchase CMS (Change Management Systems) to give them real sophistication in the area.

❖ Users. The system-supplied profile is QUSER. A user can be defined as anyone not in the computer department.

Many of the real distinctions between user types is achieved through the granting of special authorities. For additional information, see section 5.2.2.1, Special Authorities.

5.8 BIBLIOGRAPHY

OS/400 Security-Reference V3R6

AS/400 System Operation V3R6

AS/400 Programming Reference Summary V3R6

6. System Values and Security

6.1 OVERVIEW

System values are a set of values applied system wide. Security areas associated with user profiles are discussed in chapter 5, and I review them in this chapter along with object-level security.

6.2 SYSTEM VALUES

System values are global items the system needs to know. You can work with system values with these commands:

❖ dspsysval (display system value).

❖ CHGSYSVAL (CHANGE SYSTEM VALUE).

❖ WRKSYSVAL (WORK SYSTEM VALUE). This is a powerful command.

❖ RTVSYSVAL (RETRIEVE SYSTEM VALUE). This command is used within a CL program to collect a specific system value and put it into a CL variable.

System values can provide default values for command keywords. For example, the CRTUSRPRF (CREATE USER PROFILE) command has the ASTLVL parameter where you can specify the assistance level available to the user. Your choices are:

❖ *BASIC

❖ *INTERMEDIATE

❖ *ADVANCED

❖ *SYSVAL

If you specify the last option, the system will use the contents of system value QASTLVL, which will contain one of the first three choices. In this way, system values can speed up adding new users. If you want all or most of your users to have *INTERMEDIATE assistance levels, set the system value and don't do anything on the field when you create a new user profile; *SYSVAL is the default.

With system values, keep in mind that when you change one you could unwittingly affect many things on your AS/400. Appendix A contains a list of system values. The following section describe the system values (*SYSVALS) that affect security. The most commonly used values are noted in brackets.

6.2.1 QSECURITY—Security Level

The first security system value is QSECURITY. It sets the security level of the whole machine. Here are the valid values for QSECURITY and a brief description of each level:

❖ Security Level 10. This is considered no security. The user may sign on with any user ID and no password. If the user profile does not exist, the system will just create one. Usually this results in hundreds of user profiles on the system as users make errors keying their IDs. With this scenario, every user has full access to everything on the system.

❖ Security Level 20. This is a little better than SL10. The user must sign on with a valid user ID and a password. Once the user has access, however, he or she has full access—except for things reserved for SECOFR—to everything on the system.

❖ Security Level 30. [This is the security level most common with AS/400 shops.] The user must sign on with a valid user ID and password. Users have access to objects only when the objects have been designated as useable by the individual user or by *PUBLIC (anyone). Remember, objects can be commands, files, or programs. Because there can be so many objects and so many users, designating individual access rights might seem a pain. Nevertheless, the AS/400 has some features that will speed up this task. For additional information, see section 6.3.3, Authorization Lists. When files are restored, there is an option on the restore command in SL30 that isn't on SL10/SL20. This is the ALLOW OBJECT DIFFERENCES option and it is defaulted to a *YES. If you are restoring a file and the file has been changed since the backup was made, if the option is still a *YES (the default), the system will complete the restore. If the option was changed to a *NO, the system will not complete the restore.

❖ Security Level 40. The user must sign on with a valid user ID and password. Users have access to objects only when the objects have been designated as useable by the individual user or by *PUBLIC (anyone). When files are restored, the same ALLOW OBJECT DIFFERENCES option is defaulted to a *NO and must be changed if the file has been changed since the last save. This is a small thing, but it can make simple restores difficult. The biggest thing SL40 does for you that the others don't do is that it prevents applications from using "unauthorized" low-level programming techniques.

❖ Security Level 50. This level was developed for the Department of Defense and it is finding more acceptance where AS/400 systems allow open access to remote users. This level is also called C2. With the following exceptions, SL50 is the same as SL40. Users can only access objects to which they have been given explicit access. This eliminates many of the shortcuts and defaults with SL30 and SL40. Programs will blow up if they access unauthorized low-level functions. Also, programs will blow up if they access AS/400 APIs or functions and they don't pass exactly the right number of parameters. NOTE: With many of these functions, the number of parameters are optional.

6.2.2 QMAXSIGN—Maximum Sign-On Attempts

QMAXSIGN declares the number of times a user can unsuccessfully attempt to sign onto the AS/400 before that user profile is deactivated. Once the user ID has been deactivated, only the SECOFR or system administrator can reactivate it. [3]

6.2.3 QPWDEXPITV—Password Expiration Interval

QPWDEXPITV specifies how many days the system will allow a user to go without changing his or her password. After this interval, the user can still sign on, but the only option available is to access the change-password function. Once the password has been changed, the user can continue as usual. [Varies, but try 30 or 45.]

6.2.4 QPWDMINLEN—Minimum Password Length

QPWDMINLEN specifies the minimum length of a password. It can range from 1 to 10 characters. The longer a password is the harder it is to guess. [6]

6.2.5 QPWDMAXLEN—Maximum Password Length

QPWDMAXLEN specifies the maximum length of a password. It also can range from 1 to 10 characters. While this requirement might seem a little silly, the AS/400 will need this setting to match the smaller password lengths of the other machines if it is networked with other, non-AS/400 machines. [10]

6.2.6 QPWDRQDDIF—Expired Password Must Be Changed

When the maximum time for a password has expired and the user is asked to change his or her password, if SYSVAL QPWDRQDDIF is set to a 1 (instead of a 0), the new password must be different from any of the previous 32 passwords. If QPWDRQDDIF is set to a 0, the new password can be the same. [1]

6.2.7 QPWDLMTCHR—Invalid Password Characters

System value QPWDLMTCHR allows you to specify up to 10 characters that your users may never put in as a password. These can be any 10 characters (such as @, #, S, %, ^, or &) but the idea is to block special characters. [0]

6.2.8 QPWDLMAJC—Limit Adjacent Characters In Password

If system value QPWDLMAJC is set to a 1, users cannot create passwords (such as 12345) that are not very secure. [0]

6.2.9 QPWDLMREP—Limit Repeated Characters In Password

If system value QPWDLMREP is set to a 1, users cannot create passwords (such as 11111) that are not very secure. [1]

6.2.10 QPWDPOSDIP—Force All New Password Characters to Be Different

If system value QPWDPOSDIF is set to a 1, users cannot create new passwords with any character the same as the old password. This prevents passwords like FRANK01, FRANK02, etc. [0]

6.2.11 QPWDRQDDGT—Force the Use of at Least One Number In a Password

System value QPWDRQDDGT, set to a 1, requires the user to build passwords that include at least one number. The number can be in any position and more than one number can be included, but there must be at least one number. [0]

6.2.12 QPWDVLDPGM—User Program to Validate Passwords

If the system doesn't give enough controls on the construction of passwords, you can specify a user-written program to validate new passwords to some other criteria. A validation program can be used to give the user additional instructions for creating a new password. [Not used.]

6.2.13 QAUDLVL—Keeping a Security Audit

System value QAUDLVL sets up a security audit. The audit can contain many parameters that tell the system what events it should record. Also, the security audit can monitor object activity, user activity, or any combination of the two. The audit records the event, who did it, when, and from what terminal. [Used or not used as the need arises.]

The audit journal is named QAUDJRN and it lives in library QSYS. You can query its contents at any time. For additional information, see chapter 4.

6.3 SECURITY

We've covered System Values in section 6.2, and User Profiles in chapter 5. We'll cover Object-Level Security in this section.

Security on the AS/400 comes from three generic places:

- ❖ System values.
- ❖ Each user profile (chapter 5).
- ❖ Each object.

Every AS/400 object carries its own list of who can do what to it. This is referred to as its *authorities*.

6.3.1 Ownership

The first item in an object's authority is who owns it. Ownership consists of one of four categories:

- ❖ The person who created it.

- ❖ The group user profile of the creator.

- ❖ Any other user to which ownership has been transferred.

- ❖ If the user profile has been deleted, the object's owner will be set to the system default, QDFTOWN.

Wherever ownership comes from the owner automatically has all rights to any object he owns. The owner can read, write, or change records as well as delete or change the object itself.

If you have special problems with the objects group of users own, you could use group user profiles and set object ownership to OWNER(*GRPPRF). In that way, one user can easily work on another user's programs or files. For additional information, see chapter 5.

Here's a twist to object ownership. You don't want programmers changing production jobs. Therefore, when programs or files are moved from a development (or quality assurance) library into production, object ownership should be changed to some nonperson owner. When the files or programs are checked out for maintenance, they can be changed back to the developers' group user profile. Object ownership is a little complex. However, it is one of the things a good change-management system can do for you.

6.3.2 Specific Authorities

There are plenty of users on a system and only one of them (or several through a group profile) can have ownership at one time. Access to others (non-owners) is granted through specific authorities.

Specific authorities are a list (attached to the object) of user profiles or group user profiles with a specific access authority for each. Although an object can only have one owner, it can have many individual specific users, and each user has access. There are four specific authorities that can be granted to an object. See Table 6-1.

Table 6-1: Specific Authorities That Can Be Granted to an Object.

Authority	Explanation
*ALL	The user can do anything with the object
*CHANGE	The user can change the object
	➤ File objects—the user can clear, read, or change the records in the file.
	➤ Program objects and command objects—the user can use them.
	No matter what the object is, the user cannot delete it or change its attributes.
*USE	The user can only use the object.
	➤ File objects—the user can read records.
	➤ Program or command objects—the user can execute it. The user cannot delete it or change its attributes
*EXCLUDE	The user can do nothing with the object.

Object authority is granted, revoked, or changed in a real-time mode through the following commands:

❖ GRTOBJAUT (GRANT OBJECT AUTHORITY).

❖ RVKOBJAUT (REVOKE OBJECT AUTHORITY).

❖ EDTOBJAUT (EDIT OBJECT AUTHORITY).

❖ WRKOBJ (WORK WITH OBJECTS, then take options for authorities).

Note that when a user's specific authority is removed from an object—if the user is not the SECOFR or owner—the user's authority reverts to whatever *PUBLIC authority is set. Therefore, if the public can use an object and you remove a user from the object's specific authority, the user can still use the object as a member of the public. For that reason, some AS/400 customers set public authority to *EXCLUDE on all objects.

Granting, revoking, and changing object authority is done to individual objects. Because that can be quite time-consuming, the AS/400 allows generic identification of objects on the OBJECT AUTHORITY commands. It even allows the word *ALL so that all objects (usually within a library) can be changed at once. While this method can save a lot of keying time, it should be used judiciously.

6.3.3 Authorization Lists

Because adding individual users to an object can be quite cumbersome, AS/400 objects can be secured through *authorization lists*. An authorization list is a type of object itself (*AUTL). It contains lists of user IDs and authorizations for each one.

If you have an application that has hundreds of objects and hundreds of users, you can set up an authorization list of all valid users and their authorizations. You can attach the list to each of the hundreds of objects and avoid rekeying the same set of users for each object. When you create a new file in that application, you can just attach the same authorization list to it and all your security needs will be met. If a user leaves the group and is no longer eligible to access the object, you just drop that user's name from the authorization list, and you don't have to reconstruct the authorities for each object.

You can mix special authorities with authorization lists. You can even have the same users named in both places. Such practice is common but redundant. Once the system finds the user named in an authorization list, it won't look further into the specific authorities.

The contents of authorization lists are integrated with the user profiles. If you delete a user profile, it automatically will be deleted from any authorization list on which it appears.

6.3.4 Public Authority

Besides ownership, specific authorities, and authorization lists, objects have *public authority*. This is the amount of authority the object will allow someone who isn't recognized in any other category. The system default is *NONE or the public has no access to the object. Public access *EXCLUDE also leaves the public with no access.

The object owner, the SECOFR, or applications such as a change-management system can change the public authority on any object. Authorities that can be granted to *PUBLIC are shown in Table 6-2.

Table 6-2: Authorities That Can Be Granted to *PUBLIC.

Authority	Explanation
*ALL	All access to the object.
*CHANGE	The public can change the object.
	➤ File objects—the user can clear, read, or change the records in the file.
	➤ Program objects and command objects—the user can use them.
	No matter what the object is, the user cannot delete it or change its attributes.
*USE	The public can only use the object.
	➤ File objects—the user can read records.
	➤ Program or command objects—the user can execute it. The user cannot delete it or change its attributes
*EXCLUDE	The user can do nothing with the object.

6.3.4.1 Recap

Some simple system commands can be used to review what I've just covered. Figure 6-1 shows a sample authorization list named MCAUTLST.

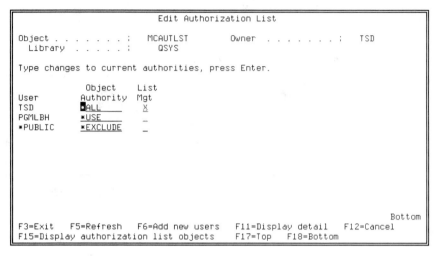

```
                      Edit Authorization List

Object . . . . . . . :   MCAUTLST        Owner  . . . . . . . :   TSD
   Library  . . . . . :   QSYS

Type changes to current authorities, press Enter.

                Object    List
User            Authority Mgt
TSD             *ALL        X
PGMLBH          *USE        _
*PUBLIC         *EXCLUDE    _




                                                             Bottom
F3=Exit    F5=Refresh    F6=Add new users    F11=Display detail   F12=Cancel
F15=Display authorization list objects       F17=Top    F18=Bottom
```

Figure 6-1: Sample authorization list, MCAUTLSt. Displayed using the EDTAUTL command.

The owner of the authorization list is TSD. TSD is not a user profile, but a group user profile for all the users in a department. Therefore, any user in that group has all access to any object that has this authorization list on it. Notice the X (to the right of TSD) under the List Mgt column. This symbol indicates this user (or, in this case, a group of users) can change the authorization list. Anyone not so marked may not change the list. On an authorization list, this is referred to as *list management rights*.

User PGMLBH, who is a programmer, can change any records on any files that use this list, but cannot delete those files or change their descriptions. In addition, the public is excluded from any access to this file. You can investigate further and see what objects use the authorization list by pressing the F15 key. See Figure 6-2.

```
┌─────────────────────────────────────────────────────────────────────┐
│█                    Display Authorization List Objects                │
│                                                                       │
│ Authorization list . . . . . . . . :    MCAUTLST                      │
│   Library  . . . . . . . . . . . . :      QSYS                        │
│ Owner  . . . . . . . . . . . . . . :    TSD                           │
│                                                                       │
│ Object      Library    Type     Owner      Text                       │
│ ASPUTLC1    @QAS4OBJ   *PGM     TSDMYD     ASP Utilization             │
│ ASPUTLR1    @QAS4OBJ   *PGM     TSDMYD     ASP Uitlization Report      │
│                                                                       │
│                                                                       │
│                                                                       │
│                                                                       │
│                                                                       │
│                                                                       │
│                                                              Bottom    │
│ Press Enter to continue.                                              │
│                                                                       │
│ F3=Exit    F12=Cancel    F17=Top    F18=Bottom                        │
└─────────────────────────────────────────────────────────────────────┘
```

Figure 6-2: Result of pressing F15 from see Figure 6-1—EDTAUTl. Objects that use the authorization list MCAUTLST.

In this case, two objects use it, and they are both programs. No one else has access because the public is excluded.

If you want to see what security is attached to an object, you can either use the EDTOBJAUT (EDIT OBJECT AUTHORITY) or WRKOBJ (WORK OBJECT) commands. Either command will produce the screen shown in Figure 6-3.

```
┌─────────────────────────────────────────────────────────────────────┐
│                         Edit Object Authority                         │
│                                                                       │
│ Object . . . . . . . :   CWXC340      Object type  . . . . :   *PGM   │
│   Library  . . . . . :   SCBIN130     Owner  . . . . . . . :   BINS   │
│                                                                       │
│ Type changes to current authorities, press Enter.                     │
│                                                                       │
│ Object secured by authorization list  . . . . . . . . . . .   MCAUTLST│
│                                                                       │
│              Object                                                   │
│ User         Authority                                                │
│ ALLONCMS     *ALL                                                     │
│ *PUBLIC      *EXCLUDE                                                  │
│                                                                       │
└─────────────────────────────────────────────────────────────────────┘
```

Figure 6-3: Object authority from object viewpoint.

At the top right, the owner is specified as BINS. I just happen to know that BINS is a group profile name. If you didn't know that, you could use the WRKUSRPRF command to see it.

The object is secured with authorization list MCAUTLST, which you have seen on Figure 6-1.

ALLONCMS is a user ID with all access. The public is excluded from the object. Because *PUBLIC was taken care of in the authorization list, this is redundant.

6.3.5 Special

Suddenly, there is a problem with security by ownership, specific, and authorization list. So far, I have addressed only simple access or no-access situations. But there are gray areas. System operators must have enough access to the payroll file to be able to back it up or restore it, but you don't want them looking at payroll records.

The solution to these scenarios is through special authorities granted on the user profile. One or more special authorities can be granted to each user. Note the exception that special authorities stay with the user ID (not the objects). Table 6-3 shows the special authorities and what they allow a user to do.

Table 6-3: Special Authorities.

Authority	Explanation
*ALL	All access to the object.
	➤ This is reserved for SECOFR. (NOTE: when the system security level is set to 10 or...
*ALLOBJ	The user can do anything to any object.
	➤ 20, all users have *ALLOBJ special authority).
*SAVSYS	Allows the user to perform backup and restore operations on all objects even if the user has no authority to an object. This authority is usually given to system operators.
*JOBCTL	Allows a user to manage jobs running on the system. He or she can change jobs to other job queues and change output to different queues. For running jobs, the user can cancel, alter, or change priorities. On the system, he or she can start or stop entire subsystems, load the operating system, and so on. This authority usually is granted to system operators.
*SPLCTL	This authority allows a user to manage output queues. Users can display, move, print, release, or cancel spooled output. This is commonly granted to all users who need to be able to browse their reports while they sit in output queues. The problem that can occur with this authority is that you don't want one user browsing another user's output. The solution is to build restricted output queues where users with *SPLCTL can browse only those output queues in which they are not restricted.
*SECADM	Allows user to create and alter user profiles. Some AS/400 shops have a person dedicated to this function.
*SERVICE	This allows service and dump functions. These are never given to someone who is not extremely knowledgeable about the system. Often, this authorization is extended to the IBM service representatives rather than anyone in house.

6.3.6 Adopted Authorities

Another way to obtain access to a file is through adopted authorities. In concept, adopted authority is a little different than the others in that it affects (and resides in) an executing program. When a program runs, it also has authority and a user ID. Typically, the user who starts the program becomes the "user" for security purposes. In this way, two people can run the same program at the same time and get different results.

Let's consider two users, Bob and Sue, who run the same program. The program needs to read the payroll master-file object. If the object has Bob on its list of those who may look at the file, Bob's program will be able to look at and read records. On the other hand, if Sue isn't on the list and she isn't an owner of the file—and the file has public access excluded—Sue's program won't be able to read the file's records and will abort. Bob's won't.

The preceding example can be a problem where an application spans departments. For example, consider two separate applications: insurance claims and policies. The first cut at security is easy. Claims files are available to claims people; some users can only read files and some can read and update files. The same procedures apply to the policy files and users.

Problems become evident when data records must be made accessible in order to verify coverage to support the claim. If you proceeded no further with security, no claims person or program would be able to look at a policy record.

One way around this problem would be to extend policy-file access to all claims people. Suddenly, the shop's security would be very watered down. It wouldn't take long before everyone had access to everyone's files, and that's not be acceptable in some shops.

The way around this problem is with *adopted authority*. Here's how it works. A developer who has access to policy files writes a simple record-retrieval program. The developer gives claims people access to the program. After the developer compiles and tests the program, he or she changes it with the CHANGE PROGRAM (CHGPGM) command.

The change the developer makes is that the authority the program uses is the authority of the program's owner (the developer) not the user running the program (the claims people). Therefore, when a claims person executes the program, he or she can read a policy record because the owner of the program has access to policies (even if the user doesn't).

This is effective because the claims person's capability to read policy records is limited to only those records he or she can get through the accessing program. The claims person isn't left with any residual authority that will allow him or her into policies using any other accessing method.

However, there is one drawback to this method. Once one program adopts authority, any programs *it calls* will adopt that authority as well. Adoption occurs even if the programs are meant only to have user authority. The exposure is small because of the controls available. The programmer who writes the accessing program should know this and not have the program call any other programs. Problems can occur in a shop with inexperienced programmers who know enough about adopted authorities to be dangerous.

6.4 BIBLIOGRAPHY

OS/400 Security Reference V3R6

AS/400 System Operations V3R6

7. Backup and Recovery

7.1 OVERVIEW

Backups on the AS/400 are done with save commands (prefix SAV). Recoveries are made with restore commands (prefix RST). You can save and restore AS/400 objects for disaster protection or to move files, objects, and libraries from one system to another.

7.2 SAVE TO...

You can save individual objects, files, libraries, or the entire system on the AS/400 to one or more diskettes, tape reels, cartridges. Individual libraries, or multiple files/objects can also be saved to a *save file*. All AS/400 objects that are saved are done so in a special file format that you cannot read or process directly. They are different from database files in that they have no individual fields and their contents are compressed so that multiple objects, files, and libraries can be stored within a single save file. They must be restored before you can access their contents.

While most of the save media are self-explanatory, save files are not. They are special AS/400 objects with object type *SAVF.

Saving objects to save files is typically faster than saving objects to tape because any write operation is faster to disk than to tape. After the save is complete and the system is restored to normal operation, the save file is stored on magnetic media and purged from the system. The down side to save files is that they can take up quite a bit of disk space until they are archived and purged.

7.3 BACKUP AND RECOVERY LOOK AND FEEL

New AS/400 customers sometimes feel that things are not progressing well when they first do a backup or a restore. Feelings of uncertainty are especially evident in customers who back up or recover to reel tapes where they can watch the tape drive's progress. The AS/400 backup and restore programs do some preliminary processing and post processing that makes the drive seem a little erratic.

When saving objects, files, and libraries, the backup process builds directories about the objects being saved. When each directory is complete, it is written to the save media and the objects follow. Many small objects take a long time (usually longer than a few large objects). If you view the tape, it advances a few inches when the process starts and then sits for several minutes before rapidly continuing. The tape might stop again for a few minutes and then continue.

Restores are similar. The tape drive will read a few inches of information and then digest it for several minutes before continuing. The same behavior happens on diskettes and tape cartridges (even save files), but there is nothing that you can watch like the older tape reels.

7.4 SAVE COMMANDS

The following sections describe the AS/400 save commands and their formats.

7.4.1 SAVSYS

SAVSYS must be run with the system in a *restricted state*. In other words, all subsystems—including the controlling subsystem—are ended. Save System (SAVSYS) saves the system libraries. It will save:

❖ OS/400.

❖ Licensed internal code.

❖ System configuration. For additional information, see section 7.3.1.1 SAVCFG.

❖ System resource management objects.

❖ Security objects. For additional information, see section 7.3.1.2 SAVSECDTA.

❖ All PTFs. For additional information, see chapter 2.

But it won't save:

❖ IBM licensed programs (such as compilers).

❖ Any optional parts of OS/400.

❖ Folders.

- ❖ Libraries QGPL and QUSRSYS. NOTE: Although they start with a Q, they are not really system libraries.

- ❖ Any user libraries.

Figure 7-1 shows the prompted version of SAVSYS.

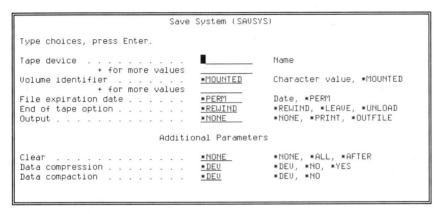

```
                          Save System (SAVSYS)

Type choices, press Enter.

Tape device  . . . . . . . . .   ▮_____       Name
                + for more values
Volume identifier  . . . . . . .  *MOUNTED        Character value, *MOUNTED
                + for more values  _____
File expiration date . . . . . .  *PERM           Date, *PERM
End of tape option . . . . . . .  *REWIND         *REWIND, *LEAVE, *UNLOAD
Output . . . . . . . . . . . . .  *NONE           *NONE, *PRINT, *OUTFILE


                       Additional Parameters

Clear  . . . . . . . . . . . .    *NONE           *NONE, *ALL, *AFTER
Data compression . . . . . . . .  *DEV            *DEV, *NO, *YES
Data compaction  . . . . . . . .  *DEV            *DEV, *NO
```

Figure 7-1: Prompted version of SAVSYS command.

7.4.1.1 SAVCFG

A SAVSYS takes a long time and, for the most part, it isn't necessary to do very often. The operating system is quite stable. However, you will routinely change parts of the operating system—such as device configurations, user profiles, and authorities—and you will probably want a current backup of them. Because backing up one part takes about 2 minutes, you don't want to spend hours doing a whole SAVSYS.

In order to save time, the AS/400 offers the SAVE CONFIGURATION (SAVCFG) command. This is similar to the SAVSYS command discussed in section 7.4.1, but it only saves device configurations. Device configurations are:

- ❖ Line descriptions.

- ❖ Controller descriptions.

- ❖ Device descriptions.

- ❖ Mode descriptions.

- ❖ Class-of-service descriptions.

- ❖ Network interface descriptions.
- ❖ Connection lists.
- ❖ Configuration lists.
- ❖ System configuration:
  - ✓ Hardware resources.
  - ✓ Token ring adapter data.

Figure 7-2 shows a prompted version of SAVCFG.

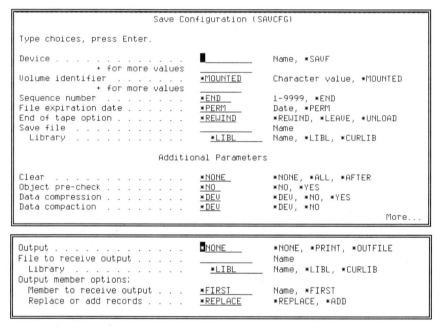

```
                      Save Configuration (SAVCFG)

Type choices, press Enter.

Device . . . . . . . . . . . . .   █_____    Name, *SAVF
              + for more values                  _____
Volume identifier . . . . . . .   *MOUNTED       Character value, *MOUNTED
              + for more values
Sequence number . . . . . . . .   *END           1-9999, *END
File expiration date . . . . . .  *PERM          Date, *PERM
End of tape option . . . . . . .  *REWIND        *REWIND, *LEAVE, *UNLOAD
Save file . . . . . . . . . . .                  Name
   Library . . . . . . . . . . .  *LIBL          Name, *LIBL, *CURLIB

                      Additional Parameters

Clear . . . . . . . . . . . . .   *NONE          *NONE, *ALL, *AFTER
Object pre-check . . . . . . . .  *NO            *NO, *YES
Data compression . . . . . . . .  *DEV           *DEV, *NO, *YES
Data compaction . . . . . . . .   *DEV           *DEV, *NO
                                                              More...
```

```
Output . . . . . . . . . . . . .  █NONE          *NONE, *PRINT, *OUTFILE
File to receive output . . . . .                 Name
   Library . . . . . . . . . . .  *LIBL          Name, *LIBL, *CURLIB
Output member options:
   Member to receive output . . . *FIRST         Name, *FIRST
   Replace or add records . . . . *REPLACE       *REPLACE, *ADD
```

Figure 7- 2: Prompted version of SAVCFG command (part 1 and 2).

7.4.1.2 *SAVSECDTA*

Similar to the SAVCFG command, SAVE SECURITY DATA (SAVSECDTA) presumes that security data is a system component that is subject to change and, rather than require you to do a complete SAVSYS each time you add or drop a user profile, SAVSECDTA will only save system security information.

The items saved are:

❖ User profiles.

❖ Private authorities to objects.

❖ Authorization lists.

For additional information, see chapter 6. Figure 7-3 shows a prompted version of SAVSECDTA.

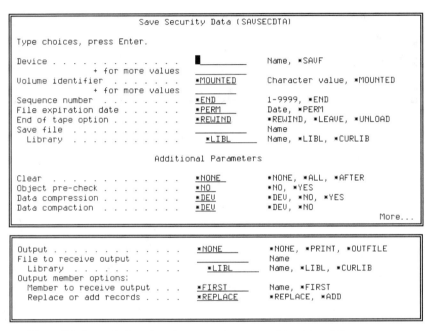

```
                    Save Security Data (SAVSECDTA)

Type choices, press Enter.

Device . . . . . . . . . . . .    █_____      Name, *SAVF
             + for more values    _____
Volume identifier . . . . . . .   *MOUNTED        Character value, *MOUNTED
             + for more values    _____
Sequence number . . . . . . . .   *END            1-9999, *END
File expiration date . . . . . .  *PERM           Date, *PERM
End of tape option . . . . . . .  *REWIND         *REWIND, *LEAVE, *UNLOAD
Save file . . . . . . . . . . .   _____       Name
  Library  . . . . . . . . . . .  *LIBL           Name, *LIBL, *CURLIB

                    Additional Parameters

Clear  . . . . . . . . . . . .    *NONE           *NONE, *ALL, *AFTER
Object pre-check . . . . . . . .  *NO             *NO, *YES
Data compression . . . . . . . .  *DEV            *DEV, *NO, *YES
Data compaction  . . . . . . . .  *DEV            *DEV, *NO
                                                                    More...
```

```
Output . . . . . . . . . . . .    *NONE           *NONE, *PRINT, *OUTFILE
File to receive output . . . . .  _____       Name
  Library  . . . . . . . . . . .  *LIBL           Name, *LIBL, *CURLIB
Output member options:
  Member to receive output . . .  *FIRST          Name, *FIRST
  Replace or add records . . . .  *REPLACE        *REPLACE, *ADD
```

Figure 7-3: Prompted version of SAVSECDTA command (part 1 and 2).

7.4.2 SAVLIB

This command is used to save the libraries that SAVSYS didn't save and any user-created libraries. Figure 7-4 shows a prompted version of that command.

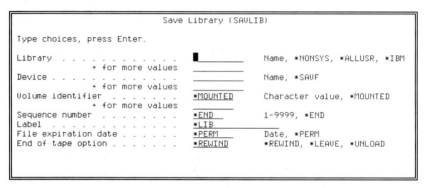

```
                          Save Library (SAVLIB)

Type choices, press Enter.

Library . . . . . . . . . . .   ▌           Name, *NONSYS, *ALLUSR, *IBM
              + for more values _____
Device . . . . . . . . . . . .  _____ Name, *SAVF
              + for more values _____
Volume identifier . . . . . .   *MOUNTED    Character value, *MOUNTED
              + for more values _____
Sequence number . . . . . . .   *END        1-9999, *END
Label . . . . . . . . . . . .   *LIB
File expiration date . . . . .  *PERM       Date, *PERM
End of tape option . . . . . .  *REWIND     *REWIND, *LEAVE, *UNLOAD
```

Figure 7-4: Prompted version of SAVLIB command.

The first parameter, LIB, is an important one. It's possible values are:

❖ The name of up to 300 libraries to save.

❖ *NONSYS

  ✓ Saves all non-system libraries in alphabetical order.

  ✓ Must be run with the system in a restricted state.

❖ *ALLUSR

  ✓ Saves including: QDSNX, QGPL, QGPL38, QPFRDATA, QRCL, QS36F, QUSER38, QUSERSYS, QUSRVXRXMX, and any other library that does not begin with a Q or #.

❖ *IBM

  ✓ Should be run when libraries it saves are not being used.

  ✓ Saves libraries starting with a "#" symbol.

  ✓ Saves all Q-libraries except the ones saved by *ALLUSR.

You cannot use SAVLIB to save these libraries:

❖ QSYS

❖ QDOC

❖ QSPL

❖ QRPLOBJ

❖ QTEMP

❖ QSRV

❖ QRECOVERY

This command has an optional parameter, OMITLIB, that appears whenever one of the three generic values (*NONSYS, *ALLUSR, *IBM) are specified. With this parameter, you can exclude up to 300 specific libraries from being saved.

Although it is necessary to have the system in a restricted state only when saving with the LIB(*NONSYS) parameter, in practice the other parameters are almost as limited. Technically, you can save a library when some of its objects are in use. The ones that are active will not be saved. You really don't want a false sense of security from believing that your save tape contains all the objects from a library when it doesn't. For that reason, when backing up any library, make sure no one is using any of its objects.

NOTE: The way around this problem is called save-while-active. For additional information see section 7.5.

7.4.3 SAVCHGOBJ

The SAVE CHANGED OBJECT (SAVCHGOBJ) command is used to save any object changed—such as a file with records added, changed, or deleted—since the previous save. Most shops specify *ALLUSR but you can identify specific libraries. If you use *ALLUSR, the optional OMITLIB parameter allows you to omit libraries. Figure 7-5 shows the prompted version.

```
┌────────────────────────────────────────────────────────────────────┐
│                 Save Changed Objects (SAVCHGOBJ)                     │
│                                                                      │
│ Type choices, press Enter.                                           │
│                                                                      │
│ Objects  . . . . . . . . . . .   █_____   Name, generic*, *ALL  │
│            + for more values     _____                          │
│ Library  . . . . . . . . . . .   _____    Name, *ALLUSR         │
│            + for more values     _____                          │
│ Device . . . . . . . . . . . .   _____    Name, *SAVF           │
│            + for more values     _____                          │
│ Object types . . . . . . . . .   *ALL___      *ALL, *ALRTBL, *BNDDIR...│
│            + for more values     _____                          │
│ Journaled objects  . . . . . .   *NO____      *NO, *YES              │
│ Reference date . . . . . . . .   *SAVLIB      Date, *SAVLIB          │
│ Reference time . . . . . . . .   *NONE__      Time, *NONE            │
│ Volume identifier  . . . . . .   *MOUNTED     Character value, *MOUNTED│
│            + for more values     _____                          │
│ Sequence number  . . . . . . .   *END___      1-9999, *END           │
│ Label  . . . . . . . . . . . .   *LIB_____                        │
│ File expiration date . . . . .   *PERM___     Date, *PERM            │
│                                                            More...    │
└────────────────────────────────────────────────────────────────────┘
┌────────────────────────────────────────────────────────────────────┐
│ End of tape option . . . . . .   *REWIND      *REWIND, *LEAVE, *UNLOAD│
│ Starting library . . . . . . .   *FIRST___    Name, *FIRST           │
│ Save file  . . . . . . . . . .   _____   Name                   │
│   Library  . . . . . . . . . .   *LIBL____    Name, *LIBL, *CURLIB   │
│ Update history . . . . . . . .   *YES___      *YES, *NO              │
│ Library to omit  . . . . . . .   *NONE_____   Name, *NONE            │
│            + for more values     _____                          │
│                                                                      │
│                     Additional Parameters                           │
│                                                                      │
│ Target release . . . . . . . .   *CURRENT     *CURRENT, *PRV, V2R3M0...│
│ Clear  . . . . . . . . . . . .   *NONE__      *NONE, *ALL, *AFTER    │
│ Object pre-check . . . . . . .   *NO__        *NO, *YES              │
│ Save active  . . . . . . . . .   *NO____      *NO, *LIB, *SYNCLIB, *SYSDFN│
│ Save active wait time  . . . .   120_____   0-99999, *NOMAX        │
│                                                            More...    │
└────────────────────────────────────────────────────────────────────┘
┌────────────────────────────────────────────────────────────────────┐
│ Save active message queue  . . .  *NONE_____   Name, *NONE, *WRKSTN  │
│   Library  . . . . . . . . . . .  *LIBL____    Name, *LIBL, *CURLIB  │
│ Save access paths  . . . . . . .  *NO__        *NO, *YES             │
│ Save file data . . . . . . . . .  *YES__       *YES, *NO             │
│ Data compression . . . . . . . .  *DEV__       *DEV, *NO, *YES       │
│ Data compaction  . . . . . . . .  *DEV__       *DEV, *NO             │
│ Output . . . . . . . . . . . . .  *NONE__      *NONE, *PRINT, *OUTFILE│
│ File to receive output . . . . .  _____   Name                  │
│   Library  . . . . . . . . . . .  *LIBL____    Name, *LIBL, *CURLIB  │
│ Output member options:                                               │
│   Member to receive output . . .  *FIRST___    Name, *FIRST          │
│   Replace or add records . . . .  *REPLACE     *REPLACE, *ADD        │
│ Type of output information . . .  *OBJ__       *OBJ, *LIB, *MBR      │
└────────────────────────────────────────────────────────────────────┘
```

Figure 7-5: Prompted version of the SAVCHGOBJ *command (parts 1-3).*

7.4.4 SAVOBJ

While not always considered part of backup or recovery, the save object (SAVOBJ) command nevertheless has an ancillary role. SAVOBJ will allow you to save individual objects within libraries. A good backup strategy will use the other commands, but this one fills a niche as a backup tool.

 Saving something on the AS/400 isn't always done for disaster-recovery reasons. SAVOBJ is often done just because its a convenient way of saving something or transporting a set of objects.

If you have two AS/400s linked as a networked, you should find it easy to save several objects in a save file, send the save file to the other machine, and restore the objects there. Don't attempt something like the SAVLIB (which will save a whole library as a minimum). SAVOBJ will allow you to save exactly the objects you want. Figure 7-6 shows a prompted view of the SAVOBJ command.

```
╔══════════════════════════════════════════════════════════════════╗
║                    Save Object (SAVOBJ)                            ║
║                                                                    ║
║  Type choices, press Enter.                                        ║
║                                                                    ║
║  Objects  . . . . . . . . . . . .   _____  Name, generic*, *ALL
║               + for more values     _____                   ║
║  Library  . . . . . . . . . . .     _____  Name             ║
║               + for more values     _____                   ║
║  Device . . . . . . . . . . . .     _____  Name, *SAVF      ║
║               + for more values     _____                   ║
║  Object types . . . . . . . . .     *ALL_____     *ALL, *ALRTBL, *BNDDIR...
║               + for more values     _____                   ║
║  Volume identifier  . . . . . .     *MOUNTED      Character value, *MOUNTED
║               + for more values     _____                       ║
║  Sequence number  . . . . . . .     *END___       1-9999, *END    ║
║  Label  . . . . . . . . . . . .     *LIB_____                    ║
║  File expiration date . . . . .     *PERM____     Date, *PERM     ║
║  End of tape option . . . . . .     *REWIND       *REWIND, *LEAVE, *UNLOAD
║  Save file  . . . . . . . . . .     _____  Name            ║
║     Library . . . . . . . . . .     *LIBL_____    Name, *LIBL, *CURLIB
║                                                         More...    ║
╚══════════════════════════════════════════════════════════════════╝
```

```
╔══════════════════════════════════════════════════════════════════╗
║  Update history . . . . . . . .     *YES          *YES, *NO       ║
║                                                                    ║
║                     Additional Parameters                          ║
║                                                                    ║
║  Target release . . . . . . . .     *CURRENT      *CURRENT, *PRV, V2R3M0...
║  Clear  . . . . . . . . . . . .     *NONE         *NONE, *ALL, *AFTER
║  Object pre-check . . . . . . .     *NO           *NO, *YES       ║
║  Save active  . . . . . . . . .     *NO____       *NO, *LIB, *SYNCLIB, *SYSDFN
║  Save active wait time  . . . .     120_____      0-99999, *NOMAX ║
║  Save active message queue  . .     *NONE         Name, *NONE, *WRKSTN
║     Library . . . . . . . . . .     *LIBL_____    Name, *LIBL, *CURLIB
║  File member:                                                      ║
║     File . . . . . . . . . . .      *ALL_____    Name, *ALL      ║
║     Member . . . . . . . . . .      *ALL_____    Name, generic*, *ALL, *NONE
║               + for more values     _____                   ║
║               + for more values _                                  ║
║                                                         More...    ║
╚══════════════════════════════════════════════════════════════════╝
```

```
╔══════════════════════════════════════════════════════════════════╗
║  Save access paths  . . . . . .     *NO___        *NO, *YES       ║
║  Save file data . . . . . . . .     *YES___       *YES, *NO       ║
║  Storage  . . . . . . . . . . .     *KEEP___      *KEEP, *FREE    ║
║  Data compression . . . . . . .     *DEV____      *DEV, *NO, *YES ║
║  Data compaction  . . . . . . .     *DEV____      *DEV, *NO       ║
║  Output . . . . . . . . . . . .     *NONE____     *NONE, *PRINT, *OUTFILE
║  File to receive output . . . .     _____  Name            ║
║     Library . . . . . . . . . .     *LIBL_____    Name, *LIBL, *CURLIB
║  Output member options:                                            ║
║     Member to receive output  . .   *FIRST____    Name, *FIRST   ║
║     Replace or add records  . . .   *REPLACE      *REPLACE, *ADD ║
║  Type of output information . . .   *OBJ____      *OBJ, *LIB, *MBR ║
╚══════════════════════════════════════════════════════════════════╝
```

Figure 7-6: Prompted version of SAVOBj command (parts 1-3).

Although it might look completely functional, there are a couple of restrictions on the command's parameters that limit its use.

❖ If you specify more than one library, you must specify all objects (OBJ(*ALL)) within those libraries to be saved.

❖ If you want to save to an outfile (a *SAVF), you can only specify a single library.

7.5 SAVE-WHILE-ACTIVE

When save commands run, they try to grab an exclusive lock on whatever object they are saving. If the SAVLIB command can't obtain a lock, it will just ignore that object. If a command can obtain a lock, it won't release it until the object is saved. The AS/400 has a nice feature that allows an object to be saved while it is being accessed (even updated) by users. The feature is called a *save-while-active*.

Journaling must be in effect before you can use save-while-active. For additional information on journaling, see chapter 8.

The system creates a *checkpoint* of the file being saved, and then relies on the journal to capture any changes made to it. First, the file is saved. Then, as part of post-processing, the journal entries that were made during that time are applied. Next, the file is unlocked for the users. The users don't notice a thing happening except that their applications might run slower while the save is in progress. You invoke save-while-active (through the SAVACT parameter) on these save commands:

❖ SAVLIB

❖ SAVOBJ

❖ SAVCHGOBJ

Possible SAVACT values are:

❖ *NO—This is the default value. Objects will not be saved if they are being used.

❖ *SYSDFN—Objects in use will be saved. Objects will not be synchronized to each other.

❖ *LIB—Objects in use will be saved. All objects will be synchronized within each library.

❖ *SYNCLIB—Objects in use will be saved. All objects will be synchronized within all libraries being saved.

If the applications that are accessing the objects you are saving make changes to several files, synchronicity could be an issue. If the system were to come down during the save, you would want all files being accessed and saved to be synchronized so that you don't end up with transactions posted to some files but not others.

These synchronization values don't imply extra object locking or extra DASD overhead. They only indicate that a checkpoint has been reached and changes have been applied to changed files.

7.6 RESTORES

The opposite of save (or backup) is restore. Most of the save commands covered so far have a counterpart with a prefix RST (for restore). For example, SAVLIB can be restored with a RSTLIB. Here is a list of the common restore commands:

❖ RSTLIB—Restores one or more libraries.

❖ RSTOBJ—Restores one or more objects from one or more libraries.

❖ Security restores:

   ✓ RSTAUT—Restores authorizations.

   ✓ RSTCFG—Restores configurations.

   ✓ RSTUSRPRF—Restores user profiles.

SAVSYS doesn't have a counterpart. And the restore commands have some overlap where they can be used to restore files saved with other SAV commands. Table 7-1 shows the save and restore command relationships.

Table 7-1: Save and Restore Command Relationships.

Objects/ Files/ Libraries Saved with:	Can be Restored with:
SAVOBJ	RSTOBJ
SAVLIB	RSTOBJ or RSTLIB
SAVCHGOBJ	RSTOBJ
SAVSYS	RSTOBJ (though limited. See chapter 6, *AS/400 Basic Backup and Recovery Guide*) also RSTUSRPRF, RSTAUT, or RSTCFG
SAVCFG	RSTCFG

These commands are fairly simple, but RSTOBJ has two parameters you need to understand. The OPTION parameter is used to control what objects are restored. Here are the possible values for OPTION:

❖ *ALL—The default. All objects on the save media requested to be restored will be restored.

❖ *NEW—Only objects that do not exist on the system will be restored.

❖ *OLD—Only objects that do exist on the system will be restored.

❖ *FREE—Only objects that exist on the system with their storage freed will be restored.

OPTION refers to the objects on the system you are restoring to. The default *ALL is usually what you want (all items you want restored will be restored). The other parameter, DATABASE MEMBER OPTION, refers to the objects on the media you are restoring from. This parameter is only in effect when restoring database files, and it will cause you some grief if you're not careful.

Here are its possible values:

❖ *MATCH—the default. Database files to be restored will only be restored if the member lists exactly match the member lists on the system. For example, if you want to restore file TRNFILE and its saved version has four members, it will only be restored if TRNFILE on the system also has four members with the same names.

❖ *ALL—All members of a saved file are restored.

❖ *NEW—Only members of a saved file that aren't members of the file on the system are restored.

❖ *OLD—Only members of a saved file that are also members of the file on the system are restored.

If you forget to override the default from *MATCH to something else, you will spend time wondering why your restores didn't take.

7.7 BACKUP STRATEGY

In the event of a disaster, basically, your backups become your system. If you've lost your system, whatever isn't on the backups isn't part of your system anymore.

But backing up the whole system takes significant media and time and can require dedicated use of libraries while the backup takes place. Some AS/400 customers can tolerate no unavailability periods. Other users only operate during the daytime. Part of your backup strategy should be to determine the amount of time the system must be available to users and balance that against the backup effort required.

Recovery parameters need to be considered as part of your backup plan. Some say backup strategy should be considered first. How quickly the system must be returned to operational status will help determine the kind of backup and the frequency of the backups.

The physical units available on your specific AS/400 also will affect backup strategy. What is the capacity and speed of media units (tape, diskette drives, DASD)? If *SAVF are considered, how much extra DASD is available? How much operator time is available for manual processes such as changing tapes?

Part of your routine backup strategy should be to rotate through several tapes. In the event you do have to restore objects, files, and libraries—and the tape is bad or becomes bad during the process—you at least have another tape. While the data will be somewhat obsolete, it will be better than nothing.

Use media rotation and store one or more of the rotated sets off site. This will ensure your backups survive an on-site disaster. A suggested backup strategy is:

❖ Whenever you install a new release of the operating system, a new licensed program, or some new PTFs, back up the system environment.

❖ Monthly—save the entire system.

❖ Weekly—save all user libraries. These include libraries for users and programmers as well as libraries for all applications. Save everything in their libraries.

❖ Daily—save all objects that were changed that day.

❖ Periodically:
   ✓ Prior to purging obsolete objects from a library, save the library.
   ✓ Prior to running a large processing cycle, save the application's libraries.

Backups take away resources from normal processing and heavy, normal processing makes a backup run slow. Therefore, backups are almost always done during the night when work on the system is at its lightest. Even at 24-hour AS/400 shops, the demand on the system is lightest during evening hours. Normal system activity and the processing required to do backups conflict with each other.

7.8 VERIFY YOUR BACKUP STRATEGY

Its rare for a shop to actually lose their AS/400 to the extent that they really need to reload their systems from the backup media. However, when it does happen, a high percentage of users find that one or more important things weren't backed up. This is not a good time to discover backup problems.

Check and double-check your backup strategy periodically to determine four points:

- ❖ Are the planned saves completing? Surprisingly, too many shops go for months with failed saves.

- ❖ Are you saving what you think you're saving? For example, are all user libraries really getting saved? How about all libraries containing source code? All developers' libraries?

- ❖ Are the save tapes readable?

- ❖ Is the tape drive in good condition?

If you automate these checks as much as you can, make them happen soon after every backup to ensure that your strategy works. At least, be as sure as you can be without going through an actual disaster.

7.8.1 Are Saves Complete?

Review the save job log the morning after the save was supposed to run. Just bring it up on your workstation and go to the bottom of the log. Quickly verify that the job completed normally and does not have an error code. Also, verify that the save wasn't canceled by the operator.

The most common exposure for incomplete saves I've seen is in small shops with night-shift operations staff. The new operators are assigned to the night shift. I've seen more than one person not recognize the message icon on the workstation and cancel the save when it requested a second tape! Even if that doesn't happen, operators are busy and aren't always alert to an abnormal termination. Perform a periodic double-check.

7.8.2 Are You Saving Everything?

When the AS/400 saves an object, it updates the date and time the object was saved. You can check this information with the DISPLAY OBJECT DESCRIPTION (DSPOBJD) or WORK OBJECT (WRKOBJ) commands. The concept is that you can do a save and then check each object to verify it was actually saved. That's maximum tedium. If you have the QUSRTOOL library, you'll find two commands, CHKSAVSTS and PRTSAVSTS, that will identify any objects that have been changed since they were last saved. If you run either of these commands soon after a save, it will list the objects that weren't saved.

If you don't have the QUSRTOOL library, it's easy enough to issue the command, DSPOBJD, specifying output to a file, and then read the file with a program or query. Just have the program or query check two dates: the last save date (ODSDAT) and last changed date (ODLDAT).

 The dates are both in MMDDYY format. Therefore, you will have to change them into YYMMDD for an easy check. Have the program or query report all objects with ODLDAT greater than ODSDAT. If you run it soon after a save, the list it prints will be the objects not saved.

7.8.3 Are the Tapes and Drives Okay?

The last weak link in any backup and recovery strategy is with the media or drives themselves. No one relies on tapes for everyday data processing like they used to. Tapes and drives have been relegated strictly to backup and recovery. If the recovery side of that equation is rare, you really can't be sure it will work.

7.8.3.1 Tapes and Diskettes

Verify that the tapes and diskettes you use for your saves are good. Shops reuse the same tapes and diskettes for repeated saves without taking into account that magnetic media wears thin over time. Unfortunately, drive units will write onto unreadable tapes.

You probably have a backup strategy that involves rotating sets of tapes and diskettes. Begin each set with new tapes or diskettes. As you save to them, the system will record any errors it encounters when writing to them. Individual errors aren't the problem, but lots of errors are a signal. Look for a trend. New, fresh tapes won't have many errors; older ones will have many. As errors increase, replace the entire set. Tapes are cheap. Don't mix old tapes with new tapes.

Verify tapes after the save. The tapes don't have to be on the drives to be verified. Any errors are already in the system. Start the SYSTEM SERVICE TOOLS (STRSST) and select option 1, START A SERVICE TOOL. From there, select option 1 again, ERROR LOG UTILITY, and then option 5, DISPLAY OR PRINT TAPE OR DISKETTE SESSION STATISTICS.

The default time period to look at errors is the previous 24 hours. Override this to the backup period. You'll get a report of each drive's read/write errors, errors corrected, as well as number of bytes written to tapes. This report can be printed and stored with the backup tape set.

7.8.3.2 Tape Drives and Diskette Drives

Again, there is a potential problem with tape drives when you only use them to create save tapes. If you have more than one tape drive and you use tapes frequently, or if you process tapes periodically from other sites, your drives are constantly being validated. Therefore, you're probably all right in this department. However, if you only have one drive that's only used to create save tapes, you might have a huge, unrecognized exposure.

Think about the kind of disasters from which you might have to recover. Isn't it possible you won't have access to the same drive that created your backup tapes? If a drive gets out of adjustment, it often can read the tapes it creates but no other drive can read them. Periodically verify your drives by taking the tapes they create and have them read on other drives.

While you're at it, borrow tapes created on other drives and read them on your primary drive. This protects you not only from out-of-adjustment drives, but also from having a drive that suddenly decides to eat tapes when you are restoring from a disaster.

7.9 BACKUP AND RECOVER TIMESAVERS

Some save commands require that the system first be in a *restricted state*. But any backup or recovery command can run faster if the system is in a restricted state. For maximum system up time for the users, objects can be backed up with the save-while-active function. While granting maximum up time to those users, this produces the slowest backups.

When saving many libraries, it will go faster if you can use a single SAVLIB command for all of them (rather than one SAVLIB for each library). Saving only changed objects daily with the SAVCHGOBJ command is faster than saving entire libraries.

Don't forget your restore requirements when planning your backup strategy. Saving access paths will definitely lengthen the backup process but it will also shorten the restore. Actually, in most cases, saving access paths will enhance the restore function many times more than it degrades the backup function.

NOTE: To be successfully saved and restored, ACCPTH(*YES) must be specified on both the save and restore commands and, if the access path belongs to a logical file, the file must have MAINT(*IMMED) or MAINT(*DELAY).

If the person doing the backups has special authority *SAVSYS or *ALLOBJ in his or her user profile, security checking on each object will be bypassed and the save operation will be faster. For more information on special authorities, see chapter 5 and chapter 6.

Data compression can reduce the amount of media required to save objects, files, or libraries but it will slow down the backup. There are three data compression choices:

❖ Software data compression done by the CPU. Slows the backups down the most.

❖ Hardware data compression performed by the AS/400 adapter (with the attachment feature). Faster save times.

❖ Hardware data compacting performed by the 3480/3490 and 3590 tape units. Fastest and most elaborate data compression; results in best save times with compression.

7.10 BIBLIOGRAPHY

OS/400 Backup and Recovery—Advanced V3R6

OS/400 Backup and Recovery V3R6

AS/400 Systems Operations V3R6

8. Journaling

8.1 OVERVIEW

Journaling is a facility that extends the AS/400 recovery capabilities beyond what can be obtained through backup or restore commands (see chapter 7). The best you can hope for from an adequate backup strategy is a crashed system restored to the last save (which is probably the prior evening). Combine journaling with the same backup strategy and a system can be restored to its condition at the moment the system was lost.

Journaling can be useful in non-disaster scenarios, for example, in the middle of a nightly batch process. If you discover a program has gone bad—provided the files it was updating were journaled—you could remove every transaction that program made to the files with a single command. If a data-entry operator made some gross error, with a simple command you could remove all the updating he or she did to any files.

Journaling comes into play indirectly as well. It enables files to be backed up while in use. Also, journaling makes commitment control possible. For additional information, see chapter 7; section 7.5, Save-While-Active; and the *OS/400 Backup and Recovery—Avanced V3R6*.

Programmatically accessing and using journal receiver records is a common, though advanced, AS/400 technique. Journaling is usually done to all database files within a library, but it is not done to all libraries.

8.2 JOURNAL RECEIVER

When one or more database files arc journaled, all changes to those files are kept in a central repository called a *journal receiver*. This is different from normal file processing where each file keeps its own records (each with their own layouts). A journal receiver keeps records for all files being journaled to it.

The two main ingredients in journaling are objects called a journal and a journal receiver. The object type for a journal is *JRN and for a journal receiver it is *JRNRCV. The journal contains the logic for capturing and storing receiver records (lots of information about what it is journaling, but no real data). The data actually gets placed, by the journal, in the journal receiver.

The journal receiver (or receiver) is like a bag of potato chips. The journal is the machine filling the bag. The chips are database records. One bag moves along a conveyor belt and stops under the journal. The journal fills the bag until it is full or something tells it to stop, and then the bag is replaced with another empty bag.

Changes to several physical files can be journaled in one receiver. However, changes for one physical file can be journaled to only one journal at a time. Therefore, if a logical file is dependent on more than one physical file, all physical files should be journaled to the same receiver.

Keeping records for all database files makes the journal's records much more complex. They contain their own fields, but they also contain a single large data field for the database record. If you want to read the contents of a database record, you have to know its field definitions that can be pretty labor intensive.

Journal records show the updating activity to each record by storing the afterimage of that record. Optionally, you can have the journal store the record's before image as well. In addition to file updating activities, journal receivers also contain many files and much system-related information.

You should change journal receivers as they reach their threshold (specified on the CRTJRN command) or once a day. Journals and receivers have names, but many shops just identify the journal as JOURNAL and the receiver as RECEIVxxxx (the xxxx is a sequential number to give the receivers unique names). The following is a list of the information the receiver can contain:

❖ Record add, change, or delete information:
  ✓ The before image.
  ✓ The after image.

❖ File information—every time a file is:
  ✓ Opened.
  ✓ Closed.
  ✓ Saved.
  ✓ Restored.
  ✓ Renamed.
  ✓ Moved.

❖ File access path information.

❖ File member information—every time a file member is:

   ✓ Cleared.

   ✓ Added.

   ✓ Removed.

❖ System information—every time the system is:

   ✓ IPLed.

   ✓ To perform dynamic tuning (per the QPFRADJ system value) for every change the system makes.

❖ Improvised information. Programmers can write their own records to the journal receiver. For example, users might want to record account balances or to process checkpoints.

Each entry in the journal receiver is sequentially numbered. When a physical file is journaled, adds, changes, or deletes made to that physical file through logical files are journaled as changes to the physical file. For example, when SWXP010 is journaled, a program that makes updates through the attached logical file, SWXP01005, will create journal entries for SWXP010 but not for SWXP01005.

Optionally, you can journal access paths. Take the option. While it will increase the amount of data journaled, it also will reduce greatly the recovery time if you must rebuild from a journal.

From being around computers, you know there is a cost associated with everything. With journaling, you will have high DASD use and a little slower response time. Therefore, not all files are journaled; just the ones deemed crucial.

By the way, I said journaling is an extension of the AS/400's backup and recovery features. Many AS/400 shops think journaling is too slow and instead use RAID-5 or data mirroring for their backup and recovery protection. However, those methods relate to data corruption at the system level. Journaling is the only method that focuses on corrupted data at the file, program, and user levels.

8.3 Journaling Strategy

There are many parts to journaling strategy. You should be able to come up with a strategy customized for your shop. You can design this strategy to give yourself journaling as well as support issues within your shop. For example, you could have a journaling strategy that uses minimal disk space. However, a recovery from journals can take a while or be somewhat limited. On the other hand, you could journal everything possible in order to ensure fully functional and rapid recovery. Remember that this method will consume considerable disk space.

Here's the quick way to develop your own journal strategy. Decide first what kind of recovery you expect: fast and functional or slow and limited. Then determine how much information you need to journal (system, file, access paths, before images) to achieve that recovery goal. Once you've decided that, determine where to place the files you want journaled, the journal, and the receiver. Here are three options:

❖ Everything goes into the same library. While this is the simplest and most common method of journaling, its not the most efficient.

❖ Files and journals in one library and receivers in another. A little better for performance and managing backup and recovery.

❖ Files and journal in the system ASP; receivers in a user ASP, preferably one with its own input/output bus. Provides best performance and maximum protection of journal entries. For additional information about user ASPs, see chapter 3.

At the end of the day, no matter where you place your files, journal, and receivers, run a CL program that will:

❖ Change journal receivers.

❖ Save the library with the SAVLIB command, or

❖ Save changed objects with the SAVCHGOBJ command, excluding journaled files and attached receivers.

❖ Save the old receivers and then delete them. If you have the disk space, try to leave the last several receivers on the system.

When journaling starts on a file, a *journal identifier* is assigned to each member. You can see it when you do a DSPFD (DISPLAY FILE DESCRIPTION) command. Figure 8-1 shows an example.

```
12/14/96              Display File Description
DSPFD Command Input
   File  . . . . . . . . . . . . . . . . . . : FILE      DWXP031
     Library . . . . . . . . . . . . . . . . :           DTASCOOT
   Type of information . . . . . . . . . . . : TYPE      *ALL
   File attributes . . . . . . . . . . . . . : FILEATR   *ALL
   System  . . . . . . . . . . . . . . . . . : SYSTEM    *LCL
File Description Header
   File  . . . . . . . . . . . . . . . . . . : FILE      DWXP031
   Library . . . . . . . . . . . . . . . . . :           DTASCOOT
   Type of file  . . . . . . . . . . . . . . :           Physical
   File type . . . . . . . . . . . . . . . . : FILETYPE  *DATA
   Auxiliary storage pool ID . . . . . . . . :           02
Data Base File Attributes
   Externally described file . . . . . . . . :           Yes
   File level identifier . . . . . . . . . . :           0950125211655
                                     .
                                     .
                                     .
   File is currently journaled . . . . . . . :           Yes
   Current or last journal . . . . . . . . . :           JOURNAL
     Library . . . . . . . . . . . . . . . . :           DTASCT
   Journal images  . . . . . . . . . . . . . : IMAGES    *BOTH
   Journal entries to be omitted . . . . . . : OMTJRNE   *OPNCLO
   Last journal start date/time  . . . . . . :           12/14/96 4:31:11
Access Path Description
   Access path maintenance . . . . . . . . . : MAINT     *IMMED
   Unique key values required  . . . . . . . : UNIQUE    Yes
   Access path journaled . . . . . . . . . . :           Yes
   Access path . . . . . . . . . . . . . . . :           Keyed
   Number of key fields  . . . . . . . . . . :           5
```

Figure 8-1: DSPFD of a file that is journaled, showing the journal identification.

This identification is crucial to successful journaling and, more importantly, to successful recovery. If you ever have to apply journal entries to a file and the journal identification isn't there, the file won't get any journal entries applied.

The journal identification gets onto the file when journaling starts. If you saved a file, started journaling, and had to recover the file, journaling wouldn't work. When you restored the saved file, the journal identification wouldn't be on it. Therefore, the system wouldn't apply any journal entries.

What you should do is time your file saves to take place immediately after journaling starts (and at any time a member is added). Another way to say it is to apply a rule: The start of journaling is always immediately followed by a save of the journaled files.

8.3.1 Duality

You can elect to journal one library's files to one journal or receiver and another set of library files to another journal or receiver. This could make journal management easier for you.

Sometimes, in crucial situations where you are worried that one journal receiver might get damaged along with the database file, you can attach two journal receivers to the same journal. Then all file updates are journaled to both receivers at once. If the system loses one journal receiver, the system will continue to write to the other. If you do this, you really should keep each receiver in its own ASP. The protection is better and the DASD load is shared more evenly.

8.3.2 Naming Journal Objects

Part of your journaling strategy should be how you name your journal objects. There is no need to get exotic. Unless you keep more than one journal and receiver set going, use the name JOURNAL and call the receiver RECEIV0001. That way they are easy to remember and, when you programmatically change receivers late at night, the system will calculate a new name for the receiver (RECEIV0002, then RECEIV0003, and so on).

8.4 USING JOURNALS

After having made a solid journal strategy, you're ready to start. First, create a journal receiver with the CRTJRNRCV command. Figure 8-2 shows the prompted version of that command.

```
┌══════════════════════════════════════════════════════════════════════┐
║              Create Journal Receiver (CRTJRNRCV)                       ║
║ Type choices, press Enter.                                             ║
║                                                                        ║
║ Journal receiver . . . . . . . .   █           Name                    ║
║   Library  . . . . . . . . . . .   *CURLIB     Name, *CURLIB           ║
║ Auxiliary storage pool ID  . . .   *LIBASP     1-16, *LIBASP           ║
║ Journal receiver threshold . . .   *NONE       1-1919999, *NONE        ║
║ Text 'description' . . . . . . .   *BLANK                              ║
║                                                                        ║
║                                                                        ║
║                     Additional Parameters                              ║
║                                                                        ║
║ Preferred storage unit . . . . .   *ANY        1-255, *ANY             ║
║ Authority  . . . . . . . . . . .   *LIBCRTAUT  Name, *LIBCRTAUT, *CHANGE... ║
║                                                                        ║
║                                                                        ║
║                                                                        ║
║                                                           Bottom       ║
║ F3=Exit   F4=Prompt   F5=Refresh   F12=Cancel   F13=How to use this display ║
║ F24=More keys                                                          ║
└══════════════════════════════════════════════════════════════════════┘
```

Figure 8-2: Prompted version of CRTJRNRCV command.

The option AUXILIARY STORAGE POOL ID allows you to specify a user ASP where your journal receivers will live. In this case, it will just reside in the same ASP the library is in.

Option JOURNAL RECEIVER THRESHOLD specifies the threshold level of the receiver. The system will send a message when the receiver becomes this size. The message will either go to the system operator or to a special message queue. You specify this on the CRTJRN command (next).

The threshold level should be set so that it is rarely encountered between receiver changes. However, if something unusual happens on the system that causes an abnormal number of entries to go to the receiver, the threshold message alerts you to it. Note that in alerting you to an exceeded threshold, the system is actually alerting you to another abnormal situation that requires your attention. Journal receivers will continue to accept journal entries way past their threshold point, but you need to determine why the system is generating so many file updates.

If you want dual journal receivers on one journal, create them both on this step by using the command twice. After you have at least one journal receiver, create the journal itself with the CRTJRN (CREATE JOURNAL) command. Figure 8-3 shows a sample of it in formatted form.

```
                    Create Journal (CRTJRN)

Type choices, press Enter.

Journal  . . . . . . . . . . .  █               Name
  Library  . . . . . . . . . .   *CURLIB        Name, *CURLIB
Journal receiver . . . . . . .                  Name
  Library  . . . . . . . . . .   *LIBL          Name, *LIBL, *CURLIB

                                 *LIBL
Auxiliary storage pool ID  . . . *LIBASP        1-16, *LIBASP
Journal threshold msgq . . . . . QSYSOPR        Name
  Library  . . . . . . . . . .   *LIBL          Name, *LIBL, *CURLIB
Text 'description' . . . . . . . *BLANK



                    Additional Parameters

Authority  . . . . . . . . . .   *LIBCRTAUT     Name, *LIBCRTAUT, *CHANGE...

                                                            Bottom
F3=Exit   F4=Prompt   F5=Refresh   F12=Cancel   F13=How to use this display
F24=More keys
```

Figure 8-3: Prompted version of CRTJRN command.

Note the space for specifying dual journal receivers and specifying an ASP number. If you use single receivers (like most AS/400 shops), you only specify the initial receiver. Don't worry about the next receiver after the initial one. The system will take care of that for you. Because you specify upon journal creation what receiver(s) it is to use, you will have created the receivers first. See the preceding paragraphs.

8.4.1 Start Journaling

After the journal and receiver are created, you're ready to start journaling. There are two commands to start journaling. START JOURNAL PHYSICAL FILE (STRJRNPF) starts journaling your physical files and START JOURNAL ACCESS PATH (STRJRNAP) starts journaling your access paths.

STRJRNPF starts journaling on one or more specified files in a library. Although files in several different libraries can be journaled together, the common practice is to journal all files in a particular library. Figure 8-4 shows a prompted version of the STRJRNPF command.

```
                    Start Journal Physical File (STRJRNPF)

Type choices, press Enter.

Physical file to be journaled  .   _____    Name
    Library  . . . . . . . . . .   *LIBL_____   Name, *LIBL, *CURLIB
                 + for more values
                                   *LIBL_____
Journal  . . . . . . . . . . . .   _____    Name
    Library  . . . . . . . . . .   *LIBL_____   Name, *LIBL, *CURLIB
Record images  . . . . . . . . .   *AFTER        *AFTER, *BOTH
Journal entries to be omitted  .   *NONE___      *NONE, *OPNCLO
```

Figure 8-4: Prompted version of the STRJRNPF *command.*

Two STRJRNPF options will dramatically affect how much data is journaled.
They are OMTJRNE(*OPNCLO) and images(*BOTH).

OMTJRNE(*OPNCLO) omits JOURNALING when each file is opened and closed
(potentially, a great many entries). IMAGES(*BOTH) journals the before images as
well as the afterimages. This method provides great recovery, but it doubles the
amount of DASD space your receivers will take.

Access paths are the key paths for physical and logical files. Recreating all the
access paths can take quite a while during recovery. Journaling access paths
will reduce this time and hasten recovery after a system crash. The system is
faster at recovering an access path from the journal than it is at rebuilding a path
from scratch.

If you want to journal an access path, keep in mind that you cannot do it unless
the related physical files are also journaled. Always start journaling in this order:
STRJRNPF followed by STRJRNAP. Figure 8-5 shows a prompted version of the
STRJRNAP (START JOURNAL ACCESS PATH) command.

```
                    Start Journal Access Path (STRJRNAP)

Type choices, press Enter.

Journaled file . . . . . . . . .    _____   Name
   Library  . . . . . . . . . . .   *LIBL         Name, *LIBL, *CURLIB
            + for more values       _____
                                    *LIBL
Journal  . . . . . . . . . . . .    _____   Name
   Library  . . . . . . . . . . .   *LIBL         Name, *LIBL, *CURLIB
```

Figure 8-5: Prompted version of the STRJRNAP command

After you've entered one or both of these commands, journaling is in effect.
You don't have to do anything to the files or the programs that update them. The
journaled files have their journal identifications attached. Therefore, it is a good
time to back them up.

8.4.2 Change Receivers

There are three times when you want to change receivers:

❖   On a regular (preferably daily) basis.

❖   When the receiver exceeds its threshold and you have to change.

❖   When you want to either reset your receiver's sequence number to one
     or change its threshold limit.

The command is CHANGE RECEIVERS (CHGJRN). Figure 8-6 shows the
prompted form.

```
                         Change Journal (CHGJRN)

 Type choices, press Enter.

 Journal  . . . . . . . . . . .                      Name
   Library  . . . . . . . . . .    *LIBL            Name, *LIBL, *CURLIB
 Journal receiver:
   Journal receiver . . . . . . .  *SAME            Name, *SAME, *GEN
     Library  . . . . . . . . . .                   Name, *LIBL, *CURLIB
   Journal receiver . . . . . . .                   Name, *GEN
     Library  . . . . . . . . . .                   Name, *LIBL, *CURLIB
 Sequence option  . . . . . . . .  *CONT            *RESET, *CONT
 Journal threshold msgq . . . . .  *SAME            Name, *SAME
   Library  . . . . . . . . . .                     Name, *LIBL, *CURLIB
 Text 'description' . . . . . . .  *SAME
```

Figure 8-6: Prompted version of the CHGJRN command.

The command shown in Figure 8-6 is grossly exaggerated. It shows all the things you can do with it. Most of the time you'll just specify the journal and the *GEN keyword on the option JOURNAL RECEIVER instead of the default *SAME. Presumably you named your receivers so that they have a trailing four digits. If so, the system will generate the next receiver name for you.

The command to change receivers can be given at any time (even while journaling is active). The old journal receiver will be detached, the new receiver will be attached, and journaling will just continue.

Also, you can use the change receivers command to set the journal entry sequence numbers to 1. Note that this is the sequence number on each entry; it is not the sequential names of the receivers. Use the keyword SEQUENCE OPTION to do this. Override the default *CONT to 1.

The maximum sequence number the system can support is 2,100,000,000. The system will alert the operator when the journal entries' sequence number reaches 2,000,000,000. This usually allows plenty of warning time.

8.4.3 End Journaling

You rarely end journaling; it essentially goes on and on. If you do need to end journaling for any reason, use the END JOURNAL PHYSICAL FILE (ENDJRNPF) and the END JOURNAL ACCESS PATH (ENDJRNAP) commands.

Because you can't journal access paths if the associated physical files aren't journaled, you also can't end journaling on physical files if their access paths are still being journaled. The sequence for ending journaling is ENDJRNAP followed by ENDJRNPF. Figure 8-7 shows the prompted format of the ENDJRNAP command and Figure 8-8 shows the prompted version of the ENDJRNPF command.

```
                    End Journal Access Path (ENDJRNAP)

Type choices, press Enter.

Journaled file . . . . . . . . .  _____    Name, *ALL
  Library  . . . . . . . . . . .  *LIBL         Name, *LIBL, *CURLIB
            + for more values     _____
                                  *LIBL
Journal  . . . . . . . . . . . .  *FILE         Name, *FILE
  Library  . . . . . . . . . . .  _____    Name, *LIBL, *CURLIB
```

Figure 8-7: Prompted version of the ENDJRNAP command.

```
                   End Journaling PF Changes (ENDJRNPF)

Type choices, press Enter.

Journaled physical file  . . . .  _____    Name, *ALL
  Library  . . . . . . . . . . .  *LIBL         Name, *LIBL, *CURLIB
            + for more values     _____
                                  *LIBL
Journal  . . . . . . . . . . . .  *FILE         Name, *FILE
  Library  . . . . . . . . . . .  _____    Name, *LIBL, *CURLIB
```

Figure 8-8: Prompted version of the ENDJRNPF command.

8.4.4 Saving Journals and Receivers

Journals and receivers are just objects. They can be saved with any of the save commands (see chapter 7.) Normally, you'll be saving old journal receivers that have been detached from their journals. You can save receivers currently attached to journals but the saved version will be a partial version.

When journal receivers are saved, they can be optionally saved with storage freed. The option and keyword is STG(*FREE). As soon as the save is complete, the storage taken up by the receiver's data (but not its description) is freed (the records are cleared). The (*FREE) option cannot be used on currently attached journal receivers.

8.4.5 Deleting Journals and Receivers

Journal receivers take up considerable disk space. You can keep your disk use down by frequently deleting old receivers. Once in a long while, you will have ended journaling on a file completely and you will have saved the journals and receivers. Then you will want to delete the journal receiver from your system.

You can delete a journal receiver with the DLTJRNRCV command. However, it's a good idea to have a backup of each journal receiver before deleting it. You cannot delete a journal receiver while a journal is using it.

Because of the importance of receiver chains, receivers can only be deleted in the order in which they were attached to the journal. The exception to this is when you have a damaged receiver. You can delete a damaged receiver at any time after you detach it from the journal. Or you can delete a receiver anytime if you are using dual receivers on a journal and its mate still exists on the system.

Although the system will allow it, it is a very bad idea to delete a journal receiver that hasn't been saved first. The system will warn you if a receiver has not been saved by sending the error message CPF7025. You can get through by taking an I (IGNORE) response.

When the rare moment comes that you have to delete a journal, you do so with the DELETE JOURNAL (DLTJRN) command. You cannot delete a journal while it is journaling files. To get an active journal and its receivers off your system, here's the sequence:

❖ End journaling of all logical files with the ENDJRNAP (END JOURNAL ACCESS PATH) command.

❖ End journaling of all files associated with the journal using the ENDJRNPF (END JOURNAL PHYSICAL FILE) command.

❖ If commitment control is active and the journal is associated with it, end it with the ENDCMTCTL (END COMMITMENT CONTROL) command.

❖ Save/delete the journal using the SAVEOBJ (SAVE OBJECT) and DLTJRN (DELETE JOURNAL) command.

❖ Save/delete the journal receiver using the DLTJRNRCV (DELETE JOURNAL RECEIVER) command.

8.4.6 Restoring Journals and Receivers

Journals and receivers can be saved with any of the restore commands (see chapter 7). That's easy enough but this gets tricky. Journals, receivers, and associated database files and logical files must be restored in order. If these items all resided on one library and were saved with a SAVLIB (SAVE LIBRARY) or RSTLIB (RESTORE LIBRARY), there is no problem. The system will ensure that all elements are restored in order.

If the objects were in different libraries (typically database files and journals in one library, receivers in another), the system cannot determine the order even if SAVLIB and RSTLIB were used.

If the system cannot determine the correct order, you have to find the sequence. Restore these items in this order:

1. Journals.

2. Physical files.

3. Logical files.

4. Journal receivers (newest to oldest).

Needless to say this can be a painful process. Most shops tend to lump all elements into one library because the system will handle restoration of the elements.

Because performance degradation occurs when elements are lumped together, it's better to keep journals, physical files, and logical files in one library and journal receivers in another. For added performance and storage protection, preferably the two libraries should be in different ASPs. However, you must have some solid restoration procedures in place to ensure that everything gets restored in the correct order.

8.5 APPLYING AND REMOVING JOURNAL CHANGES

Once you've collected all these journal entries, there are two ways of using them. One way is to look at them yourself on your workstation or you can access them with a program you write. These methods are covered in the *OS/400 Backup and Recovery—Advanced V3R6* and *OS/400 CL Programming V3R6*. This book only deals with using the system to apply or remove journal entries.

Before you can either apply or remove journaled changes, the database file to which you will do this must have journal identification. See section 8.3, Journaling Strategy.

Applying journaled changes to a database file and removing journaled changes from a database file are two ways of using journaled changes to fix corrupted files. If you want to remove journaled changes, you must have been journaling both before images and afterimages on the physical file.

If a database file gets corrupted in the system sense (something like a disk going bad), whatever is on the disk will not be useable. You must restore your last good version of the file, ensure that the receiver chain is present, and then apply changes from that last date forward.

However, if a database file was corrupted in a non-system way, you could use a little different method. For example, a file can be damaged because of a programming bug (it's unusual, but it happens). The database file is not damaged in the system sense, but say several thousand records are bad. Because you know specifically what program and during what time period those records were corrupted, you don't have to go back to old versions of the file. You can just remove the changes made to the file by the bad program.

8.5.1 Applying Journal Changes

Journal changes are applied from an old date forward. The implication is that a file restore must have taken place in order for you to end up with an old version of the file and more current journal entries. Here's what you do:

❖ Restore the latest uncorrupted version of the file.

❖ Restore all the journal receivers that were used from the date of that save and are currently not on the system or were saved with their storage freed. Do this restore in order from the newest (today) to the oldest (the date of the save).

❖ Ensure that you have exclusive use of the database file and the receivers (ALCOBJ—ALLOCATE OBJECT).

❖ Apply the JOURNALED CHANGES (APYJRNCHG). Specify the journal receiver from which the system should start applying. This journal receiver should be the one that was in effect when the database file was saved.

Figure 8-9 shows the prompted version of the APYJRNCHG command.

```
              Apply Journaled Changes (APYJRNCHG)

Type choices, press Enter.

Journal  . . . . . . . . . . . .   _____    Name
  Library  . . . . . . . . . . .   *LIBL_____    Name, *LIBL, *CURLIB
Journaled physical file:          _
  Journaled physical file  . . .   _____    Name, *ALL
    Library  . . . . . . . . . .   *LIBL_____    Name, *LIBL, *CURLIB
  Member . . . . . . . . . . . .   *FIRST____    Name, *FIRST, *ALL
               + for more values  _
Range of journal receivers:
  Starting journal receiver  . .   *LASTSAVE_    Name, *LASTSAVE, *CURRENT
    Library  . . . . . . . . . .   _____    Name, *LIBL, *CURLIB
  Ending journal receiver  . . .   _____    Name, *CURRENT
    Library  . . . . . . . . . .   _____    Name, *LIBL, *CURLIB
Starting sequence number . . . .   *LASTSAVE_    Number, *LASTSAVE, *FIRST
Ending sequence number . . . . .   *LASTRST__    Number, *LASTRST, *LAST

                                                                More...
```

```
Ending date and time:
  Ending date  . . . . . . . . .   _____    Date
  Ending time  . . . . . . . . .   _____    Time
Fully qualified job name . . . .   _____    Name
  User . . . . . . . . . . . . .   _____    Name
  Number . . . . . . . . . . . .   _____    000000-999999
Fully qualified job name . . . .   _____    Name
  User . . . . . . . . . . . . .   _____    Name
  Number . . . . . . . . . . . .   _____    000000-999999
Commitment boundary  . . . . . .   *NO__        *NO, *YES
```

Figure 8-9: Prompted version of the APYJRNCHG command (part 1 and 2).

This command requests the qualified journal name that is the source of journal entries. The next set of parameters wants to know to which file it should apply journals. You can specify a file, or multiple files, or the generic *ALL.

The next parameter, RANGE OF JOURNAL RECEIVERS, is where you specify the receiver to start. You could tell the system where the receiver should end. However, common practice is to start with the first journal receiver after the last save of the file and continue through the receiver chain until applying the current receiver's changes.

If you want to restore just the changes within a range of entry sequence numbers, you can specify the start and end numbers in the STARTING SEQUENCE NUMBER and ENDING SEQUENCE NUMBER parameters. If you don't know these numbers, you can find them by using the DSPJRN (DISPLAY JOURNAL) command. For additional information, see the *OS/400 Backup and Recovery—Advanced V3R6*.

If you don't want to apply all journal changes from all receivers, you probably want to apply journal changes for a specific time period. You can specify any date and time range.

If you know the specific job user or job number to apply changes from, you can specify them. If your files are updated with programs that use commitment control, you have the option of adhering to those boundaries or not. If you are recovering from a system crash and you use commitment control, you probably will want to adhere to those boundaries. When the system applies journaled changes, it applies them in order from oldest to current. For additional information, see the *OS/400 Backup and Recovery—Advanced V3R6*.

8.5.2 Removing Journal Changes

Depending on your journaling skill and strategy and the nature of the problem you're trying to recover from, it might be easier to remove journaled changes than try to restore the file and apply lots of changes. There are three advantages to removing journal changes rather than applying journal changes:

- ❖ You don't have to reload your last saved version of the damaged file.

- ❖ Generally, you don't have to reload receivers; the current one is usually sufficient.

- ❖ The remove uses considerably fewer records and goes faster.

There are several details in removing journal entries that you must be concerned about that aren't a concern when you apply journal changes:

- ❖ Your must have been journaling before images and afterimages of changed records.

❖ When you specify where the system should stop removing journaled changes, you cannot specify a certain time (such as 7:30 A.M.). You must specify the sequence number. That's an extra step. You have to use the DISPLAY JOURNAL (DSPJRN) command to determine what sequence number was in effect at 7:30 A.M.

❖ The current receiver is generally far enough back in the sequence, but you should check to see if the current receiver goes back to the time where you want to stop removing entries. If it doesn't go back far enough (in the example, receivers were changed sometime between 7:30 A.M. and 10:00 A.M.), make sure the previous receiver is on the system.

❖ You cannot use this command to rebuild a database file damaged from a system problem. The command works on files corrupted by a bad program or a crazed user.

Figure 8-10 shows the prompted REMOVE JOURNAL CHANGES (RMVJRNCHG) command.

```
                  Remove Journaled Changes (RMVJRNCHG)

Type choices, press Enter.

Journal  . . . . . . . . . . .                   Name
  Library  . . . . . . . . . .    *LIBL         Name, *LIBL, *CURLIB
Journaled file identification:    _
  Journaled physical file  . . .                 Name, *ALL
    Library  . . . . . . . . .    *LIBL         Name, *LIBL, *CURLIB
  Member . . . . . . . . . . .    *FIRST        Name, *FIRST, *ALL
              + for more values _
Range of journal receivers:
  Starting journal receiver  . .  *CURRENT      Name, *CURRENT
    Library  . . . . . . . . .                  Name, *LIBL, *CURLIB
  Ending journal receiver  . . .                Name
    Library  . . . . . . . . .                  Name, *LIBL, *CURLIB
Starting sequence number . . . .  *LAST         Number, *LAST, *LASTSAVE
Ending sequence number . . . . .  *FIRST        Number, *FIRST
```

```
Fully qualified job name . . . .  █             Name
  User . . . . . . . . . . . . .                Name
  Number . . . . . . . . . . . .                000000-999999
Commitment boundary  . . . . . .  *NO           *NO, *YES
```

Figure 8-10: Prompted version of the RMVJRNCHG command (part 1 and 2).

for STARTING JOURNAL RECEIVER of *CURRENT (as opposed to *LASTSAV). The sequence numbers are from the *LAST to *FIRST. Note that if you change nothing, the system will apply all changes in the current receiver only. When the system removes journaled changes, it removes them in order from current to oldest.

8.5.3 Receiver Chains

Except for the first receiver you attached to a journal when you started journaling, every receiver has a predecessor. Also, every receiver except for the current one has a next receiver. These entries are made when receivers are attached and detached to journals. When you start recovering from the receivers, you need to make sure the complete chain is online. In that way, when the system applies changes, it will go from the starting receiver right through the other ones.

For example, consider a shop that changes receivers every evening—starting with RECEIV0010 on the current Monday night—and loses a database file on Thursday. That shop would restore the last saved version of the file. Let's presume it was made on Sunday.

If you were doing the restore, you would start applying journal entries with the RECEIV0010 receiver. Before you start applying changes, RECEIV0010 must be on the system as well as RECEIV0011 and RECEIV0012. The system will walk through consecutive receivers until it gets current.

On the other hand, if you were restoring receivers and couldn't find RECEIV0011, you would have a problem. Not only would you have lost the changes for Tuesday, but the system couldn't apply changes after RECEIV0010 (at least not automatically—you could re-request RECEIV0012 be applied after RECEIV0010 completes). Good journal management is necessary to make the whole thing work.

This is one example of what causes a *broken chain*. Another broken chain can occur when a receiver is backed up while it is still attached to the journal. While this is theoretically possible, actually what happens is that the receiver is only partially saved and, therefore, does not complete the restore. Aside from broken chains, other causes of journal chain problems are:

- ❖ Restoring a receiver from another system.

- ❖ Restoring a receiver that has not had its storage freed by a save operation.

- ❖ Saving or freeing a receiver and then trying to use it without restoring it.

8.6 BIBLIOGRAPHY

OS/400 Backup and Recovery—Advanced V3R6

OS/400 Backup and Recovery V3R6

OS/400 CL Programming V3R6

AS/400 CL Reference

AS/400 System Operations V3R6

9. Performance

9.1 OVERVIEW

Nothing gets users angrier than waiting on a computer. When the performance of your AS/400 isn't up to par, users will make your life miserable. More importantly, access and performance generally becomes the basis by which people judge the quality of the AS/400 and your shop's service. There's hardly an area that presses more hot buttons than performance.

9.2 AS/400—PERFORMANCE COMPONENTS

References to AS/400 performance implies any or all of six major areas:

* ❖ Emergencies. The performance just degrades for some reason.
* ❖ Tuning. Is the AS/400 optimally set up for your job mix?
* ❖ Monitoring. The ongoing capture of performance data.
* ❖ Reporting. Periodic reporting from captured performance data.
* ❖ Capacity planning. Measuring where you are and where you will be on the AS/400.
* ❖ Stress tests and individual program and application measurements.

All these areas come together eventually. If you tune the computer correctly, you will encounter fewer emergencies. If you monitor and report adequately, you avoid unexpectantly outgrowing the AS/400's capacity. If you stress test applications before they go into production, you will avoid performance surprises.

9.2.1 Emergencies

Computers spoil people. The feeling of quick response times only lasts for two weeks past any upgrade (even to a RISC processor). After that, there's an underlying feeling that the computer is slow. That feeling gets prodded every once in a while when an errant program suddenly gobbles up too much of the computer's resources and you really do experience a sharp increase in response time.

Quite often these performance emergencies are transitory, but you really can't make that assumption. You have to look into the system on the chance that the initial symptom (slow response time) isn't going to suddenly escalate into an overflowed ASP or a locked CPU.

Although anyone can look into a performance problem, I prefer to have one person (not everyone in the Information Systems Department) do the investigation on the system console. The console is set to run at a very high priority (10). Therefore, it's better able than other workstations to grab system resources from a runaway program.

The primary command to isolate an emergency is WORK WITH ACTIVE JOBS (WRKACTJOB). Figure 9-1 shows the screen from that command.

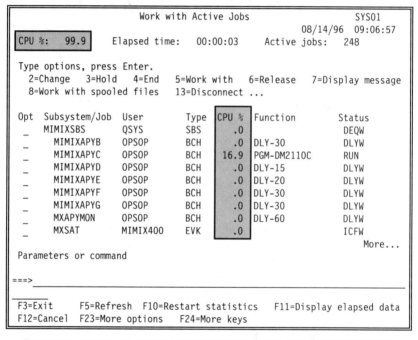

```
                         Work with Active Jobs                        SYS01
                                                       08/14/96  09:06:57
 CPU %:    99.9      Elapsed time:   00:00:03    Active jobs:   248

 Type options, press Enter.
   2=Change   3=Hold   4=End   5=Work with   6=Release   7=Display message
   8=Work with spooled files   13=Disconnect ...

 Opt  Subsystem/Job  User      Type   CPU %   Function        Status
   _   MIMIXSBS       QSYS      SBS      .0                    DEQW
   _     MIMIXAPYB    OPSOP     BCH      .0    DLY-30          DLYW
   _     MIMIXAPYC    OPSOP     BCH    16.9    PGM-DM2110C     RUN
   _     MIMIXAPYD    OPSOP     BCH      .0    DLY-15          DLYW
   _     MIMIXAPYE    OPSOP     BCH      .0    DLY-20          DLYW
   _     MIMIXAPYF    OPSOP     BCH      .0    DLY-30          DLYW
   _     MIMIXAPYG    OPSOP     BCH      .0    DLY-30          DLYW
   _     MXAPYMON     OPSOP     BCH      .0    DLY-60          DLYW
   _     MXSAT        MIMIX400  EVK      .0                    ICFW
                                                                  More...
 Parameters or command

 ===>
 _____
 F3=Exit    F5=Refresh  F10=Restart statistics   F11=Display elapsed data
 F12=Cancel  F23=More options   F24=More keys
```

Figure 9-1: Display screen for the WORK WITH ACTIVE JOBS (WRKACTJOB) command.

With my first pass at an emergency, I am most interested in two areas. First, I want to know the overall CPU percentage in the upper left corner. Second, I want to know the CPU percentage down the middle of the screen. Those areas are highlighted in Figure 9-1.

The CPU percentage will often be around 99.9% (perhaps even over 100%, which is indicated by the symbol ++++). Check the percentage figure first. Primarily, this gives you a quick look at the overall health of the system.

If the percentage is high, continue looking for a problem. If you see 75 percent indicated, it might be a good indication that you have lost a device on the LAN. For example, if a gateway goes down and strands its users, the users will still have their screens up and will be getting tired of waiting. The AS/400 is happily cruising because it just lost 100 or so users. Seeing a response-time problem and a low CPU percentage, I would immediately dispatch someone to look at the LAN. Because it could still be a program problem, I would continue investigating the problem from the AS/400 side.

9.2.1.1 Work with Active Jobs

After checking the overall CPU percentage, I want to quickly know who is taking up the largest CPU percentage. A nice feature of the WORK WITH ACTIVE JOBS command is that you can use the arrow keys to move the cursor onto the CPU percentage column, press the F16 (Shift + F4) key, and the information will be redisplayed sorted with the highest percentage user on the top. Figure 9-2 shows a sample.

```
┌─────────────────────────────────────────────────────────────────────┐
│                    Work with Active Jobs                    SYS01      │
│                                                    08/14/96  09:14:03  │
│  CPU %:   99.6     Elapsed time:   00:07:09     Active jobs:   249     │
│                                                                       │
│  Type options, press Enter.                                           │
│    2=Change   3=Hold   4=End   5=Work with   6=Release   7=Display message │
│    8=Work with spooled files   13=Disconnect ...                      │
│                                                                       │
│  Opt  Subsystem/Job  User       Type  CPU %  Function       Status    │
│    _    SQLEXEC       PGMABC     INT   35.5   CMD-EXECUTE    RUN       │
│    _    BRM_MAINT     OPC        BCH   23.2   PGM-RBT164     RUN       │
│    _    ESFR176       PGMDEF     BCH   11.4   PGM-RBT096     RUN       │
│    _    ROSE05V1      PGMDEF     BCH   10.9   PGM-RBT096     RUN       │
│    _    SQLEXEC       USRRGC     BCH    7.1   CMD-EXECUTE    RUN       │
│    _    MIMIXAPYC     OPSOP      BCH    5.6   PGM-DM2110C    RUN       │
│    _    XTRA0202      QUSER      EVK    3.3                  ICFW      │
│    _    SQLEXEC       PGMXYZ     BCH    3.1   CMD-EXECUTE    RUN       │
│    _    SERVICE       QSVCDRCTR  BCH    3.0   PGM-ANCONTROL  RUN       │
│                                                               More...  │
│  Parameters or command                                                │
│                                                                       │
│  ===>                                                                 │
│                                                                       │
│  F3=Exit     F5=Refresh    F10=Restart statistics   F11=Display elapsed data │
│  F12=Cancel  F23=More options   F24=More keys                         │
└─────────────────────────────────────────────────────────────────────┘
```

Figure 9-2: Display screen for WORK WITH ACTIVE JOBS command after the display has been sorted by using the cursor and the F16 key.

There are some jobs that don't run all the time, but when they do run they take a lot of resources until they are complete. For example, if you use BRMS (Backup and Recovery Media Services) a job called BRM_MAINT, runs periodically and takes about 20 percent of the CPU. You wouldn't do anything in this case.

Figure 9-2 reveals that user PGMABC is running a structured query language (SQL) and taking 35 percent of the CPU. When a program or a user is killing the system, it will appear at the top with a CPU percentage of 30 percent or higher—after you've sorted with the cursor and F16 key.

Once I've identified a problem program, I put it on hold by putting a 3 on the OPTION line to the left of the job. In this example, the options I have access to are highlighted with shading in Figure 9-2.

After holding the job, entering a 5 on the OPTION line will look into the job to see what program it is running and what files it is updating. Also, I can see any system messages the SQL has encountered. I would note the job program, any open files, and any messages. Next, I would call the user or programmer responsible (preferably the programmer) to confer. While this is going on, the emergency is fading away because the offending program is being held.

If the job's user or programmer confirms that the job must run, the job can be released from hold by entering a 6 on the OPTION line. In addition, the SQL's priority can be reduced to give other users a chance to complete their work.

In addition to CPU percentage, you can view the impact of the jobs on the system by monitoring how much disk IO each is doing. You can do this with the F11 key. Figure 9-3 shows the same set of jobs from Figure 9-2 after F11 has been pressed.

```
                        Work with Active Jobs                     SYS01
                                                      08/14/96  09:14:03
 CPU %:   99.6     Elapsed time:   00:07:09     Active jobs:   249

 Type options, press Enter.
   2=Change   3=Hold   4=End   5=Work with   6=Release   7=Display message
   8=Work with spooled files    13=Disconnect ...
                                            --------Elapsed--------
 Opt  Subsystem/Job  Type  Pool  Pty    CPU  Int   Rsp  AuxIO  CPU %
   _    SQLEXEC       INT    4    20   3120.9               238   35.5
   _    BRM_MAINT     BCH    4    40    892.9              3540   23.2
   _    ESFR176       BCH    4    50    718.9              5268   11.4
   _    ROSE05V1      BCH    4    50   2097.9                77   10.9
   _    SQLEXEC       BCH   10    50    345.3              3312    7.1
   _    MIMIXAPYC     BCH    9    25   9162.1              5593    5.6
   _    XTRA0202      EVK    5    19     29.3               112    3.3
   _    SQLEXEC       BCH    4    50     88.0             21386    3.1
   _    SERVICE       BCH    2    51    221.3                 0    3.0
                                                               More...
 Parameters or command
 ===> _____
 F3=Exit      F5=Refresh        F10=Restart statistics   F11=Display status
```

Figure 9-3: Display screen for WORK WITH ACTIVE JOBS command after the F11 key has been pressed.

In most shops, interactive queries and SQLs are discouraged. Programmers should use good judgment and only submit SQLs and interactive queries when they are very small or when the system is lightly loaded. Neither pattern applies in the preceding example. If the programmer really needs the SQL to run, I would lower its priority to a 50. The normal priority for a batch job is 50 and that is where this SQL should run.

To change a priority, use the screen displayed in Figure 9-3. Put a 2 (change) on the OPTION line and press Enter. You'll get the screen shown in Figure 9-4.

```
                           Change Job (CHGJOB)

 Type choices, press Enter.

 Job name . . . . . . . . . . . . > SQLEXEC      Name, *
   User . . . . . . . . . . . . . >   PGMABC     Name
   Number . . . . . . . . . . . . >   905191     000000-999999
 Job priority (on JOBQ) . . . . .   *SAME        0-9, *SAME
 Output priority (on OUTQ)  . . .   5            1-9, *SAME
 Print device . . . . . . . . . .   PRT01        Name, *SAME, *USRPRF...
 Output queue . . . . . . . . . .   RELOUTQ      Name, *SAME, *USRPRF, *DEV...
   Library  . . . . . . . . . . .     QGPL       Name, *LIBL, *CURLIB
 Run priority . . . . . . . . . .   50           1-99, *SAME




                                                                    Bottom
 F3=Exit   F4=Prompt   F5=Refresh   F10=Additional parameters   F12=Cancel
 F13=How to use this display        F24=More keys
```

Figure 9-4: Screen to change a job's priority. Just overwrite the value in the RUN PRIORITY parameter.

Changing the job's priority is as simple as putting the 50 (its new priority) on the last parameter, RUN PRIORITY. After you change a priority like that, give the job 10 to 20 minutes to give up its hold on the system. Built-in delays are one reason why you want to react quickly to these situations.

This example has a clear offender, an interactive SQL, that is probably causing a response-time problem. If changing the SQL's priority does not return the system to normal or if that job hadn't been there, I would focus on the third and fourth jobs in the list shown in Figure 9-2.

Although each job is taking only about 11 percent and 10 percent, together they are taking 22.3 percent, and they both belong to the same user. Cases like these, two fairly significant programs fired off by the same user, often will require the same resources and will be in constant conflict for those resources. Conflicts degrade the system. The solution could be to hold one of the programs until the other finishes.

9.2.1.2 Sorting Priorities

Sometimes you won't find any jobs taking high CPU percentages and you have to look elsewhere. The next items to look for are unusually low or unusually powerful priorities where they shouldn't be. Like the CPU percentages, you can position the cursor on the priority column and press the F16 key for a quick sort. Figure 9-5 shows a sample of sorted priorities.

```
                    Work with Active Jobs                        SYS01
                                                     08/14/96  09:37:20
 CPU %:   99.8     Elapsed time:   00:30:26    Active jobs:   251

 Type options, press Enter.
   2=Change   3=Hold   4=End   5=Work with   6=Release   7=Display message
   8=Work with spooled files   13=Disconnect ...
                                          --------Elapsed---------
 Opt  Subsystem/Job  Type  Pool  Pty     CPU  Int    Rsp  AuxIO  CPU %
       MONJRN         BCH    2    10       .1                0    .0
   _   MONSYSSTS      BCH    2    10      30.1               2    .0
   _   MONTAPSTSD     BCH    2    10      40.6              18    .0
   _   QBRMRCY        BCH    2    10       .5                0    .0
   _   QSYSSCD        BCH    2    10      1.0                0    .0
   _   QMLMAIN        PJ     2    11      68.1               0    .0
   _   QMLRS232       PJ     2    11      35.0               0    .0
   _   QMLTRACE       PJ     2    11     165.2               0    .0
   _   RBCMANAGER     BCH    2    11     568.8              37    .0
                                                              More...
 Parameters or command
 ===>
 F3=Exit      F5=Refresh         F10=Restart statistics    F11=Display status
 F12=Cancel   F23=More options   F24=More keys
```

Figure 9-5: Display screen for WORK ACTIVE JOBS command after using the cursor position and the F16 key to sort by priorities.

You should know what jobs have legitimate high priorities. Scan this list for examples of high priorities that don't belong. Be particularly alert for high priorities where they shouldn't be when either of the following situations exist:

❖   You're running any kind of automatic tuner (either the third-party ones or the AS/400 itself) and it has gotten out of control.

❖   Users or programmers have special authority for job control in their user profile. For additional information, see chapter 5.

If you can't find any jobs taking large CPU percentages or priorities (and you have determined the LAN is not the problem), you need to look deeper into the system using the command WORK WITH SYSTEM ACTIVITY (WRKSYSACT). Figure 9-6 shows an example of that command's display.

```
                          Work with System Activity

Automatic refresh in seconds  . . . . . . . . . . . . . . . :      5
Elapsed time . . . . :    00:00:05
CPU 1 util . . . . . :     99.9
CPU 2 util . . . . . :     99.9


                                              Total  Total
   Job or                               CPU   Sync   Async    PAG    EAO
   Task       User      Number  Pty  Util    I/O    I/O     Fault   Excp
   QBRMNET    QPGMR     161530   30  30.6    827    452      68      0
   HAL25V6    PGMDEF    161609   50  15.3     48    154       0      7
   SQLEXEC    PGMABC    161585   50  13.9      2    219       0      0
   ESFR176    PGMDEF    161460   50   9.6     70     16       0      0
   TSFR680    OPC       161604   50   8.7     32     32       0      0
   ROSE05V1   PGMDEF    161255   50   8.6      0    222       0      0
   ISLWES4    PGMGHI    161495   20   1.2      7      1       2      0
   SERVICE    QSVCDRCTR 161488   51    .3      0      0       0      0

Attn=Terminate automatic refresh
Or press Sys Req and option 2 to end automatic refresh and WRKSYSACT
```

Figure 9-6: Work with system activity.

This screen refreshes itself every 5 seconds. Therefore, you can monitor transitory situations. Another benefit from this screen is that it will show system tasks and their CPU percentages (which don't normally appear on the WRKACTJOB display). System tasks will have the user identification label "SYS" (notice the second column, "User").

Any AS/400 job can have two components: a user component and a system component. The user component is what WRKACTJOB displays. System components don't appear there because they have a very high priority and are very transitory (lasting less than a second). However, you can start a system-intensive job where the system component is long and consumes the CPU. The user component on WRKACTJOB will show a very low CPU percentage usage because it isn't doing anything. The system component of the job will be using 40 percent of your CPU and you won't see it.

A prime example of out of sight problems occurs with a large library save during the day. The user portion of the SAVLIB job will show 0-3 percent CPU utilization, yet the system will be pegged. If you look at the system with the WRKSYSACT command, you'll see USER SYS (the system portion) taking 40 percent of the CPU. And talk about abnormally high priorities, user SYS's task will run at a priority of 1! It takes some creativity (but not much) to associate such a SYS task with a user job. The solution is twofold:

❖ Cancel the user job (the system task will go with it).

❖ Institute a rule that the user job (like a large save library) won't be started during the production day unless an emergency exists.

9.2.1.3 Emergency Aftermath

The recovery period following an emergency has the potential to cause worse damage than the original emergency. Changing almost anything in the system, at a time when the system is getting hit hard, causes it to really flop. When you change a runaway job's priority to 55 in order to minimize its impact, the first thing the system seems to do is start running at about 150 percent. Depending on how deep the program was into the system, sometimes even a simple hold will be delayed for 30 or more minutes. New priorities always require time to take effect. Meanwhile, the system performance degrades further. All you can do during this time is wait. And tell your users to take a break.

Earlier, I mentioned the potential for a LAN problem. Sometimes a gateway or a bridge will fail and, thereby, knock a large percentage of your users off the AS/400. Depending on many variables, the only way users are alerted to such a problem is by sitting on a AS/400 screen for a really long time.

There is another problem with LANs and AS/400s. LANs tend to be a little flaky all the time. Many AS/400 customers customize their computers slightly to accommodate that instability. From time to time, due to transient signal losses from the LAN equipment, the AS/400 doesn't recognize someone who is logged in and active. The AS/400 will react to this by canceling the user's interactive job. So users randomly get disconnected all the time. This isn't good. Therefore, most AS/400 customers eventually modify system value QDSCJOBITV (DISCONNECT JOB INTERVAL) to keep interactive jobs active until 10 or 15 minutes has elapsed.

Now imagine a significant LAN hardware problem on an AS/400 that has this system value set. Assume a gateway crashes and that the AS/400 has QDSCJOBITV set to 10 (minutes). At first gateway users are relatively unaffected, but 10 minutes later the AS/400 is going to disconnect all of them at once. The result will be a major problem on the AS/400 (dumping logs and cleaning up the jobs). Would you be surprised to know that good old USER SYS does this dumping and cleaning and anything that USER SYS does runs at a very high priority?

If the gateway can be brought back up within 10 minutes, theoretically there should be no problem. But that isn't what happens.

Most help desks and many individual users feel that, when a failed piece of LAN hardware is recovered, everyone has to sign off and then back onto the AS/400. Now you have several bottlenecks: the LAN goes down; the LAN comes up; 100 users sign off; and then 100 users sign on. Even on a powerful AS/400, you're going to see performance die for 15 to 45 minutes, and there is nothing you can do about it.

Quite often, the aftermath to a performance emergency is so severe that many shops just cross their fingers and hope any response-time degradation is transitory. That strategy works about half the time. As with many problems that are not addressed immediately and intelligently, you can dig yourself a hole you can't get out of quickly.

Every AS/400 shop needs to develop emergency guidelines. Depending on your job mix and LAN usage, your emergency procedures should include the following:

- ❖ First indications of problems (calls from users, monitoring programs, etc.).
- ❖ Initial steps to identify the type of problem:
  - ✓ Who takes action. Assign one person, usually someone with ready access to the system console.
  - ✓ What to look for.
  - ✓ Specific things to do.

- ❖ Problem identification:
  - ✓ Who must be notified:
    - ➤ LAN administration.
    - ➤ Programming.
    - ➤ Management.
  - ✓ Action taken:
    - ➤ Hold programs.
    - ➤ Contact developers.
    - ➤ Change job priorities.
    - ➤ Cancel jobs.
    - ➤ Get hardware back up.

- ❖ Recovery:
  - ✓ What is the status of the AS/400?
    - ➤ Is the AS/400 suffering from heavy user disconnections?
    - ➤ Have all job changes taken effect?
    - ➤ Have high-hitting jobs released their holds on the system?
  - ✓ Are users to sign off and then sign on or just be patient?

9.3 PERFORMANCE TUNING

While an emergency can happen to any AS/400, getting your AS/400 into tune and keeping it there will allow your shop to be generally a more pleasant place to work.

The art of performance tuning an AS/400 is almost a lost art. No one really bothers anymore and that's too bad. Most AS/400s being considered for upgrade really only need a good tune-up.

There really aren't too many specific tasks to tuning, but there is a definite lack of what's right for any particular system. The problem is that the AS/400 gets tuned to support a job mix. As the mix changes, the tuning requirements change. And guess what? Because the mix is always changing, users try to strike a happy medium. Gathering the data for that happy medium is the challenge.

A lightly loaded AS/400 always runs well and looks relatively healthy. Don't waste your time doing performance tuning during those times. Always monitor AS/400s during the busiest time for any job mix. Take note of what I'm saying here. The busiest time for interactive job mixing is from 10:00 A.M. to 2:00 P.M. (excluding lunch hour). The busiest time for a batch job mix is generally during nightly processing. Some 24-hour shops are even more complex. For example, the job mix might not completely change from interactive to batch, but the emphasis on either could change.

There are two performance tuning tasks: monitoring and modifying. Monitoring tasks should be done during busy, stressful times. Modifying system parameters—such as changing memory or activity levels—should be done, if possible, during less busy times. Because monitoring is boring, consider writing a program to do it.

9.3.1 Monitoring Tasks

There are two AS/400 monitoring issues of concern to users.

- ❖ Wait-to-ineligible ratio.
- ❖ Non-database faults:
    - ✓ Non-machine pool.
    - ✓ Machine pool.
    - ✓ All pools.

9.3.1.1 Wait-to-Ineligible Ratio

The wait-to-ineligible ratio is the primary factor you want to monitor. Here's what that means. Jobs have three run states.

- ❖ Active—currently running.
- ❖ Wait—waiting for something.
    - ✓ A disk access, which could be a page retrieval or some record retrieval.
    - ✓ A user's response to a screen.
- ❖ Ineligible—the job is ready to run, and just waiting for the system to allocate resources to it.

From these three states, IBM defines three transition states (or the act of a job going from one state to another). The three transitions are:

- ❖ Active-to-wait.
- ❖ Active-to-ineligible.
- ❖ Wait-to-ineligible.

The AS/400 takes these transition states and measures them as a ratio of them to each other . Transition ratios are used to define what you want to see in a healthy system. Valid ratios are available for each AS/400 model and each version of the operating system. The ratios are found in the IBM Redbook, *AS/400 Performance Management* (GG24-3723-02).

Keep in mind that the text and examples in this chapter all use acceptable values for an AS/400, but the samples shown might not be anything like yours. Follow the discussion but don't take any of my values for your AS/400. Before you start tuning, check the Redbook for your AS/400's values.

For this example, the primary transition ratio is the wait-to-ineligible to active-to-wait. Expect the ratio to be around 10 percent. In other words, 10 percent of the jobs that went from active-to-wait states are unable to start right away when they are done waiting.

To understand why the preceding is a good situation, consider what happens when no jobs wait to run. When there are no jobs waiting, it is an indication that not too much is running on the system or that you have an overtuned system. In other words, so many system resources are allocated that no jobs ever have to wait. That's great for individual jobs and it's usually the way customers new to the AS/400 tune their machines. Nevertheless, with an overtuned system, you will discover that random jobs just degrade for no reason.

The monitoring command for these ratios is WORK WITH SYSTEM STATUS (WRKSYSSTS). Figure 9-7 shows a sample.

```
                          Work with System Status                  SYS02
                                               08/14/96  11:27:42
% CPU used . . . . . . . :      99.9   System ASP . . . . . . . :    22368 M
Elapsed time . . . . . . :   00:00:07  % system ASP used . . . :    84.6376
Jobs in system . . . . . :     22892   Total aux stg . . . . . :   131468 M
% perm addresses . . . . :    27.612   Current unprotect used . :     4260 M
% temp addresses . . . . :     9.307   Maximum unprotect  . . . :     4265 M


Sys    Pool    Rsrv    Max   -----DB-----   ---Non-DB---  Act-   Wait-  Act-
Pool   Size K  Size K  Act   Fault  Pages   Fault  Pages  Wait   Inel   Inel
 1      90741   40932  +++     .1     .1     3.2    7.5   67.0    .0     .0
 2      70547       0   32    1.2   191.9   26.6   298.0  33.5    .0     .0
 3       3000       0    4     .0     .0      .0     .0     .0    .0     .0
 4      60000       0    3     .4   +++++    2.5    27.3    .0    .0     .0
 5      20000       0    3     .0     .0     5.3   213.9   33.5   .0     .0
 6     120000       0    9    1.8   315.0    4.4    19.9   83.7   .5     .0
 7     160000       0   17    6.2   143.9   44.9   429.0  326.6   4.0    .0
```

Figure 9-7: Work with system status.

You can monitor and change two things on this screen: the MAX ACT and the POOL SIZES. To change either field, just position the cursor on the field and type in the new figure.

To *monitor* for good transition, you must focus on two columns: ACTIVE-TO-WAIT and WAIT-TO-INELIGIBLE. You want to see WAIT-TO-INELIGIBLE at approximately 10 percent or less, but greater than 0 percent of the ACTIVE-TO-WAIT value.

As a result of monitoring these columns, the next step is to *modify* information. The only way you can make the WAIT-TO-INELIGIBLE column change is to change the MAX ACT figure. You lower the figure in increments of 2, until the WAIT-TO-INELIGIBLE number drops to almost 0, and then increase the figure by 2 one time.

9.3.1.2 Non-Database Faults (Non-Machine Pool)

As shown in Figure 9-7, non-database faults are another crucial point to monitor. Any pool other than pool 1 is a user pool. User pools are what this section is about. Database faults can be an application issue, but non-database faults are a way of saying that there isn't enough memory to adequately load the program.

Monitor the non-database (NON-DB) value on the screen as shown in Figure 9-7. You can modify the value by changing the POOL SIZE value. Raising the pool size makes more memory available and lowers the non-database faulting rate.

These pools should have non-database faults of between 10 and 20 pages per minute. Actually, don't worry too much about the ones that are below 10. In the example shown in Figure 9-7, the faults are for non-interactive jobs. During the day, you would expect to be very lightly loaded. Therefore, the fault rate for non-interactive jobs would be low. If a pool supporting interactive jobs needed some extra memory, however, you could get it from one of these batch pools.

As shown in Figure 9-7, pool 7 is an interactive pool and has a fairly high non-database fault rate of 44. You should adjust this value. For specific information on what to modify, see section 9.3.2, What to Modify.

9.3.1.3 Non-Database Faults (Machine Pool)

Pool 1 is always called the *machine pool*. The machine pool is where the system does its system tasks. Its non-database fault rate should be between 3 and 5 pages per minute and you can adjust pool 1 until you get that rate.

9.3.1.4 Non-Database Faults (All Pools)

Another activity to monitor is the total of all non-database faults for all pools (including the machine pool). As shown in Figure 9-7, the value for this specific AS/400 should be between 180 and 300.

If the value isn't between 180 and 300, it could mean that one or more pools are seriously out of tune. If all pools are tuned or there are no further steps you can take (such as no inactive pools from which to draw memory), your AS/400 could be out of capacity and in need of an upgrade.

9.3.1.5 When to Monitor

If the AS/400 is lightly loaded, you'll get zeros for your key monitoring points. If you make adjustments based on those values, your AS/400 will not function when any serious work load hits it. Always monitor when the AS/400 is getting hammered.

Take several monitor samples and don't worry about reacting to all of them. On the best-tuned AS/400s, you will get periods where the monitored values are not good. What you want is a trend where you can say they're acceptable most of the time. Remember, you can tune any AS/400 for any job mix, but job mixes change. So tune yours for its most representative mix.

Approach performance monitoring like stock brokers advise you to approach investing. Establish a goal—such as 10 percent growth in a year—and check it periodically. As with a financial investment, if you check performance hourly or daily, you'll go crazy. With performance tuning set a goal. During your busiest hours, your ratios and faults will be this and that. Look only at the big picture. Don't seriously consider individual monitoring samples.

9.3.2 What to Modify

Refer to Figure 9-7 again. Its second and fourth left-side columns represent the things you can change:

❖ Pool size.

❖ Max act.

The preceding are both poorly named columns. Read them this way:

❖ Memory.

❖ Activity level. (It is definately not the maximum active jobs.)

9.3.2.1 Memory

Pool size or memory is the amount of memory a set of jobs has available to play in. You will see a memory pool for all interactive jobs and one for all batch jobs. The more memory a set of jobs has the faster the jobs will run. But they will do so at the expense of other jobs.

Notice from the display shown in Figure 9-7 that you cannot modify the memory for pool 2. That pool is also called the base pool, *BASE, or "star-base." The memory in it is all the system memory not used in any other pool. For additional information on memory storage pools, see chapter 3.

When you decrease the memory in any pool, the extra amount of memory you don't need anymore goes into pool 2. When you increase the memory in any pool, the amount you need comes from pool 2.

When you want to modify the system to take memory from one storage pool that isn't using it and put it in another that needs it, you do so by:

❖ Decreasing the first pool's memory.

❖ Increasing the second pool's memory.

9.3.2.2 Activity Level

Activity level is hard to explain. Primarily because it is called MAX ACT on the WRKSYSSTS display, people confuse it with MAXACT jobs on the subsystem description and job-queue descriptions. First, those MAXACTS refer to how many jobs can be running at any one time.

The MAX ACT on the WRKSYSSTS display is really the activity level and is quite different. The activity level doesn't affect how many jobs can run at one time. It affects how many jobs can be active at one time. Remember the three job states mentioned in the section on wait-to-ineligible ratio?

Jobs are always going into waits when they return from a wait. Whether the job can become active again or have to wait for another job to go into a wait is determined by the activity level (or MAX ACT) setting for the storage pool.

You could have a storage pool with MAXACT jobs at 6, but an activity level of 3. Theoretically, you set it that way because you know that the six jobs running will have a certain amount of waiting activities every minute. If you ever set the activity level to 6 for six active jobs, no job would ever have a problem when it returned from a wait because it would just go active again. But it would go active at the expense of another active job that would suddenly go ineligible. The effect is a kind of drive-by faulting.

You don't want this to happen to an otherwise healthy job. You want the job to run until it normally goes to wait. Then your job would be allowed to start.

How do you know that level of detail about any of your jobs? You don't. That's why you use the ratios to tell you what you need to know.

Monitoring and modifying this area has a look and feel that is very different from batch and interactive pools. Interactive pools go into waits when they display a screen to a user. In computer-use time, those waits are small eternities.

You could have a storage pool supporting 100 interactive users, with an activity level of 6, because you expect the others to be waiting on screens anyway. Batch programs do a lot of waiting, but only for the system to get something for them. This process is very fast. The wait time is minimal. Therefore, you will have a batch storage pool with the activity level around 50 percent of the maximum active jobs.

Adjust activity levels in sets of 2 at a time and wait until you can monitor before you make another adjustment. If you're new to the AS/400, the Redbook, *AS/400 Performance Management,* has the recommended initial values for activity-level settings.

9.3.2.3 *When to Modify*

When you change either the memory level or the activity level, your system must go through a fairly intensive rearranging of the jobs in those pools. This can get intensive when you are taking memory from one or more pools and putting it into one or more other pools. When you make these changes, you can watch your CPU activity light go steady for anywhere from several seconds to several minutes. For this reason, don't make modifications when your system is heavily loaded.

9.3.3 Performance Tuning Summary

Performance tuning must be an ongoing activity. It's not a real good task to start doing when your system is crashing. Remember the rules:

- ❖ Monitor when the system is at its busiest (for the job mix).
- ❖ Modify when the system is at its lightest.
- ❖ When reassigning memory among pools, do so in the following order:
  - ✓ Decrease memory in all pools.
  - ✓ Increase memory in all pools.

Also, remember that monitoring is an ongoing process, and that it is a fairly boring task. Consider writing a program to monitor your system at known busy times and just collect data that you can scan periodically. Then make modifications when the time is right. If you're good about making performance tuning an ongoing activity, you'll never be backed into a corner where your system is limping along with a tuning problem and you must make a change in the middle of a busy period.

9.4 PERFORMANCE MONITORING AND REPORTING

The AS/400 comes with a powerful performance-monitoring tool call Performance Monitor/400 (PM/400). Like the name says it monitors performance. This product writes thousands of records to hundreds of files. There is more information here than you could ever want. IBM has a subscription service that takes this data monthly and produces more reports than you could ever use.

Try collecting the data and producing your own reports. With PM/400 data you can eliminate a lot of confusing analysis. I make references to what I do in this section, but keep in mind that you should review the files and information and decide what you need to collect for your shop.

Try focusing on one file, QAPMJOBS, in library QPFRDATA. Use the display file field definitions (DSPFFD) to see what its fields capture: Even it has too much data. Write a program or programs to sift it down to something reasonable.

In all the performance monitor files, every day's transactions are captured in unique *members* within the files. By the end of the month, this file and all its members is in the gigabyte range. That's why I like to extract it into a form that is meaningful and I can keep online for a while.

I like to have this data handy for trend analysis. Also, I will review individual programs or applications to see if their hit on the system is reasonable or not. When a new application goes live, this collected data can be compared to new data to see if the change has caused an application to suddenly adversely impact the system. Here's the sifting process I use:

❖ Many members to one (or one per month).

❖ Many, many job types are monitored. I only extract the interactive and batch jobs because they are typically the only ones I have control over.

❖ I don't collect for non-working days.

❖ Only QPFRDTA/QAPMJOBS file.

Within the records I do collect, I only include:

❖ Response time—interactive programs only. The response time is the amount of time the system takes to process a transaction. An example of response time is the amount of time elapsed from when the user presses the Enter key until a screen is returned. However, you lose the time the transaction spends in the network.

❖ CPU utilization—batch and interactive. The amount of CPU seconds used.

❖ CPU percent utilization—batch and interactive. The percentage of CPU used by both batch and interactive jobs.

❖ Number of transactions—interactive programs only. The number of times the Enter key was pressed.

❖ Cost per transaction—interactive programs only. My own measurement. Pure CPU seconds can be misleading because a program can legitimately take a lot of CPU seconds. Also, transactions can be misleading because lots of transactions with little processing behind them don't impact the system. I divide the CPU used by the number of transactions in order to come up with a cost (in CPU seconds) per transaction. This is much more meaningful for uncovering problem applications.

❖ Asynchronous Database IO—batch and interactive. Asynchronous DASD IO is good IO because they are DASD IO that programs don't have to wait for. For example, when reading records sequentially, if they were read from disk in blocks, the program doesn't wait for the next record when it comes from the input buffer.

❖ Wait for asynchronous Database IO—batch and interactive. These are very bad IO because—although the program shouldn't have to wait—it does. An example would be a program that is sequentially reading records. The system expects the records to be blocked and expects not to have to wait. If it does wait, you get that information here. In the blocked records example, a program legitimately has to wait whenever the buffer is exhausted and the system has to get another set of records from the disk. So some activity in here is acceptable. However, if the program had a problem and the system had to wait on every record, this count would go way up, and you would know to take a look at it.

❖ Synchronous DASD IO—batch and interactive. These are not so good IO because the programs have to wait. Random record reads and screen displays are examples of valid synchronous DASD IOs.

I extract these to the EXCEL product and graph them to review each day of the previous month. These are kept together to present graphs of long-term trends. These trending graphs track a year or more history of:

❖ Average response time per job.

❖ Average number of jobs per day.

❖ Total number of interactive jobs.

❖ Average number of transactions per interactive job.

❖ Average CPU utilization per interactive job.

❖ Total number of interactive transactions.

❖ Total CPU used by interactive jobs.

9.5 CAPACITY PLANNING

The AS/400 comes with a built-in capacity planning product called BEST/1. Unfortunately, I've never had it tell me anything other than "buy more hardware."

That is not to say the conclusion is invalid. Most people don't run it when they have lots of capacity. Therefore, the conclusion is probably valid. Given just that conclusion, I would have to do a lot of support work before I would use it alone to make a board-level recommendation for a major upgrade.

Look at capacity planning as the ultimate culmination of the other techniques covered in this chapter. Performance activities and measuring must ultimately result in capacity planning information. You must be able to provide evidence that you've done all you reasonably can accomplish. You must have a track record of:

- ❖ Performance tuning. Have you done all you can?
  - ✓ What have you monitored?
  - ✓ What have you modified?
  - ✓ Why can't you keep on modifying?

- ❖ You've kept monthly graphs of the key items the AS/400 uses. Over time, these graphs should reflect a trend to higher:
  - ✓ Response times.
  - ✓ CPU utilization.
  - ✓ DASD utilization.

- ❖ Your staff handles emergencies as efficiently as anyone. At some point, you need to be able to demonstrate:
  - ✓ Your performance-related emergencies have grown in number.
  - ✓ Your performance-related emergencies have grown in frequency.
  - ✓ The emergencies are caused by:
    - ➤ Growth in applications on the system.
    - ➤ Growth in the number of users on the system.
    - ➤ Growth in transaction levels.

If you really have all the preceding, capacity issues are easy to spot and easy to document.

9.6 BIBLIOGRAPHY

AS/400 Performance Management (GG24-3723-02) (Redbook).

10. Communications: SNA, APPC, and APPN

10.1 OVERVIEW

The AS/400 will support almost any communication protocol in the world. And, the way that support is growing, it will probably support any new ones that come along in the future.

But AS/400 communications does not come from a purebred ancestry. That's not a knock on the AS/400. Remember that IBM's midrange communications were years ahead of their time in speed and multiple platform support.

But over time the rest of the world connected and IBM blessed the AS/400 with openness. The AS/400 still supports the original 5250 protocol, but you can do much better with Ethernet, IPX, or token ring.

With openness, some of the new and old technologies get pretty mixed up. Here's the code I use to help me keep everything straight. If IBM merely supports a protocol, it will probably run under APPC or APPN. If IBM offers *native support* for a protocol, it will run on its own, not under APPC/APPN.

The whole subject of communications on any platform is very complex. As a handbook, this book describes the high points. If you get overwhelmed (and you probably will) remember that just by relying on IBM-supplied defaults and automatic configuration, you can do a pretty fair job of bringing up a network. If you're interested in more detail on any of the specific areas, refer to the IBM manuals referenced in this chapter.

In order to build a foundation of the basic features of the "old" AS/400 communications, this chapter covers SNA, APPC, and APPN. The chapters cover LANs, TCP/IP, IPX, token ring, and Ethernet.

10.2 SYSTEMS NETWORK ARCHITECTURE

Systems Network Architecture (SNA) is at the highest level of IBM communication. SNA isn't as simple as a protocol. SNA is a collection of descriptions of logical structures, protocols, and instruction sequences that handle all parts of IBM communications.

SNA is omnipresent over all IBM platforms, but relatively unknown in the LAN world. An exception is the servers designed specifically for SNA communications.

10.2.1 Advanced Peer-to-Peer Communications

Under SNA is the *advanced peer-to-peer communications* (APPC) that handles AS/400 communications. Another way to put it is that APPC uses what it needs of SNA to support AS/400 communications. For those of you so inclined, it does so as an implementation of SNA logical unit 6.2 and node type 2.1 architectures.

A key thing to remember about APPC is that it is a peer-to-peer architecture. You can have one platform act as the master to the other hosts if you want to, but that's not required. You can write programs on one system that start, control, and end jobs on other systems.

APPC isn't a protocol; it supports protocols.

10.2.2 APPC Functions

Most AS/400 customer contact with APPC is through the following nine functions it offers. For all the functions, you must have APPC or APPN in effect to use them.

❖ Distributed data management (DDM). Allows a program or user on one system to access database files on another system. See section 10.9, Distributed Data Management.

❖ SNA distribution services (SNADS). Allows electronic mail and files to be sent to another system. See section 10.10, SNA Distribution Services.

❖ Display station pass-through. Allows a user signed onto one AS/400 to pass through it into another AS/400 and sign on there as a "local" workstation. See section 10.11, Display Station Pass-Through.

❖ Electronic Customer Support (ECS). Allows a customer to access question-and-answer, problem-solving databases at IBM. Also, a customer can use ECS to order OS releases and PTFs. PTFs also can be delivered via ECS. See section 10.12, Electronic Customer Support.

❖ SNA pass-through. Allows SNA data to be passed between applications.

❖ File transfer support. Moves file members from one system to another.

❖ CA/400. Provides system access and functions to an attached personal computer.

❖ Alert support. When a problem or impending problem is detected by the system, it alerts the operator.

❖ CICS/400. Allows developers to write programs to process workstation transactions.

10.2.3 Programming for APPC

If you write programs that use communication links, they will use APPC interfaces. You must have APPC or APPN in effect to use the three APPC communications interfaces available to your programs:

❖ Interprogram communications function (ICF).
  ✓ Make ICF calls through DDS.
  ✓ Can be used in RPG, COBOL, C/400, and FORTRAN.

❖ Common programming interface communications (CPI-C):
  ✓ Make CPI-C calls through CPI communications CALLS.
  ✓ Can be used in the ICF languages plus REXX.

* CICS:
  * ✓ Make CICS calls through EXEC CICS commands.
  * ✓ Can be used in COBOL programs.

10.2.4 Communication Lines Support

APPC will support the following types of communications lines (a line adapter for each must be installed on the AS/400):

* Distributed data interface (DDI).
* Frame-relay network (FR).
* ISDN data line control (IDLC):
  * ✓ Switched.
  * ✓ Non-switched.

* Synchronous data link (SDLC):
  * ✓ Point-to-point switched.
  * ✓ Point-to-point non-switched.
  * ✓ Multiple-point non-switched.

* X.25.
* Token ring.
* Ethernet.

10.2.5 System Names in APPC/APPN

Whether you're using APPC (two AS/400s per network line) or APPN (multiple AS/400s networked), you should give serious consideration to meaningful system names.

If your connected AS/400s are within one local facility, you could make their departments or buildings the prefix to the system names. If you are supporting multiple AS/400s scattered around the city, make their streets or areas the name prefix. If you have AS/400s around the country, make their cities the name prefix. Follow each prefix with a rotating number.

Here are examples of three AS/400s each:

- ❖ Local facility:
  - ✓ ACTRCV01
  - ✓ ORDENT01
  - ✓ ORDENT02

- ❖ Local city:
  - ✓ SOUTH01
  - ✓ BEVHIL01
  - ✓ WODHIL01

- ❖ Nationwide:
  - ✓ LOSANG01
  - ✓ NEWYRK01
  - ✓ NEWYRK02

The preceding system might seem simplistic now, but location-based system names will save you hours of frustration later as you manage your APPC/APPN network.

10.3 ADVANCED PEER-TO-PEER NETWORKING (APPN)

Advanced peer-to-peer networking (APPN) is an enhanced APPC. Where as APPC is concerned with two AS/400s connected by a single line, APPN is concerned with multiple AS/400s, multiple lines, and even multiple APPN networks. APPN offers enough added functionality that many AS/400 customers use APPN to support a simple, two-AS/400 network instead of APPC.

You could support a network solely with APPC. You would have an APPC session for each line, but the work to use it could be prohibitive. On the other hand, APPN takes on the network-support chores for you.

APPN will control your transmissions, in complex networks, where multiple AS/400s are attached. Not all AS/400s have direct routes between them. APPN automatically will choose AS/400s (or nodes) it can use as intermediate systems to get to a target AS/400. If all systems and lines are under APPN control, no operator on the system has to worry about how a transmission will get to its destination. An APPN network can support any mixture of:

* ❖ AS/400s.

* ❖ Personal computers.

* ❖ S/36s.

* ❖ S/370s (running CICS or ACF/NCP with VTAM).

* ❖ S/38s.

* ❖ S/390s (running CICS or ACF/NCP with VTAM).

In addition to the nine APPC functions already discussed in 10.2.2, APPN provides:

* ❖ Distributed directory services. APPN, given a remote system name, will search the network to locate that system.

* ❖ Dynamic route selection based on user-defined rules. APPN will determine the best route to take to send a transmission to a remote system. You define the parameters it will use. For example, you can specify lowest cost or fastest route.

* ❖ Intermediate session routing. Any AS/400 can be used as an intermediate station for routing objects to a final destination.

* ❖ Automatic creation and vary on of APPN controller descriptions on token-ring or Ethernet networks. APPN dynamically determines the remote system's LAN address.

* ❖ Automatic creation and starting of remote device descriptions necessary to complete a network transmission.

10.3.1 Nodes, Control Points, and Class-of-Service

AS/400s on APPN are referred to as *nodes*. There are basically two types of nodes:

❖ *Network nodes*. An AS/400 running APPN and fully participating by providing intermediate-session routing, route-selection services, and distributed-directory services. These are network links between other nodes.

❖ E*nd nodes*. An AS/400 on the end of a network line, connected to a single network node.

✓ Low-entry networking node. Basically an AS/400 on an APPN network, but only running APPC.

✓ APPN end node. An AS/400, on an APPN network, running APPN, but it can receive some additional automatic configuration benefits from APPN.

When end nodes are attached to network nodes, the network node must be configured as a *network node server*. APPN allows you to have up to five network node servers per APPN network. They are created within the CHANGE NETWORK ATTRIBUTES (CHGNETA) command. These servers provide services for the attached end nodes:

❖ Directory searches.

❖ Route calculations.

❖ Remote locations do not have to be configured on the end nodes; the network node servers will do that.

❖ The end nodes are able to inform the network server node of all their local locations. That information stays within the network server node for its use in routing transmissions.

Note that the designations of the nodes have nothing to do with the quality or type of the AS/400s. They are only configuration decisions.

When APPN is up, *control points* are established. A simple control point is the directory and route information between two nodes. Network nodes build control-point information about themselves and all attached nodes.

End node control points only contain their own information, and that comes from the control point on the attached network *server node*. Once the connection is established and this information is obtained, it becomes part of the *network topology database* that is kept on each network node (but not end nodes). Each network node always contains complete system information. It uses the information to route transmissions.

When a network link goes down, the adjacent control points reconfigure themselves and update all nodes' network topology databases so each network node is aware that the network configuration has changed. Each network node always has a real-time network topology with which to work.

APPN uses a so-called *class-of-service* to determine the best routing (by your definition) for a transmission. Any network node knows (from its network topology database) all the links and nodes between it and the destination node. But the user can add value to that simple database by specifying a preference for each link and node. These preferences are kept in what are called classes-of-service. APPN will apply class-of-service rules to each topology entity to come up with what should be the most desirable routing for any transmission.

You create a class-of-service with the CREATE CLASS-OF-SERVICE DESCRIPTION (CRTCOSD) command. The APPN session locates the class-of-service through the mode description specified on each session initiation. For additional information, see section 10.4.6, Mode Descriptions.

Where class-of-service is line-related, each network node (AS/400) also has two characteristics you can use for force routing: *route addition resistance* (RAR) and *route congestion*. RAR makes a particular node more or less desirable as an intermediate network node.

If you have a smaller AS/400 on your network, you might not want to have APPN use it much for intermediate routing. You can set a number (0 through 255, the higher the number the less likely it is to be used) on the node that will discourage APPN from using it. Also, the node's link congestion can be taken into consideration. If a link is 90 percent or higher utilized, APPN will try to route away from that link. You can lower that value to have APPN look for alternative links sooner. Change either of these values with the CHANGE NETWORK ATTRIBUTES (CHGNETA) command.

10.4 APPC/APPN Configuration

Each AS/400 pair and the line between them is an APPC configuration. You can have more than one APPC configuration up at a time, but each must have a unique name. You have to configure several objects to make one APPC configuration. Here are the items and the order they must be created in:

- ❖ Connection list (for ISDN only).

- ❖ Network interface (for ISDN or frame relay only).

- ❖ Lines:
  - ✓ SNA pass-through requires two lines (one to send and one to receive).
  - ✓ Non-SNA pass-through only requires one line.

- ❖ Controller:
  - ✓ SNA pass-through requires two controllers (one for each line).
  - ✓ Non-SNA pass-through only requires one controller.

- ❖ Device:
  - ✓ SNA pass-through requires type *SNPT.

- ❖ Mode.

10.4.1 Creating a Connection List (ISDN Only)

The ISDN lines and controllers can refer to entries on the connection list to obtain information on managing calls sent or received across the network. First, you create the list and then you manage the entries in it. The commands to work with the list are:

- ❖ WRKCNNL   WORK WITH CONNECTION LISTS

- ❖ CRTCNNL   CREATE CONNECTION LIST

- ❖ CHGCNNL   CHANGE CONNECTION LIST

- ❖ DSPCNNL   DISPLAY CONNECTION LIST

- ❖ DLTCNNL   DELETE CONNECTION LIST

The commands to work with communications list entries are:

- ❖ WRKCNNLE   WORK WITH CONNECTION LIST ENTRIES
- ❖ ADDCNNLE   ADD CONNECTION LIST ENTRIES
- ❖ CHGCNNLE   CHANGE CONNECTION LIST ENTRIES
- ❖ RNMCNNLE   RENAME CONNECTION LIST ENTRIES
- ❖ RMVCNNLE   REMOVE CONNECTION LIST ENTRIES

10.4.2 Creating a Network Interface Description (ISDN/Frame Relay Only)

The network interface description is an object the system will refer to when it needs information about how the AS/400 and the network should interface. The commands to work with the description are:

- ❖ WRKNWID   WORK WITH NETWORK INTERFACE DESCRIPTION
- ❖ CRTNWI*xxxx*   CREATE NETWORK INTERFACE DESCRIPTION
- ❖ CHGNWI*xxxx*   CHANGE NETWORK INTERFACE DESCRIPTION
- ❖ DSPNWID   DISPLAY NETWORK INTERFACE DESCRIPTION
- ❖ DLTNWID   DELETE NETWORK INTERFACE DESCRIPTION

Some of these commands are specific to ISDN networks and some are specific to frame relay. Where the commands have *xxxx*, substitute:

- ❖ "ISDN" for ISDN.
- ❖ "FR" for frame relay.

10.4.3 Creating a Line Description

The line description will describe to the system the physical line connection and the data link protocol to be used between the AS/400 and the network. The commands to work with lines are:

- ❖ WRKLNID   WORK WITH LINE DESCRIPTION
- ❖ CRTLIN*xxxx*   CREATE LINE DESCRIPTION

Some of these commands are particular to specific line types. Where the commands have *xxxx*, substitute:

- ❖ "DDI" for DDI.

- ❖ "ETH" for Ethernet.

- ❖ "FR" for frame relay.

- ❖ "IDLC" for IDLC.

- ❖ "SDLC" for SDLC.

- ❖ "TRN" for token ring.

- ❖ "X25" for X.25.

When you work with a line for an APPC connection, you don't have much more to do than the basic command. However, when you configure an APPN line, you can use more of the command parameters:

- ❖ LINK SPEED (LINKSPEED). The speed of the link. The default is *INTERFACE and it provides automatic speed setting. In most cases, just use this default. If you need to, you can specify a line speed.

- ❖ COST PER CONNECT TIME (COSTCNN). Cost per connect times is the relative (not the actual) cost of being connected on the line. The default *CNN bases relative cost on the type of connection. You can override this with any number from 0 through 255. The lower numbers represent lower costs.

- ❖ COST PER BYTE (COSTBYTE). Cost per byte is the relative (not the actual) cost per byte of being connected on the line. The default *CNN BASES relative cost on the connection type. You can override this with any number from 0 through 255. The lower numbers represent lower costs.

❖ SECURITY USED ON THE LINE (SECURITY). Security on the line does not apply to AS/400 user identification, passwords, or object security. This parameter's possible values are:

✓ *NONSECURE—No security.

✓ *PKTSWTNET—Packet-switched network. Security is through packets' random routing through the network.

✓ *UNDGRDCBL—Underground cable in secured conduit.

✓ *SECURECND—Secured conduit; not guarded.

✓ *GUARDCND—Guarded conduit; protected against physical tampering.

✓ *ENCRYPTED—Data flowing on line is encrypted.

✓ *MAX—Guarded conduit; protected against physical tampering and radiation tapping.

❖ PROPAGATION DELAY (PRPDLY). Propagation delay is the amount of time you expect a transmission to take to travel from one end of a link to another. Possible values are:

✓ *MIN—Minimum delay.

✓ *LAN—Less than .48 milliseconds. Specifies local area network delay.

✓ *TELEPHONE—From .48 milliseconds to 49.152 milliseconds. Specifies telephone network delay.

✓ *PKTSWTNET—From .49.152 milliseconds to 245.76 milliseconds. Specifies packet-switched network delay.

✓ *SATELLITE—Greater than 245.76 milliseconds. Specifies satellite network delay.

✓ *MAX—Maximum delay.

❖ User-defined value 1, 2, 3 (USRDFN1, USRDFN2, USRDFN3). You can specify a numeric value from 0 through 255. The default is 128. The values can be changed during operations to indicate various activities on the network.

❖ Automatically create controller (AUTOCRTCTL). Specifies whether the system is to automatically create controller descriptions when incoming calls are received. Possible values are *YES and *NO (with *NO being the default).

❖ Automatically delete controller (AUTODLTCTL). Specifies whether and for how long the APPC controller can remain idle (status VARIED ON PENDING) before the controller description is varied off and deleted. These values are the number of minutes. The default is 1440 (24 hours). However, any values from 1 to 10,000 can be used.

10.4.4 APPC/APPN Controller Descriptions

One important key to creating an APPC/APPN environment is simply creating a controller with the appropriate options. You can start with the WORK WITH CONTROLLER DESCRIPTION (WRKCTLD) command. It will take you to the CREATE CONTROLLER APPC (CRTCTLAPPC) command. This command, which can be used directly if you want, creates an APPC controller, and it has a parameter that allows you to turn it into an APPN controller. Figure 10-1 shows the prompted version of the WRKCTLD command.

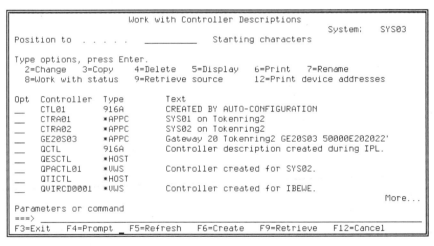

```
                    Work with Controller Descriptions
                                                    System:   SYS03
 Position to  . . . . .  _____      Starting characters

 Type options, press Enter.
   2=Change   3=Copy    4=Delete   5=Display   6=Print   7=Rename
   8=Work with status   9=Retrieve source     12=Print device addresses

 Opt  Controller  Type     Text
  __   CTL01       916A     CREATED BY AUTO-CONFIGURATION
  __   CTRA01      *APPC    SYS01 on Tokenring2
  __   CTRA02      *APPC    SYS02 on Tokenring2
  __   GE20S03     *APPC    Gateway 20 Tokenring2 GE20S03 50000E202022'
  __   QCTL        916A     Controller description created during IPL.
  __   QESCTL      *HOST
  __   QPACTL01    *VWS     Controller created for SYS02.
  __   QTICTL      *HOST
  __   QVIRCD0001  *VWS     Controller created for IBEWE.
                                                              More...
 Parameters or command
 ===>
 F3=Exit   F4=Prompt  F5=Refresh   F6=Create   F9=Retrieve   F12=Cancel
```

Figure 10-1: Prompted version of the WRKCTLD *command.*

This is the list of all the controllers on a sample system. If you press COMMAND 6, you can create a new controller description. Figure 10-2 shows the prompted version of that screen:

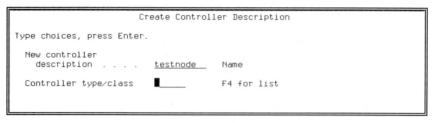

```
                         Create Controller Description
Type choices, press Enter.

  New controller
    description  . . . .    testnode     Name
  Controller type/class    █____         F4 for list
```

Figure 10-2: Resulting screen after pressing F6 (Create) from the WRKCTLD command.

Notice that the description starts off simply with just two parameters. Enter the controller name, in this case TESTNODE, and the type/class of the controller. If you position the cursor on this parameter and press F4, you'll get all possible values for the type/class:

❖ *APPC   ADVANCED PROGRAM-TO-PROGRAM COMMUNICATIONS.

❖ *ASYNC   ASYNCHRONOUS COMMUNICATIONS.

❖ *BSC   BINARY SYNCHRONOUS COMMUNICATIONS.

❖ *FNC   FINANCE.

❖ *HOST   SNA HOST.

❖ *LWS   LOCAL WORKSTATION.

❖ *NET   NETWORK.

❖ *RTL   RETAIL.

❖ *RWS   REMOTE WORKSTATION.

❖ *TAP   TAPE.

❖ *VWS   VIRTUAL WORKSTATION.

As shown in Figure 10-2, I selected *APPC as the type of controller. When I press Enter, I get a new command, CRTCTLAPPC, with the controller name and type/class filled in, but with new, specific APPC parameters added. See Figure 10-3.

```
                    Create Ctl Desc (APPC) (CRTCTLAPPC)

Type choices, press Enter.

Controller description . . . . . > TESTNODE      Name
Link type  . . . . . . . . . . .    _____      *ANYNW, *FAX, *FR, *IDLC...
Online at IPL . . . . . . . . .     *YES          *YES, *NO
```

Figure 10-3: Prompted version of the CRTCTLAPPC command.

If you've done this command a few times, you know you could have just invoked the command directly instead of going through WRKCTLD. This command has a couple of presentations. The first one, displayed in the Figure 10-3, requests three types of information:

❖   The name of the controller (already provided and it was carried over).

❖   The link type.

❖   Whether the controller will be automatically online anytime the
      AS/400 IPLs.

Let's focus on the link type. If you put the cursor on the parameter and press F4, you'll get a list of valid link types:

❖   *ANYNW

❖   *FAX

❖   *FR

❖   *IDLC

❖   *ILAN

❖   *LAN

❖   *LOCAL

❖   *SDLC

❖   *TDLC

❖   *X25

I selected the *LAN link type. When you press the Enter key, the command will expand as shown in Figure 10-4.

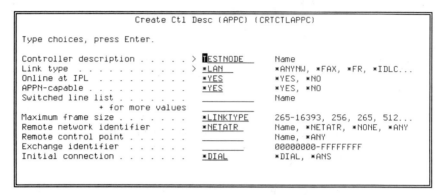

```
                    Create Ctl Desc (APPC) (CRTCTLAPPC)

Type choices, press Enter.

Controller description . . . . . > TESTNODE        Name
Link type  . . . . . . . . . . . > *LAN            *ANYNW, *FAX, *FR, *IDLC...
Online at IPL  . . . . . . . . .   *YES            *YES, *NO
APPN-capable . . . . . . . . . .   *YES            *YES, *NO
Switched line list . . . . . . .                   Name
                + for more values
Maximum frame size . . . . . . .   *LINKTYPE       265-16393, 256, 265, 512...
Remote network identifier  . . .   *NETATR         Name, *NETATR, *NONE, *ANY
Remote control point . . . . . .                   Name, *ANY
Exchange identifier  . . . . . .                   00000000-FFFFFFFF
Initial connection . . . . . . .   *DIAL           *DIAL, *ANS
```

Figure 10-4: Prompted version of the CTLCTLAPPC command.

The significant parameter for this is APPN CAPABLE. The default is *YES. This is what differentiates a controller as APPC or APPN. If you leave the default and press Enter, the command will again expand as shown in Figure 10-5.

```
                    Create Ctl Desc (APPC) (CRTCTLAPPC)

Type choices, press Enter.

Controller description . . . . . > TESTNODE        Name
Link type  . . . . . . . . . . . > *LAN            *ANYNW, *FAX, *FR, *IDLC...
Online at IPL  . . . . . . . . .   *YES            *YES, *NO
APPN-capable . . . . . . . . . .   *YES            *YES, *NO
Switched line list . . . . . . .                   Name
                + for more values
Maximum frame size . . . . . . .   *LINKTYPE       265-16393, 256, 265, 512...
Remote network identifier  . . .   *NETATR         Name, *NETATR, *NONE, *ANY
Remote control point . . . . . .                   Name, *ANY
Exchange identifier  . . . . . .                   00000000-FFFFFFFF
Initial connection . . . . . . .   *DIAL           *DIAL, *ANS
Dial initiation  . . . . . . . .   *LINKTYPE       *LINKTYPE, *IMMED, *DELAY
LAN remote adapter address . . .                   000000000001-FFFFFFFFFFFF
LAN DSAP . . . . . . . . . . . .   04              04, 08, 0C, 10, 14, 18, 1C...
LAN SSAP . . . . . . . . . . . .   04              04, 08, 0C, 10, 14, 18, 1C...
APPN CP session support  . . . .   *YES            *YES, *NO
                                                                     More...
```

Figure 10-5: CTLCTLAPPC expanded for APPN information.

The last parameter in Figure 10-5, APPC CP SESSION SUPPORT, defines the node as capable of being a control point on the network. The command has now expanded to the point where it continues onto a second screen. See Figure 10-6.

```
                    Create Ctl Desc (APPC) (CRTCTLAPPC)

Type choices, press Enter.

APPN node type . . . . . . . .   *ENDNODE      *ENDNODE, *LENNODE...
APPN/HPR capable . . . . . . .   *YES          *YES, *NO
APPN transmission group number   1             1-20, *CALC
APPN minimum switched status . . *URYONPND     *URYONPND, *URYON
Autocreate device . . . . . . .  *ALL          *ALL, *NONE
Autodelete device . . . . . . .  1440          1-10000, *NO
User-defined 1 . . . . . . . . . *LIND         0-255, *LIND
User-defined 2 . . . . . . . . . *LIND         0-255, *LIND
User-defined 3 . . . . . . . . . *LIND         0-255, *LIND
Model controller description . . *NO           *NO, *YES
```

Figure 10-6: Second screen of the CTLCTLAPPC command.

APPN NODE TYPE is where you designate the node as an end node or a network node. Remember that, when you create a controller description, you are creating it for the AS/400 you are signed onto and not for other AS/400s on the network.

For more detailed descriptions of the controller description parameters, see the *OS/400 APPN Support V3R2..*

10.4.5 APPC/APPN Device Descriptions

The APPC/APPN device is the local AS/400 served by APPC or APPN. The command, CREATE DEVICE DESCRIPTION FOR APPC (CRTDEVAPPC), creates a description for an APPC device. Figure 10-7 shows a prompted version of that command.

```
                    Create Device Desc (APPC) (CRTDEVAPPC)

Type choices, press Enter.

Device description . . . . . . .  _____    Name
Remote location . . . . . . . .  _____    Name
Online at IPL . . . . . . . . .  *YES          *YES, *NO
Local location . . . . . . . . . *NETATR       Name, *NETATR
Remote network identifier . . .  *NETATR       Name, *NETATR, *NONE
Attached controller . . . . . .  _____    Name
Mode . . . . . . . . . . . . . . *NETATR       Name, *NETATR
               + for more values  _____
Message queue . . . . . . . . .  QSYSOPR       Name, QSYSOPR
  Library . . . . . . . . . . .  *LIBL         Name, *LIBL, *CURLIB
APPN-capable . . . . . . . . . . *YES          *YES, *NO
Single session:
  Single session capable . . . . *NO           *NO, *YES
  Number of conversations . . .  _____         1-512
```

Figure 10-7: Prompted version of the CRTDEVAPPC command.

Communications: SNA, APPC, and APPN ❖ *211*

The parameter, REMOTE LOCATION NAME (RMTLOCNAME), is the name the remote AS/400 assigns to the local one. This name can be:

❖ The LCLLOCNAME of the remote AS/400 (APPC only).

❖ A name specified in the local location list of the remote AS/400 (APPN only).

❖ The local location name specified on the remote AS/400's network attributes (controlled through the CHGNETA command (APPN only)).

❖ The local control-point name (APPN only).

The LOCAL LOCATION NAME (LCLLOCNAME) is the name of the local AS/400. The default *NETATR tells APPC to take the local name from the network attributes. Alternatively, you can specify the local network name.

The REMOTE NETWORK IDENTIFIER (RMTNETID) is the name of the remote network where the location resides. The default *NETATR tells APPC to take the name from the network attributes.

MODE NAME (MODE) tells both ends of the network which mode to use. Unless the SINGLE SESSION LOCATION (SNGSSNLOC) is set to one, a maximum of 14 modes are allowed. If the SINGLE SESSION LOCATION is set to one, only 1 mode may be specified.

The USE APPN FUNCTION (APPN) specifies whether or not the device (the AS/400) will be used on an APPN network. The default is *YES but you can specify *NO.

The SINGLE SESSION LOCATION (SNGSSNLOC) allows you to specify if the communications over the network will be limited to one session or not. Valid values are *YES (only one session will be allowed) and *NO (multiple sessions will be allowed).

For more detailed information on the other parameters, see the *OS/400 APPN Support V3R2.*

10.4.6 Mode Descriptions

Mode descriptions describe the session characteristics and numbers of communications sessions that will be allowed between network nodes. When considering a mode in the device or network description, remember that a mode of the same name must exist on both local and remote AS/400s in order for a session to happen. The mode does not need to exist on an intermediate session because the communication is being routed to another network. When you have low-entry networking nodes as remote locations, their modes must exist on the network node server that services them. To help you, every AS/400 comes shipped with five predefined modes:

❖ BLANK. The name really is blank. You can specify this name (BLANK) and APPN will look for the default mode named with eight blank characters.

❖ #BATCH. A mode tailored for batch communications.

❖ #BATCHSC. The same as #BATCH except it has security built-in for packets (*PKTSWTNET).

❖ #INTER. A mode tailored for interactive communications.

❖ #INTERSC. The same as #INTER except it has security built-in for packets (*PKTSWTNET).

Use one of the preceding modes. If you feel you need to create your own mode, at least display these to see how IBM has set up parameters. For a detailed description of the IBM-Supplied modes, see the *OS/400 APPN Support V3R2*.

If you still want to create your own mode, do so with the CREATE MODE DESCRIPTION (CRTMODD) command. Figure 10-8 shows a prompted version of that command.

```
                  Create Mode Description (CRTMODD)

Type choices, press Enter.

Mode description . . . . . . . .                    Name
Maximum sessions . . . . . . . .    8_____         1-512
Maximum conversations  . . . . .    8_____         1-512
Locally controlled sessions  . .    4_____         0-512
Pre-established sessions . . . .    0_____         0-512
Maximum inbound pacing value . .    *CALC           1-32767, *CALC
Inbound pacing value . . . . . .    7_____         0-63
Outbound pacing value  . . . . .    7_____         0-63
Maximum length of request unit      *CALC           241-32767, *CALC
Data compression . . . . . . . .    *NETATR_____   1-2147483647, *NETATR...
Inbound data compression . . . .    *RLE            *RLE, *LZ9, *LZ10, *LZ12...
Outbound data compression  . . .    *RLE            *RLE, *LZ9, *LZ10, *LZ12...
Text 'description' . . . . . . .    *BLANK_____
```

```
                       Additional Parameters

Class-of-service . . . . . . . .    #CONNECT        Name, #CONNECT, #BATCH...
Authority  . . . . . . . . . . .    *LIBCRTAUT      Name, *LIBCRTAUT, *CHANGE...
```

Figure 10-8: Prompted version of the CRTMODD command (parts 1 and 2).

Put the name of the mode you are creating in the MODE DESCRIPTION NAME (MODD) parameter.

MAXIMUM NUMBER OF SESSIONS (MAXSSN) specifies how many sessions can be active at one time through the mode. The maximum in this parameter is 512 and the default is 8. The value for this parameter should be equal to the number specified for the locally controlled sessions (LCLCTLSSN) parameter on the local system—plus the value specified for the remote system.

The MAXIMUM NUMBER OF CONVERSATIONS (MAXCNV) specifies how many conversations can be active at one time over this mode. The maximum is 512 and the default is 8. Conversation are temporary transmissions sent over a session while the session is active. For an APPC AS/400, the maximum total conversations for all modes cannot exceed 512.

The LOCALLY CONTROLLED SESSIONS (LCLCTLSSN) parameter specifies the minimum number of sessions this local AS/400 will establish and control. The PREESTABLISHED SESSIONS (PREESTSSN) parameter specifies the number of concurrent sessions that will be established automatically when the mode is started. Others can be established after the mode is started, as they are needed, so long as their number doesn't exceed the number specified in the MAXSSN parameter.

Specify the class of service of the mode in the CLASS OF SERVICE (COS) parameter. Possible values are:

❖ #CONNECT—The default.

❖ #BATCH.

❖ #INTER.

❖ #BATCHSC.

❖ #INTERSC.

Class-of-service name. The class-of-service name must have been created on your system with the CRTCOSD command.

For more detailed information on the other parameters, see the see the *OS/400 APPN Support V3R2.*

10.4.7 Class-of-Service Descriptions

Class-of-service descriptions are used to select the nodes and groups to be included in the APPC/APPN session routes. If you have a small, two- or three-node network, don't worry too much about class of service. Just use one of the IBM-supplied descriptions. If you have a large and complex network—especially if your network is international and you must deal with multinational telephone regulations—you should analyze how you want to set up your classes of service.

Every AS/400 comes with five classes of service already configured for you by IBM. They are:

❖ #CONNECT—The default.

❖ #BATCH—A class of service for batch communications.

❖ #BATCHSC—The same as #BATCH except that it has a data link security for switched packets (*PKTSWTNWK).

❖ #INTER—A class of service for interactive communications.

❖ #INTERSC—The same as #inter except that it has data link security for switched packets (*PKTSWTNWK).

If you need to create your own classes of service, use the CREATE CLASS OF SERVICE DESCRIPTION (CRTCOSD) command. With this command, you can dictate many routing rules for communicating by APPN. With these rules, APPN can save you communications dollars and maximize communications throughput.

With class of service, if you aren't using the defaults, you're probably going to want to specify all the classes of service on your networks. Through class of service, you can specify routing rules to reflect:

- ❖ Link speed.
- ❖ Cost per connect time.
- ❖ Cost per byte.
- ❖ Line performance.
- ❖ Security.

As you specify each class of service, you will indicate your preference through weighting factors. The lower the weighting factor the more desirable the factor. Each class of service has eight rows in order of weight (1 is the smallest weight and 8 is the largest). Therefore, what you specify in row 1 should be more desirable than what you specify in row 2 (which would be more desirable than what is in row 3, and so on).

When specifying link speed and security, the higher speeds should be near the bottom rows because higher is better. When specifying link costs, the higher costs should be near the higher rows because higher costs are less desirable.

You don't have to knock yourself out coming up with eight rules for every item. You can specify one or two values in the tables. However, putting those one or two in rows 1 or 2 or in rows 7 or 8 will weight the overall result when that decision table is compared to others.

Use the CREATE CLASS OF SERVICE DESCRIPTION (CRTCOSD) command to create a class of service. Figure 10-9 shows a prompted version of the command.

```
                    Create Class-of-Service Desc (CRTCOSD)

Type choices, press Enter.

Class-of-service description . .   _____      Name
Transmission priority . . . . .   *MED          *LOW, *MED, *HIGH
```

```
                    Create Class-of-Service Desc (CRTCOSD)

Type choices, press Enter.

Row 1 for lines:
  Line row weight . . . . . . .   30            0-255
  Minimum link speed . . . . . .  4M            *MIN, 1200, 2400, 4800...
  Maximum link speed . . . . . .  *MAX          *MIN, 1200, 2400, 4800...
  Minimum cost/connect time  . .  0             0-255
  Maximum cost/connect time  . .  0             0-255
  Minimum cost/byte  . . . . . .  0             0-255
  Maximum cost/byte  . . . . . .  0             0-255
  Minimum security for line  . .  *NONSECURE    *NONSECURE, *PKTSWTNET...
  Maximum security for line  . .  *MAX          *NONSECURE, *PKTSWTNET...
  Minimum propagation delay  . .  *MIN          *MIN, *LAN, *TELEPHONE...
  Maximum propagation delay  . .  *LAN          *MIN, *LAN, *TELEPHONE...
  Minimum user-defined 1 . . . .  0             0-255
  Maximum user-defined 1 . . . .  255           0-255
  Minimum user-defined 2 . . . .  0             0-255
```

```
                    Create Class-of-Service Desc (CRTCOSD)

Type choices, press Enter.

  Maximum user-defined 2 . . . .  255           0-255
  Minimum user-defined 3 . . . .  0             0-255
  Maximum user-defined 3 . . . .  255           0-255
Row 1 for nodes:
  Node row weight  . . . . . . .  5             0-255
  Min route addition resistance   0             0-255
  Max route addition resistance   31            0-255
  Minimum congestion for node  .  *LOW          *LOW, *HIGH
  Maximum congestion for node  .  *LOW          *LOW, *HIGH
```

Figure 10-9 continues

Figure 10-9 continued

```
┌─────────────────────────────────────────────────────────────────────┐
│              Create Class-of-Service Desc (CRTCOSD)                    │
│                                                                        │
│  Type choices, press Enter.                                            │
│                                                                        │
│  Row 8 for lines:                                                      │
│    Line row weight  . . . . . . .   240      0-255                     │
│    Minimum link speed . . . . . .   *MIN     *MIN, 1200, 2400, 4800... │
│    Maximum link speed . . . . . .   *MAX     *MIN, 1200, 2400, 4800... │
│    Minimum cost/connect time  . .   0        0-255                     │
│    Maximum cost/connect time  . .   255      0-255                     │
│    Minimum cost/byte  . . . . . .   0        0-255                     │
│    Maximum cost/byte  . . . . . .   255      0-255                     │
│    Minimum security for line  . .   *NONSECURE  *NONSECURE, *PKTSWTNET... │
│    Maximum security for line  . .   *MAX     *NONSECURE, *PKTSWTNET...  │
│    Minimum propagation delay  . .   *MIN     *MIN, *LAN, *TELEPHONE...  │
│    Maximum propagation delay  . .   *MAX     *MIN, *LAN, *TELEPHONE...  │
│    Minimum user-defined 1 . . . .   0        0-255                     │
│    Maximum user-defined 1 . . . .   255      0-255                     │
│    Minimum user-defined 2 . . . .   0        0-255                     │
└─────────────────────────────────────────────────────────────────────┘
```

```
┌─────────────────────────────────────────────────────────────────────┐
│              Create Class-of-Service Desc (CRTCOSD)                    │
│                                                                        │
│  Type choices, press Enter.                                            │
│                                                                        │
│    Maximum user-defined 2 . . . .   255      0-255                     │
│    Minimum user-defined 3 . . . .   0        0-255                     │
│    Maximum user-defined 3 . . . .   255      0-255                     │
│  Row 8 for nodes:                                                      │
│    Node row weight  . . . . . . .   150      0-255                     │
│    Min route addition resistance    0        0-255                     │
│    Max route addition resistance    255      0-255                     │
│    Minimum congestion for node  .   *LOW     *LOW, *HIGH               │
│    Maximum congestion for node  .   *HIGH    *HIGH, *LOW               │
│  Text 'description' . . . . . . .   *BLANK                             │
│                                                                        │
│                                                                        │
│                        Additional Parameters                           │
│                                                                        │
│  Authority  . . . . . . . . . . .   *LIBCRTAUT  Name, *LIBCRTAUT, *CHANGE... │
└─────────────────────────────────────────────────────────────────────┘
```

Figure 10-9: Prompted version of the CRTCOSD command (parts 1-5).

Name your class of service on the CLASS-OF-SERVICE DESCRIPTION NAME (COSD) parameter. On the TRANSMISSION PRIORITY (TMSPY) parameter, specify the priority any transmission under this class of service will have. Possible values are:

❖ *LOW.

❖ *MED—The default.

❖ *HIGH.

Things get interesting on the ROW N FOR LINES (ROW1LINE through ROW8LINE) parameters. You don't see the table you're building. Instead, you only use these parameters to enter data into the table. When you put in values for multiple rows, you must specify them in ascending sequence: row 1 first, row 8 last. Most rows have minimum and maximum values. When they do have values, the minimum value you enter cannot be greater than the maximum value. Additionally, the maximum values cannot be less than the minimum value.

10.5 NETWORK ATTRIBUTES

Your AS/400 system comes with IBM-supplied values for AS/400 network attributes. Most of the time these defaults will work for you, but you ought to know what they are. Take a look at them with the DISPLAY NETWORK ATTRIBUTES (DSPNETA) command.

If you feel you need to make a change, use the CHANGE NETWORK ATTRIBUTES (CHGNETA) command. Unfortunately, you can't both display and change from the same command. The CHGNETA command just shows *SAME for all the network attributes. Therefore. you must use DSPNETA to get an idea of what you're changing.

Controlling network attributes is something you do with both APPC and APPN networks. There are only four parameters you can specify with APPC-only networks:

❖ Local network ID (LCLNETID).

❖ Local control-point name (LCLCPNAME).

❖ Default local location name (LCLLOCNAME).

❖ Default mode name (DFTMODE).

On APPN networks, you can also use the CHGNETA command to change:

❖ LOCAL NETWORK ID (LCLNETID). IBM supplies APPN for this value, but you should change it to a network ID of your own. Later, if you end up with a large APPN network, management and configuration will be easier.

❖ Local control-point name. IBM supplies Snnnnnnn where nnnnnnn is the serial number of your machine. You can override this value but its not necessary. Make note of this name. When you later configure the connected AS/400's (the remote one's) controller description, you must enter this name as the remote control-point name (RMTCPNAME).

❖ Default local location name. IBM supplies Snnnnnnn where nnnnnnn is the serial number of your machine. This is adequate; just leave it intact.

❖ Default mode. The IBM default is a mode called BLANK. This mode is also supplied by IBM. If you want to specify your own default mode, you must have defined it already with the CREATE MODE (CRTMOD) command.

❖ APPN node type. The APPN node specifies whether the local system (the one you're working on) is an end node (*ENDNODE) or a network node (*NETNODE). This must agree with the APPN NODE TYPE parameter of the CRTCTLAPPC command you use to create the APPC/APPN controller.

❖ Maximum number of intermediate sessions allowed. Only used for APPN network nodes, intermediate sessions determine the congestion level for your node. Intermediate sessions are APPN sessions that have started to receive or resend network traffic not addressed to the local AS/400. The valid values for this parameter are 0-9999. The IBM-supplied default is 2000. When the number of intermediate sessions reaches 90 percent of the number in this parameter, APPN considers the node congested and starts routing traffic around it until its number of intermediate sessions falls below 80 percent of this value.

❖ Route addition resistance (RAR). Only used for APPN network nodes, a RAR is a relative number, between 0 and 255, indicating how desirable the node is as a intermediate traffic handler. The default from IBM is 128. Increase the number on a node and it becomes less desirable. Decrease the number on a node and it is more desirable.

❖ Network node service provider list. Only used for end nodes, the list contains the names of up to five network node servers. Each name is a combination network ID and control-point name of each network node server. IBM supplies *LCLNETID and *ANY. These generic values give the most flexibility and, unless you're really into control, these should suffice.

10.6 LOCATION LISTS

Location lists contain the local and remote names of all the systems APPC/APPN supports. Not all users need to be in a location list, but those that are have a weak spot you need to consider. Many of the APPN-related commands use a default of *NETATR or network attribute. Logically enough, *NETATR gets information from the network. However, if any network attribute is changed (through the CHGNETA) after the location list is prepared, changes will not be reflected in the location list. If you use location lists and you make any changes to the network attributes, always review the location lists and change any information that is no longer current.

Local and remote locations are kept on separate location lists for APPN networks. A local list contains the names of the locations defined on the local system. This sounds really complex but it isn't. Just enter the name of the local system. Use the CREATE CONFIGURATION LIST (CRTCFGL) command. Figure 10-10 shows a prompted version of it.

```
                    Create Configuration List (CRTCFGL)

Type choices, press Enter.

Configuration list type  . . . . > *APPNLCL      *APPNLCL, *APPNRMT...
Configuration list . . . . . . . > QAPPNLCL      Name
Text 'description' . . . . . . . > 'LOcal location list'


                        Additional Parameters

APPN local location entry:      _
  Local location name  . . . . .   PHX01        Name, *PROMPT
  Entry 'description'  . . . . .                _____
                   + for more values _

                                                            More...
```

Figure 10-10: Prompted version of the CRTCFGL command.

There are lots of parameters to this command, but for creating a local list keep it simple. Enter *APPNLCL as the type of list. Naming the list QAPPNLCL is typical. Give a brief description of the list. Then enter the local system name as the APPN local location entry.

Most of the time this is all you would do. However, if you had a system (PHX01 in the example) that, for whatever reason, was to receive objects for PHX99, you would add PHX99 to the local location list on system PHX01. That step ensures APPN recognizes incoming mail as something PHX01 should receive.

Similarly, location names remote to the local system need to be defined in lists. The same command, CRTCFGL, is used but the list type must be *APPNRMT. Instead of simply entering the local system name, you must enter three things:

❖ Remote location name. The remote location name can be the actual name of the remote system, a generic name, or the generic *ALL. The following are valid values:

    ✓   PHX02

    ✓   PHX*

    ✓   *ALL

❖ Network ID. The name of the network that the remote location resides on is the network identification.

❖ Local location name. The location name of the local AS/400. APPN links the local and remote location names to make a unique pair name.

That's about all you need for identifying remote locations. If you'll be using directory entries, you also should enter the:

❖ Control-point name. The name of the control point providing network functions for the remote location.

❖ Control-point network ID. The name of the network on which the control point resides.

If the remote location is going to provide transparent access, the password to that system must be defined on a remote location list. To do that enter the:

❖ Location password.

❖ Secure location. The secure location determines where password verification occurs. If a *YES is specified and a remote location wants to start a program on the local location, it can verify the password before starting the program. If *NO (the default) is specified, the remote location may not verify the password. The local location must verify the password.

When defining a single-session connection, you must enter the:

❖ Single session location. The option is *YES.

❖ Locally controlled location. For this local and remote pair network, is the session controlled locally? Options are *YES and *NO (with *NO being the default).

❖ Preestablished session. Will the session be automatically started when the mode is started between the two systems? Options are *YES and *NO (with *NO being the default).

❖ Number of conversations. How many conversations will be allowed? Valid values are 1 through 512 (with the default being 10).

10.7 CL COMMANDS FOR COMMUNICATIONS

There are lots of CL commands for controlling communications, but CL's construction makes them easy to remember:

❖ Lines:
   ✓ Can be created or changed with the CRT or CHG prefix attached to the noun LIN (CHGLIN..., CRTLIN...).

✓ Both commands must have a suffix of one of the following:
   ➤ ddi (ddi).
   ➤ ETH (ETHERNET).
   ➤ FR (FRAME RELAY).
   ➤ idlc (idlc).
   ➤ net (network).
   ➤ sdlc (sdlc).
   ➤ tdlc (tdlc).
   ➤ trn (token-ring network).
   ➤ x25 (x.25).

❖ Controllers:

   ✓ Can be created or changed with the CRT or CHG prefix attached to the noun CTL (CHGCTL..., CRTCTL...).

   ✓ Both commands must have a suffix of one of the following:
   ➤ APPC (for APPC or APPN).
   ➤ HOST.

❖ Device descriptions:

   ✓ Can be created or changed with the CRT or CHG prefix attached to the noun dev (CHGDEV..., CRTDEV...)

   ✓ Both commands must have a suffix of one of the following:
   ➤ ddi (ddi).
   ➤ eth (Ethernet).
   ➤ fr (frame relay).
   ➤ idlc (idlc).
   ➤ net (network).
   ➤ sdlc (sdlc).
   ➤ tdlc (tdlc).
   ➤ trn (token-ring network).
   ➤ x25 (x.25).

- ❖ Mode descriptions:
  - ✓ Can be created or changed with the CRT or CHG prefix attached to the noun MOD (CHGMOD, CRTMODD).

- ❖ Class-of-service (COS) descriptions:
  - ✓ Can be created or changed with the CRT or CHG prefix attached to the abbreviation COS (CHGCOSD, CRTCOSD).

10.8 USING APPN

After all that configuration effort, using the APPN network is simple. You will:

- ❖ Vary the configuration on and off.
- ❖ Control modes.

Vary the configuration on and off with the VRYCFG command. The STATUS (STATUS) parameter will accept a *YES or *NO for an on operation or an off operation. Specify the description of the object you are varying with the CFGOBJ parameter. Also specify its type with the CFGTYPE parameter.

There are a lot of objects that make up an APPC/APPN network. You don't have to vary them all on or off. You can specify RANGE(*NET) to automatically vary on all objects downstream from the one description you specified.

A mode must be started after the APPC/APPN configuration is varied on. There can be many modes for one configuration. Once the mode is started, individual sessions can be established between locations. Modes get started in four ways:

- ❖ For device descriptions automatically created by APPN, a mode is started when a request to start a session is received.

- ❖ For device descriptions created with appn(*YES), a mode is started when a request to start a session is received.

- ❖ For device descriptions manually created with appn(*NO), a mode is started when the device description is varied on.

- ❖ You can start a mode with the START MODE (STRMOD) command.

Once a mode is started (with the command or automatically), you can end it with the END MODE (ENDMOD) command. You can check on any mode with the DISPLAY MODE STATUS (DSPMODSTS) command.

Occasionally, sessions will fail to be established. You can look at the number of sessions on a mode as well as its maximum number of sessions value. You can use the CHANGE SESSIONS MAXIMUM (CHGSSNMAX) command to increase the number of sessions that may be active over an individual mode.

10.9 DISTRIBUTED DATA MANAGEMENT

Distributed data management (DDM) is a way for a program or user on one system to access database files on another system. Through DDM, you can also submit a command from a local machine to do something to a file on a remote machine.

DDM is for accessing the file's records to read, add, change, and delete them. Although it can be used to move files from one system to another, you are better off using SNADS to move files. See section 10.10, SNA Distribution Services. The five commands to work with DDM files are:

❖ WRKDDMF   WORK WITH DDM FILES (an easy way to get
                   to the other DDM commands).

❖ CRTDDMF   CREATE DDM FILE.

❖ CHGDDMF   CHANGE DDM FILE.

❖ DSPDDMF   DISPLAY DDM FILE.

❖ DLTF   DELETE DDM FILE.

It is a common but not necessary practice to create a special library for DDM files. Name the library something like DDMLIB. The prompted version of the commands (except DLTF) are similar. I will go through the CRTDDMF to explain the parameters. Figure 10-11 shows the prompted version:

```
                        Create DDM File (CRTDDMF)

Type choices, press Enter.

DDM file . . . . . . . . . . .   █                Name
  Library  . . . . . . . . . .   *CURLIB          Name, *CURLIB
Remote file:
  File . . . . . . . . . . . .   _____        Name, *NONSTD
    Library  . . . . . . . . .   _____        Name, *LIBL, *CURLIB
  Nonstandard file 'name'  . . . _____


Remote location . . . . . . . .  _____        Name
Text 'description' . . . . . . . *BLANK
```

```
                        Create DDM File (CRTDDMF)

Type choices, press Enter.

                         Additional Parameters

Device:
  APPC device description  . . .  *LOC            Name, *LOC
Local location . . . . . . . .   *LOC            Name, *LOC, *NETATR
Mode . . . . . . . . . . . . .   *NETATR         Name, *NETATR
Remote network identifier  . . . *LOC            Name, *LOC, *NETATR, *NONE
Access Method:
  Remote file attribute  . . . . *RMTFILE        *RMTFILE, *COMBINED...
  Local access method  . . . . .                 *BOTH, *RANDOM, *SEQUENTIAL
Share open data path . . . . .   *NO             *NO, *YES
Record format level check  . . . *RMTFILE        *RMTFILE, *NO
Authority  . . . . . . . . . .   *LIBCRTAUT      Name, *LIBCRTAUT, *ALL...
Replace file . . . . . . . . .   *YES            *YES, *NO

                                                               Bottom
```

Figure 10-11: Prompted version of the DDM command (part 1 and 2).

The DDM FILE parameter is the local name you will use to refer to the file. That
doesn't have to be the real name of the file. The REMOTE FILE parameter is the
library and name of the file on the remote system. If you just want to access an
AS/400 file, enter its file and library name on this parameter. If you want to
access a S/38 or S/36 file or just one member of an AS/400 file, enter
*NONSTD as the remote file name and the name of the remote file (enclosed
in single apostrophes) on the NONSTANDARD FILE "NAME" parameter. The
REMOTE LOCATION NAME parameter is the name of the remote system on which
the file resides.

That's about it for the first of the CRTDDMF screens. The additional parameter's
screen has a couple of interesting items in it. The device, location, and mode are
APPC related and are usually left to *LOC (or the values used when APPC is set

up). The RECORD FORMAT LEVEL CHECK parameter allows you to continue level checking the remote file. A value of *NO will disable level checking. You can use this to give yourself more latitude on level checks when accessing DDM files.

DDM files are extremely simple. Once you've created a DDM file, you can start using it right away. Think of DDM files as files on your system. Not only are they easily accessible by application programs, you can run almost any database file-related CL command against them, and you can use them as outfiles to CL commands.

The command to submit other commands to a remote system is the SUBMIT REMOTE COMMAND (SBMRMTCMD). It is similar to the SUBMIT JOB (SBMJOB) command in that it contains a command embedded within itself. This command can be an OS/400 command, your own command, or a CALL to start a program running.

10.10 SNA DISTRIBUTION SERVICES

Systems Network Architecture Distribution Services (SNADS) is a method to distribute objects to other systems. Think of SNADS as an application program that runs on both the local and remote AS/400s that are connected with APPC.

The purpose of the SNADS programs is to route, send, and receive objects. Before you can use them, objects must be received out of the SNADS application into the remote machine. The SNADS program features are dependent on the APPC device's description. In addition, you need three system objects on each system to make SNADS work. Fortunately, every AS/400 comes loaded with one of each of these objects, and they are all named QSNADS:

❖ QSNADS subsystem. The subsystem comes with an autostart job entry of qzdstart. For more information on autostart jobs, see chapter 3.

❖ QSNADS job queue.

❖ QSNADS user ID.

Along with the three system objects, you'll need three SNADS objects:

❖ System Distribution Directory:

   ✓ User ID/Address. The user identification and address are used as a pair to create a unique name. The address is the name of the remote system. The new SNADS request must make a match on this pair.

   ✓ System Name/Group. The system name and group are used as a pair to create a unique name. The system name is the name of the remote system. Group is optional and can be left off. This pair is used to make a match on the System Distribution Routing Table.

❖ System Distribution Routing Table

   ✓ System Name/Group. The system name is used to find an entry in the System Distribution Queue.

❖ System Distribution Queue. The following four items are used together to locate an APPC device configuration:

   ✓ Remote location name.

   ✓ Mode.

   ✓ Remote network ID.

   ✓ Local location name.

The requesting user's identification and address is sent along with the objects being transmitted and the remote machine uses that to find a match in its own system distribution directory. From that match, it assigns a local (to it) user ID.

Note that, if two machines can both send and receive each other's objects, each directory must contain two entries for each user ID: user ID/local system name, and user ID/remote system name. One entry will be used when the machine is sending and the other when it is receiving.

When SNADS is receiving an object, it doesn't presume that object is for it. It's first decision is to match the object's destination user ID/address to one in its system distribution directory. If it finds a match, it delivers the object to the recipient. If it does not determine a match, it attempts to route the object to its intended destination.

The CLs to work with these SNADS items are:

- ❖ System Distribution Directory:
  - ✓ WRKDIR—Work with directory.

- ❖ System Distribution Routing Table:
  - ✓ ADDDSTRTE—Adds an entry.
  - ✓ CHGDSTRTE—Changes an entry.
  - ✓ RMVDSTRTE—Removes an entry.

- ❖ System Distribution Queue:
  - ✓ ADDDSTQ—Adds an entry.
  - ✓ CHGDSTQ—Changes an entry.
  - ✓ HLDDSTQ—Holds the distribution queue.
  - ✓ INZDSTQ—Initializes the distribution queue, optionally deleting entries.
  - ✓ RLSDSTQ—Releases the distribution queue.
  - ✓ RMVDSTQ—Removes an entry.
  - ✓ SNDDSTQ—Sends an entry.
  - ✓ WRKDSTQ—Work with distribution queues or entries. Allows you to check the status of distribution.

- ❖ All items:
  - ✓ CFGDSTSRV—Adds, changes, removes, and displays distribution queue or routing-table entries.
  - ✓ DSPDSTSRV—Displays the distribution queues and routing tables.

SNADS is basically an application of three programs called router, sender jobs, and receiver jobs.

- ❖ Router. The program name for router is QROUTR. Only one router program is used in a SNADS subsystem. Router should be an autostart job so it will start when the subsystem starts. If the router fails, SNADS communication is impossible and error CPC8803 is sent to the operator.

❖ Sender jobs. While the program name varies, it assumes the RMTLOCNAME specified on the distribution queue. Sender jobs is active as long as the SNADS subsystem is active. If you suspect problems, check it with the WORK WITH DISTRIBUTION QUEUES (WRKDSTQ) command. This program sends objects or mail from the distribution queue to the remote system.

❖ Receiver jobs. The program name is determined by the device you use to connect to the remote system. This job starts as soon as you start the APPC/APPN conversation and stays up until you end that conversation or an error occurs.

10.10.1 Setting Up SNADS

Here are the steps for bringing up SNADS on your system:

❖ Have APPC or APPN up.

❖ Make sure subsystem QCMN is up. This is supplied by IBM. It is also supplied with one communications entry. Make sure the communications entry is present. If you use your own communications subsystems or prefer your own communications entry, you must have a communications entry in one or more communications subsystem for each communications line SNADS will use.

❖ Start the QSNADS subsystem. This is supplied by IBM. In addition, you could have created your own SNADS subsystem with the same or a different name.

❖ With the CONFIGURE DISTRIBUTION SERVICES (CFGDSTSRV) command,
  ✓ Define the distribution queue(s).
  ✓ Define the routing table.

❖ With the WORK WITH DIRECTORY (WRKDIR) command, enroll network users in the system distribution directory.

❖ With the WORK WITH DISTRIBUTION LISTS (WRKDSTL) command, set up distribution lists.

❖ Save the SNADS configuration. Saving the configuration now will make it easy to restore later.

10.10.2 SNADS Miscellaneous

You can gain more flexibility in user IDs with *ANY for identification in your distribution directory. Any transmission bound for that AS/400 will be received and routed. You can use *ANY with legitimate user IDs. Include it at the bottom of the distribution directory for incoming objects or mail for anyone (such as visitors from other locations) not on the list.

The WRKDIR command is quite powerful. If you are in a large shop and your distribution directory is set up with the following, you can press the F10 key and search for user IDs based on:

❖ User name.

❖ Department.

❖ User ID.

❖ Address.

❖ Network user ID.

❖ Telephone number.

❖ Location.

❖ Building.

❖ Company.

10.11 DISPLAY STATION PASS-THROUGH

Display station pass-through is a method of signing onto a remote AS/400 through a local AS/400. This accessing method is slightly different from other AS/400 accessing methods. With other accessing methods, a display station can be attached to one or more AS/400s at one time. With display station pass-through, the display station is signed onto one AS/400. Subsequent AS/400s that the first AS/400 signs onto are passed through the first AS/400.

Display station pass-through gets really interesting when you have an APPN network with lots of AS/400s and routes. With pass-through, you can sign onto any remote AS/400 from your local AS/400. Depending on the number of sessions allowed at one time on your workstation, you can even pass through to many remote AS/400s at one time. The key factor is that every pass-through takes up one session.

Start display station pass-through with the START PASS-THROUGH (STRPASTHR) command. Figure 10-12 shows the prompted form.

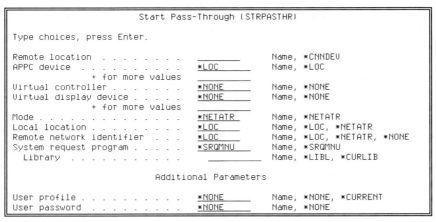

```
                    Start Pass-Through (STRPASTHR)

Type choices, press Enter.

 Remote location  . . . . . . . .                  Name, *CNNDEV
 APPC device  . . . . . . . . . .   *LOC           Name, *LOC
            + for more values
 Virtual controller . . . . . . .   *NONE          Name, *NONE
 Virtual display device . . . . .   *NONE          Name, *NONE
            + for more values
 Mode . . . . . . . . . . . . . .   *NETATR        Name, *NETATR
 Local location . . . . . . . . .   *LOC           Name, *LOC, *NETATR
 Remote network identifier  . . .   *LOC           Name, *LOC, *NETATR, *NONE
 System request program . . . . .   *SRQMNU        Name, *SRQMNU
   Library  . . . . . . . . . . .                  Name, *LIBL, *CURLIB

                    Additional Parameters

 User profile . . . . . . . . . .   *NONE          Name, *NONE, *CURRENT
 User password  . . . . . . . . .   *NONE          Name, *NONE
```

```
                    Start Pass-Through (STRPASTHR)

Type choices, press Enter.

 Initial program to call  . . . .   *RMTUSRPRF     Name, *RMTUSRPRF, *NONE
 Initial menu . . . . . . . . . .   *RMTUSRPRF     Name, *RMTUSRPRF, *SIGNOFF
 Current library  . . . . . . . .   *RMTUSRPRF     Name, *RMTUSRPRF
 Display option . . . . . . . . .   *YES           Character value, *YES, *NO
```

Figure 10-12: Prompted version of the STRPASTHR command (part 1 and 2).

Most of the time, you just need to specify the remote AS/400 name on the RMTLOCNAME parameter. This will suffice in every case unless you're running APPN and supporting multiple networks. In that case, you also need to specify the network ID on the remote network identifier (RMTNETID) parameter.

What constitutes a system name can be confusing. In this case, it is the local name of the remote system. As such, the system name can be one of these three choices:

❖ As defined on the remote system's APPN configuration list (as a local location).

❖ The local location name of the remote system.

❖ Local control point name (APPN only).

If you're not certain about the system name, use one of the following commands at the remote system to determine what location names are valid:

❖ WORK WITH CONFIGURATION LIST (WRKCFGL).

❖ DISPLAY NETWORK ATTRIBUTES (DSPNETA).

❖ DISPLAY APPN INFORMATION (DSPATTNINF).

Most of the time, you'll just use the remote system's name and your own user ID/password. The next thing you'll see is a logon menu from the remote system. Sign on and continue as if it were your primary machine. If you want to go back to the other AS/400, you must issue the TRANSFER PASS-THROUGH (TRFPASTHR) command or use one of these command keys:

❖ While on the target AS/400:

    ✓ System Request, option 10.

    ✓ System Request, option 13.

    ✓ System Request, option 14.

❖ While on the source AS/400:

    ✓ System Request menu, F3.

    ✓ System Request, option 15.

When you're through, terminate the session with the END PASS-THROUGH (ENDPASTHR) command.

10.11.1 Configuring Display Station Pass-Through

Before you start a display station pass-through, you must have APPC/APPN up and you must do some additional configuration on both systems. You need to make two decisions regarding the remote system before configuring display station pass-through:

❖ Whether to have the remote system configure your controller automatically or you configure them manually yourself.

❖ Whether to allow remote sign-on capability.

10.11.2 Automatic or Manual Configuration

Although the remote system has its own devices and controllers for its communications, it needs a set configuration in order to support communication between it and the local system. You can have the remote system set configurations automatically or manually.

These devices and controllers are virtual devices. If they are to be configured automatically, they are controlled by the QAUTOVRT system value. If QAUTOVRT is set to 0, autoconfig for virtual devices is turned off. If QAUTOVRT is set to any number between 1 and 9999, autoconfig is on until it has configured as many devices as is specified in the system value. To get started, use the CHANGE SYSTEM VALUE (CHGSYSVAL) command to set QAUTOVRT to 10.

If you are relying on autoconfig (you haven't configured any devices or controllers) and either QAUTOVRT is set to 0 or it has already configured the number of devices specified on the system value, display station pass-through will fail.

Virtual devices configured automatically by the system do not automatically get deleted. If you want them off the system, you have to delete them. Automatic configuration will create one controller for the first 250 devices. It will not create a second controller until it needs to attach device 251.

This might seem like a lot of devices on a controller, but everything is virtual. Therefore, its really no big deal. However, from a management perspective, 250 devices on one controller doesn't help you when you have system problems. The main reason for manually configuring controllers and devices is that you can group smaller numbers of devices to individual controllers.

Create device and controller descriptions manually with the CREATE CONTROLLER DESCRIPTION (VIRTUAL WORKSTATION) (CRTCTLVWS) command. Figure 10-13 shows the prompted version of the command.

```
                    Create Ctl Desc (Virtual WS) (CRTCTLVWS)

 Type choices, press Enter.

 Controller description . . . . .   ▮_____      Name
 Online at IPL  . . . . . . . . .   *YES          *YES, *NO
 Text 'description' . . . . . . .   *BLANK _____


                            Additional Parameters

 Attached devices . . . . . . . .   _____      Name
               + for more values
 Authority  . . . . . . . . . . .   *LIBCRTAUT    Name, *LIBCRTAUT, *CHANGE...
```

Figure 10-13: Prompted version of the CRTCTLVWS *command.*

One device must be assigned to the virtual controller when you create the controller and that device must already exist. It may have been created automatically or manually. If you are using automatic configuration, it will just be there for you. With manual configuration, you must have done it previously.

Virtual controllers and devices on the remote system must match physical devices on the local system. If a like device is not available, an alternate virtual device can be used, but the VRTDEV parameter must have been specified on the STRPASTHR command. For a chart of matching displays and acceptable alternatives, see the *OS/400 Remote Work Station Support V3R6.*

Personal computers can be used as terminals to emulate physical devices. Use the DISPLAY DEVICE DESCRIPTION (DSPDEVD) to find out what physical terminal any PC is emulating.

10.11.3 User Profile Configuration

User profiles must exist on the remote system for users who are passing through. Use the CREATE USER PROFILE (CRTUSRPRF) command to create the pass-through profiles.

When you initially set up display station pass-through, relax security temporarily so that you can work out connection issues without getting confused by security issues. But when you're up, seriously consider security. A user entering a system from another AS/400 is not "local" and should probably (but not necessarily) have limited access.

When a user starts a pass-through, you need to decide if that user will be presented with a sign-on screen or if the pass-through will be transparent (automatic sign on). If a program (or menu option) automatically starts pass-through for its own use, you could allow it automatic sign-on capability, but you also should specify that it automatically signs-off when its job ends.

If you want a sign-on screen to appear, use the CHANGE SYSTEM VALUE (CHGSYSVAL) command to change system value QRMTSIGN to *FRCSIGNON. Set it to *SAMEPRF when you want automatic sign-on to occur. Its easier if you use *FRCSIGNON when setting up a pass-through. Change it after you're confident of the connection.

With system value QRMTSIGN set to *SAMEPRF, you'll get automatic sign-on capability when you use the user profile and user password parameters of the STRPASTHR command. Even with automatic sign-on, the user will see system messages as the pass-through is accomplished. You can suppress those from the user's screen by specifying PASTHRSCN(*NO) on the STRPASTHR command.

10.12 ELECTRONIC CUSTOMER SUPPORT (ECS)

Electronic Customer Support (ECS) comes with every AS/400. The ECS feature allows you to contact IBM directly and inquire about current PTFs, log problems, and even order PTFs or operating-system upgrades. Also, when your AS/400's internal self-diagnostics senses a problem developing, your AS/400 will use the ECS line to initiate a service call to IBM.

You received an ECS modem with your AS/400 and you should have connected an outside phone line to it when you installed your machine. The ECS lines, controllers, and device are already configured for you. Most customers just use the equipment as delivered.

The lines and controllers IBM defined for your ECS are:

- ❖ For non-service related issues (problems, PTFs, OS/400, and product information):

  - ✓ Line—QTILINE.
  - ✓ Controller—QTICTL.
  - ✓ Device—QTIDA.

- ❖ For IBM service:

  - ✓ Line—QESLINE.
  - ✓ Controller—QESCTL.
  - ✓ Device—QESPAP.

You'll almost never need to change any of the preceding items, but if you do change something use one of the following commands:

- ❖ WORK WITH LINE DESCRIPTION (WRKLIND).

- ❖ WORK WITH CONTROLLER DESCRIPTION (WRKCTLD).

- ❖ WORK WITH DEVICE DESCRIPTION (WRKDEVD).

Although it's never happened yet, you might have to change the phone number for the IBM Service Department. If so, type either CALL QESPHONE or CALL QTIPHONE on any command and press Enter. You'll be presented with a screen to change the phone number.

The AS/400 contains contact information about products, service, and PTFs. You will need to keep this contact information updated. To do so, go to the AS/400 main menu and take option 7 (DEFINE OR CHANGE THE SYSTEM), and then take option 4 (WORK WITH SUPPORT CONTACT INFORMATION). You'll have an opportunity to change one of six contact areas:

- ❖ Q & A database.

- ❖ Local service.

- ❖ IBM product.

- ❖ Technical information exchange.

- ❖ Upgrade order.

❖ Service providers.

If you need more information on the ECS, refer to the *OS/400 Communication Configuration V3R6.*

10.13 BIBLIOGRAPHY

OS/400 APPC Programming V3R2

OS/400 APPN Support V3R2

OS/400 Communication Manager V3R2

OS/400 Remote Work Station Support V3R1

OS/400 Communications Configuration V3R6

OS/400 SNA Distribution Services

11. Communications: LANs, Frame Relay, and TCP/IP

11.1 OVERVIEW

Although SNA, APPC, and APPN provide the basis for most AS/400
communication support today, you will see most AS/400s supporting
workstations attached through local area networks (LANs). This chapter
explains how AS/400s and LANs connect.

11.2 PROTOCOLS

The LAN protocols the AS/400 supports are:

❖ Token ring.

❖ Ethernet.

❖ DDI.

❖ Frame relay.

❖ TCP/IP (transmission control protocol/Internet protocol).

Of the preceding, Ethernet is the most "native." Ethernet has a single layer, the
medium access control (MAC), between the hardware and the network. The
other three have two layers,

❖ MAC is the layer closest to the hardware. It provides the adapter
address. Sometimes this address is simply referred to as the MAC
address. The MAC layer does frame transmission and reception,
recognition, and error detection.

❖ The logical link control (LLC) provides logical connection,
disconnection, flow control, and error handling.

11.3 AS/400 LAN OVERVIEW

Protocol support for the AS/400 LAN falls into two broad categories:

- ❖ Acknowledged—provides better error handling capability, but must run under SNA.

- ❖ Unacknowledged—provide data transfer without SNA, but error handling is minimal.

The LAN devices attached to an AS/400 are logically switched. That's a little confusing at first because a dial-up remote device is considered switched. In this case, *switched* simply means that a workstation can connect to the AS/400 and expect that a communication session will be started for it, then disconnect (the session will be ended), and again reconnect.

Connecting any device to a LAN requires a LAN adapter card. Introducing an AS/400 to a LAN is no exception. To connect a LAN, you will need one or more adapter cards, and each of those cards supports a specific number of SNA connections.

AS/400 support of PC LANs can be treated with one of two strategies. With the first option, the AS/400 supports all devices directly. This requires a device con-figuration for each personal computer. Configuring each PC can be a pain, but the nice part is that LAN support is under the AS/400 umbrella. The other option is to separate the PC LAN from the AS/400 with a gateway. Using a gateway can be advantageous in a large shop where the AS/400 staff doesn't do LAN work and the LAN staff doesn't do AS/400 tasks. Set up your AS/400(s) on a small network with the AS/400(s) and a few gateways as nodes. Each gateway will support its own section of a much larger LAN.

Bridges connect dissimilar LANs. If you have this kind of situation, be espe-cially aware of addressing issues. Ethernet addresses are slightly different from token-ring and DDI addresses. For more information about this configuration, see *AS/400 LAN and Frame Relay V3R2,* Appendix C.

One thing you'll see over and over when configuring LAN objects is the *resource name*. This term indicates a concatenation of the adapter and port of that adapter the object will use. Use the WRKHDWRSC *CMN command to find the input/output adapter (IOA) you'll use, and then the port number. Concatenate the port number onto the IOA name and you'll have a resource name. For example, if the IOA name is LIN01, and you'll be using the second port on the adapter, your resource name is LIN012.

11.3.1 LAN Addresses

Every device on the LAN, including any AS/400s, requires a LAN adapter card. The adapter address, or MAC address, can be found on that card. While the MAC address is a 6-byte address, it is more frequently known by the 12 hexadecimal characters that make up the 6 bytes. Although many AS/400 customers think of the MAC address as a 12-character address, it has only 6 bytes.

Every adapter comes out of the factory with a unique address called the *preset address*. You can assign your own additional address when you configure the LAN line description. You don't have to, but it's a good idea for later LAN maintenance. If an adapter card has to be replaced, you'll have to change its configuration if you have relied on the preset address. If you have used your own address, you only have to change it for the new adapter.

An adapter for a frame relay network does not come with a preset address. If you are configuring a bridged frame-relay environment (see section 11.7 Frame Relay) that will connect to a remote token-ring, Ethernet, or DDI LAN through a network processor, you must assign an adapter address for each line description you create.

When working with LAN devices, you will often need to know adapter addresses. To quickly find them for all devices on a varied-on line, use the DISPLAY LINE DESCRIPTION (DSPLIND) command.

Another set of addresses associated with adapters are *service access points* (SAPs) that come in pairs: the source SAP (SSAP) and the destination SAP (DSAP). LAN communication flows from a SSAP address on one device to a DSAP address on another device. SSAP and DSAP addresses must be the same for a communication direction and destination to be established. The AS/400 will provide default SAP addresses and most customers just accept them.

If you like to define your own SAP addresses, you can define up to 24 SSAPs per token-ring or Ethernet adapter. Acknowledged services require that the addresses you use have SAP addresses in the range of hex 04 to hex 9C. The ones you specify must end in a 0, 4, 8, or C. If you are using TCP/IP, use hex AA as a SAP. Unacknowledged services can use any address from hex 02 through hex FE (as long as it is divisible by 2). If you really want to adjust these addresses, see *AS/400 LAN and Frame Relay V3R2* section 1.2.5, Assigning a Logical Address, and section 1.2.5.1, Service Access Points.

11.3.2 General Notes on Configurng LANs

Before you attempt any configurations commands, make sure you are doing so with a user profile that has *IOSYSCFG special authority. Many of the configuration commands are restricted from anyone without this authority.

I'll walk you through configuring the line descriptions and controller descriptions on each LAN type. In reality, many shops let the AS/400 do most of the work by accepting the default values and using autoconfiguration.

The only thing you must create is the line description (CRTLIND). On that line description, specify that you want APPC CONTROLLERS CREATED AUTO-MATICALLY (AUTOCRTCTL(*YES)). You can get to this parameter when you create the line description or change it (CHGLIND), but you won't see it when you display the line description (DSPLIND). When a workstation attempts to connect, if a controller doesn't exist, the system will create one for you. Also, the system will specify the default on the controller to automatically create its device descriptions (AUTOCRTDEV(*YES)) for you. Therefore, even devices will be created for you.

To accommodate logically switched devices, the description for the LAN controller on an AS/400 always has the INITIAL CONNECTION (INLCNN) parameter set to *DIAL. The setting is to *DIAL even if *APPN automatically creates your controller descriptions. This parameter has more to do with when polling occurs than when anything is dialed.

Another parameter, DIAL INITIATION (DIALINIT), can be set to *IMMED. This setting initiates polling as soon as the controller is varied on or *DELAY, which delays polling until the first program attempts to access the link. Again, just use the default *LINKTYPE and you'll be fine.

Another parameter you'll see but you should just leave alone is the DATA LINK ROLE (ROLE). Its default is negotiable (*NEG) and that's where you should leave it. This parameter merely allows the AS/400 to determine what stations are primary and secondary for communications.

11.4 TOKEN RING

A token-ring LAN supports the IEEE 802.5 standard. A token ring uses a token to pass data. Using a ring topology—tokens go around the ring and pass through every workstation—each workstation either passes the token on (if it isn't the addressee) or receives it.

Several workstations on a token ring can be attached to a concentrator called a multistation access unit (MAU). IBM's 8228 MAU supports seven workstations. A token-ring LAN supports two transmission speeds: 4 megabytes per second (Mbps) and 16 Mbps. A token-ring LAN uses shielded-twisted pair cabling.

11.4.1 Token-Ring Adapter Addressing

The token-ring adapter address is a 6-byte or 48-bit address. Read it like it's transmitted: from bit0/byte0 to bit7/byte5. There are two addresses—the destination address and the source address—on a token. Figure 11-1 shows the destination address. Note that three bits are reserved:

Byte 0							
0	1	2	3	4	5	6	7
IG	UL						

Byte 1							
0	1	2	3	4	5	6	7
FAI							

Byte 2							
0	1	2	3	4	5	6	7

Byte 5							
0	1	2	3	4	5	6	7

Figure 11-1: Token-ring destination address.

- ❖ IG—Individual/group:
  - ✓ The 0 means the address is an individual address or one associated with a particular station on the network.
  - ✓ The 1 means the address is a group address or that it is destined for more than one destination.
- ❖ UL—Universal/local:
  - ✓ The 0 means the address is universally administered.
  - ✓ The 1 means the address is locally administered.
- ❖ FAI—Only refers to locally administered addresses:
  - ✓ The 0 means the locally administered address is a functional address.
  - ✓ The 1 means the locally administered address is a group address.

Figure 11-2 shows the token-ring source address (two bits reserved):

Byte 0							
0	1	2	3	4	5	6	7
						U	UL

Byte 1							
0	1	2	3	4	5	6	7

Byte 2							
0	1	2	3	4	5	6	7

Byte 5							
0	1	2	3	4	5	6	7

Figure 11-2: Token-ring source address.

❖ U:

  ✓ The 0 means routing information is present in the frame.

  ✓ The 1 means routing information is not present in the frame.

❖ UL—Universal/local:

  ✓ The 0 means the address is universally administered.

  ✓ The 1 means the address is locally administered.

These bits must be considered when assigning or working with token-ring addresses because their use limits the range of numbers available for addressing.

❖ Bit0/byte0 has two implications:

  ✓ Destination addresses:

    ➤ Individual token-ring addresses can be 000000000000 through 7FFFFFFFFFFF.

    ➤ Group addresses can be 800000000000 through FFFFFFFFFFFF.

  ✓ Source addresses:

    ➤ Routing information present. The range of token-ring addresses will be 800000000000 through FFFFFFFFFFFF.

    ➤ No routing information present, token-ring addresses will be in the range 000000000000 through 7FFFFFFFFFFF.

❖ Bit1/byte0. If the address (destination or source) is locally administered, the range is limited to 400000000000 through 7FFFFFFFFFFF.

  ✓ If the address is locally administered, bit0/byte2 further limits the address.

    ➤ Group address. The adapter's address range is limited to the range 400080000000 through 7FFFFFFFFFFF.

    ➤ Functional address. The adapter's address range is limited to the range C00000000000 through C00040000000. There are some dedicated functional addresses and some that can be user defined. For a list of the addresses, see OS/400 Communications Configuration V3R2, section 2.3.2.50.

11.4.2 Token-Ring Considerations

A token-ring network requires a token-ring adapter card on each device (AS/400 and workstations) and every device's adapter card must connect to a multistation access unit (MAU). Each MAU attaches up to eight devices to the ring. There are two factors to plan for before starting to configure your token-ring network:

❖ Speed.

❖ Maximum frame size.

Token-ring networks have the option to run at two speeds: 4 Mbps or 16 Mbps. However, once you've chosen a speed, all token-ring adapter cards must be set to the same speed.

Token-ring data is stored in the token as a frame. A frame can be from 265 through 16,393 bytes (where 1,994 is the default), and this is called the *frame size*. The larger the frame size, the more efficiently data can be moved. There are four areas where the frame size is determined:

❖ You set the frame size on the CREATE TOKEN-RING LINE DESCRIPTION (crtlintrn) command with the MAXIMUM FRAME SIZE *(MAXFRAME)* parameter.

❖ You set it on the CREATE TOKEN-RING CONTROLLER DESCRIPTION (crtctltrn) command with the MAXIMUM FRAME SIZE (MAXFRAME) parameter.

❖ You set it on SSAP MAXIMUM FRAME SIZE (MAXFRAME) parameter on the CREATE TOKEN-RING LINE DESCRIPTION (CRTLINTRN) command.

The system may override your selected frame size at any time with the smallest of the large frame sizes any individual adapter can handle. If most of your adapters can handle a 16,393-byte frame size (and that is what you specified on one of the MAXFRAME parameter fields), but one adapter can only handle a 4096 frame size, you will get the 4096 size frame.

If a token-ring network passes its frames across a bridge, you must take that into consideration in your frame-size calculation. If you define a frame size too large for the bridge, that frame will be discarded when the network tries to send it through the bridge. Unfortunately, the network doesn't automatically incorporate the bridge frame size in its calculations. You must do that calculation for it. Just ensure that your bridge size is at least as large as the smallest of one of the three frame sizes listed in the preceding description.

11.4.3 Configuring a Token-Ring Network

Before you configure a token-ring network, decide four things:

❖ Resource name. For a discussion of how to determine the resource name, see section 11.1, LAN Overview. This is the second parameter of the CRTLINTRN command.

❖ Adapter address. The adapter address you'll use must have 12 characters and start with 40000.

❖ Speed. For additional information about the speed of the network, see section 11.4.2, Token-Ring Considerations.

❖ Frame size. For additional information about frame sizes, see section 11.4.2, Token-Ring Considerations.

After completing the preceding four steps, do the following commands in sequence. See Figure 11-3.

11.4.3.1 CREATE LINE DESCRIPTION—CRTLINTRN

```
                    Create Line Desc (Token-Ring) (CRTLINTRN)

Type choices, press Enter.

Line description . . . . . . . > TOKENRING1     Name
Resource name  . . . . . . . . > LIN012         Name, *NWID, *NWSD
Online at IPL  . . . . . . . .   *YES           *YES, *NO
Vary on wait . . . . . . . . .   *NOWAIT        *NOWAIT, 15-180 (1 second)
Maximum controllers  . . . . .   40             1-256
Line speed . . . . . . . . . . > 16M            4M, 16M, *NWI
Maximum frame size . . . . . . > 16393          265-16393, 265, 521, 1033...
Local adapter address  . . . . > 40000A010111   400000000000-7FFFFFFFFFFF...
Exchange identifier  . . . . .   *SYSGEN        05600000-056FFFFF, *SYSGEN
```

```
                    Create Line Desc (Token-Ring) (CRTLINTRN)

Type choices, press Enter.

SSAP list:                           _
   Source service access point . > 04             02-FE, *SYSGEN
   SSAP maximum frame . . . . . . > *MAXFRAME      *MAXFRAME, 265-16393
   SSAP type  . . . . . . . . . . > *CALC          *CALC, *NONSNA, *SNA, *HPR

   Source service access point . > 08             02-FE
   SSAP maximum frame . . . . . .   *MAXFRAME      *MAXFRAME, 265-16393
   SSAP type  . . . . . . . . . .   *CALC          *CALC, *NONSNA, *SNA, *HPR
               + for more values _
Text 'description' . . . . . . .   TOKEN RING 1 LINE DESCRIPTION


                          Additional Parameters

Network controller . . . . . . .  _____    Name
TRLAN manager logging level  . .   *OFF           *OFF, *MIN, *MED, *MAX
                                                                    More...
```

```
                    Create Line Desc (Token-Ring) (CRTLINTRN)

Type choices, press Enter.

TRLAN manager mode . . . . . . .   *OBSERVING     *OBSERVING, *CONTROLLING
Log configuration changes  . . .   *LOG           *LOG, *NOLOG
Token-ring inform of beacon  . .   *YES           *YES, *NO
Functional address . . . . . . .   *NONE          *NONE, C00000000001...
               + for more values  _____
Early token release  . . . . . .   *LINESPEED     *YES, *NO, *LINESPEED
Error threshold level  . . . . .   *OFF           *OFF, *MIN, *MED, *MAX
Link speed . . . . . . . . . . .   4M             *MIN, 1200, 2400, 4800...
Cost/connect time  . . . . . . .   0              0-255
Cost/byte  . . . . . . . . . . .   0              0-255
Security for line  . . . . . . .   *NONSECURE     *NONSECURE, *PKTSWTNET...
Propagation delay  . . . . . . .   *LAN           *MIN, *LAN, *TELEPHONE...
User-defined 1 . . . . . . . . .   128            0-255
User-defined 2 . . . . . . . . .   128            0-255
User-defined 3 . . . . . . . . .   128            0-255
Autocreate controller  . . . . > *YES            *YES, *NO
```

Figure 11-3: CREATE LINE DESCRIPTION for token-ring network (part 1, 2, and 3).

11.4.3.2 CREATE CONTROLLER DESCRIPTION (optional).

If you specify the AUTOCREATE CONTROLLER parameter on the line description as *YES, you will not have to do this step at all. When you attempt to establish a communication session, the line will create the controller for you. By specifying AUTOCREATE DEVICE(*YES), the system also will automatically create your device description for you.

For an AS/400-to-AS/400 network you will use CRTCTLAPPC. See Figure11-4.

```
                    Create Ctl Desc (APPC) (CRTCTLAPPC)

Type choices, press Enter.

Controller description . . . . . >  TRAS400      Name
Link type  . . . . . . . . . . . >  *LAN         *ANYNW, *FAX, *FR, *IDLC...
Online at IPL  . . . . . . . . .    *YES         *YES, *NO
APPN-capable . . . . . . . . . .    *YES         *YES, *NO
Switched line list . . . . . . . >  TOKENRING1   Name
             + for more values      _____
Maximum frame size . . . . . . .    *LINKTYPE    265-16393, 256, 265, 512...
Remote network identifier  . . .    *NETATR      Name, *NETATR, *NONE, *ANY
Remote control point . . . . . .    LANAPPN      Name, *ANY
Exchange identifier  . . . . . .    _____     00000000-FFFFFFFF
Initial connection . . . . . . .    *DIAL        *DIAL, *ANS
Dial initiation  . . . . . . . .    *LINKTYPE    *LINKTYPE, *IMMED, *DELAY
LAN remote adapter address . . . >  40000A020222 000000000001-FFFFFFFFFFFF
LAN DSAP . . . . . . . . . . . .    04           04, 08, 0C, 10, 14, 18, 1C...
LAN SSAP . . . . . . . . . . . . >  08           04, 08, 0C, 10, 14, 18, 1C...
APPN CP session support  . . . .    *YES         *YES, *NO
                                                                   More...
```

```
                    Create Ctl Desc (APPC) (CRTCTLAPPC)

Type choices, press Enter.

APPN node type . . . . . . . . .    *ENDNODE     *ENDNODE, *LENNODE...
APPN/HPR capable . . . . . . . .    *YES         *YES, *NO
APPN transmission group number      1            1-20, *CALC
APPN minimum switched status . .    *VRYONPND    *VRYONPND, *VRYON
Autocreate device  . . . . . . .    *ALL         *ALL, *NONE
Autodelete device  . . . . . . .    1440         1-10000, *NO
User-defined 1 . . . . . . . . .    *LIND        0-255, *LIND
User-defined 2 . . . . . . . . .    *LIND        0-255, *LIND
User-defined 3 . . . . . . . . .    *LIND        0-255, *LIND
Model controller description . .    *NO          *NO, *YES
```

Figure 11-4: CREATE CONTROLLER DESCRIPTION for AS/400-AS/400 token-ring network (part 1 and 2).

The remote-control point parameter is the same as the local control point of the remote AS/400. If you are in doubt, use the DISPLAY NETWORK ATTRIBUTE (DSPNETA) command on the remote machine to determine this. The adapter address is the address of the adapter on the remote AS/400.

For an AS/400-to-PC network you will use CRTCTLAPPC. See Figure 11-5.

```
                    Create Ctl Desc (APPC) (CRTCTLAPPC)

Type choices, press Enter.

Controller description . . . . . CTLD        > TRLAN01
Link type  . . . . . . . . . . . LINKTYPE    > *LAN
Online at IPL  . . . . . . . . . ONLINE        *YES
APPN-capable . . . . . . . . . . APPN          *YES
Switched line list . . . . . . . SWTLINLST   > TOKENRING1
                   + for more values
Maximum frame size . . . . . . . MAXFRAME      *LINKTYPE
Remote network identifier  . . . RMTNETID      *NETATR
Remote control point . . . . . . RMTCPNAME   > GE01S01
Exchange identifier  . . . . . . EXCHID
Initial connection . . . . . . . INLCNN        *DIAL
Dial initiation  . . . . . . . . DIALINIT      *LINKTYPE
LAN remote adapter address . . . ADPTADR     > 10004A00512B
LAN DSAP . . . . . . . . . . . . DSAP          04
LAN SSAP . . . . . . . . . . . . SSAP          04
APPN CP session support  . . . . CPSSN       > *NO
```

```
                    Create Ctl Desc (APPC) (CRTCTLAPPC)

Type choices, press Enter.

APPN node type . . . . . . . . .    *ENDNODE      *ENDNODE, *LENNODE...
APPN/HPR capable . . . . . . . .    *YES          *YES, *NO
APPN transmission group number      1             1-20, *CALC
APPN minimum switched status . .    *URYONPND     *URYONPND, *URYON
Autocreate device  . . . . . . .    *ALL          *ALL, *NONE
Autodelete device  . . . . . . .    1440          1-10000, *NO
User-defined 1 . . . . . . . . .    *LIND         0-255, *LIND
User-defined 2 . . . . . . . . .    *LIND         0-255, *LIND
User-defined 3 . . . . . . . . .    *LIND         0-255, *LIND
Model controller description . .    *NO           *NO, *YES
```

Figure 11-5: CREATE CONTROLLER DESCRIPTION for AS/400-PC token-ring network (part 1 and 2).

The remote-control point is the name assigned to the remote PC. You should have a naming convention for this to make device status checks easy. For example, you could name every device something starting with the letters PC. Then, when you run WORK WITH CONFIGURATION STATUS (WRKCFGSTS), you could specify the generic name PC* and isolate devices to just personal computers. You could go one step further and follow the PC label with some kind of designation for the department or location. An example would be the phone extension where the device is located.

The adapter address parameter is the manufacturer's address of the adapter on the PC.

11.4.3.3 Create Device Description for APPC— CRTDEVAPPC (Optional)

```
                     Create Device Desc (APPC) (CRTDEVAPPC)

Type choices, press Enter.

Device description . . . . . . . > TR400HOST     Name
Remote location  . . . . . . . . > SYS01         Name
Online at IPL  . . . . . . . . .   *YES          *YES, *NO
Local location . . . . . . . . . > SYS02         Name, *NETATR
Remote network identifier  . . .   *NETATR       Name, *NETATR, *NONE
Attached controller  . . . . . . > TRAS400       Name
Mode . . . . . . . . . . . . . . > BLANK         Name, *NETATR
                + for more values
Message queue  . . . . . . . . .   QSYSOPR       Name, QSYSOPR
  Library  . . . . . . . . . . .     *LIBL       Name, *LIBL, *CURLIB
APPN-capable . . . . . . . . . .   *YES          *YES, *NO
Single session:
  Single session capable . . . .   *NO           *NO, *YES
  Number of conversations  . . .                 1-512
Text 'description' . . . . . . .   APPC DEVICE FOR SYS01
```

Figure 11-6: CREATE DEVICE DESCRIPTION for a token-ring network.

If you specified the AUTOCREATE DEVICE parameter as *ALL when you created the controller description (Figure 11-4 and Figure 11-5), the system creates the device description for you, and you can skip this step.

If you specify AUTOCREATE CONTROLLER(*YES) on the line description and the line description creates the controller description for you, it creates it WITH AUTOCREATE DEVICE(*ALL) and you can still skip this step.

11.4.4 Token-Ring LAN CL Commands

To work with the token-ring LAN adapters, use the WRKHDWRSC command with *TRN as the first parameter. Figure 11-7 shows how it looks.

```
                   Work with Hardware Resources (WRKHDWRSC)

Type choices, press Enter.

Type . . . . . . . . . . . . . . > *LAN          *CMN, *CSA, *LAN, *LWS...
Line type  . . . . . . . . . . . > *TRN          *ALL, *DDI, *TRN
```

Figure 11-7: WRKHDWRSC command for token-ring adapters.

Pressing the Enter key gives you the screen shown in Figure 11-8.

```
                     Work with LAN Adapter Information
                                                        System:    SYS01
      Type options, press Enter.
       1=Add entry    2=Change    4=Remove entry    7=Rename


                                    Line
      Opt   Address      Name       Type   Description
       _    _____     _____
       _    50000E919111 GE91S01   *TRN   E/400 Gateway 91
       _    40000A010111 TOKENRING1 *TRN   SYS01 -- Token Ring 1
       _    40000A020211 TOKENRING2 *TRN   SYS02 -- Token Ring 2
       _    50000E909011 GE90S01   *TRN   E/400 Gateway 90
       _    50000E171711 GE17S02   *TRN   E/400 Gateway 17
       _    50000E131311 GE13S02   *TRN   E/400 Gateway 13
       _    50000E111111 GE11S02   *TRN   E/400 Gateway 11
       _    50000E010122 GE01S01   *TRN   E/400 Gateway 01

                                                               Bottom
```

Figure 11-8: Formatted version of the WRKHDWRSC command used for token-ring adapters.

From this screen, you can display information about an adapter, remove or add an adapter, or change an adapter. This is a somewhat limited command for working with adapters. A more potent alternative is the WORK WITH LAN ADAPTER (WRKLANADPT) command. Figure 11-9 shows the WRKLANADPT command setup.

```
                   Work With LAN Adapters (WRKLANADPT)

      Type choices, press Enter.

      Line description . . . . . . . . > TOKENRING1    Name
      Output . . . . . . . . . . . .   *              *, *PRINT
```

Figure 11-9: WRKLANADPT command setup.

```
                        Work with LAN Adapters
                                                System:   SYS01
      Line description . . . . . . . . :   TOKENRING1
      Line type  . . . . . . . . . . . :   *TRN

   Type options, press Enter.
     1=Add entry   2=Change   4=Remove entry   5=Display profile   6=Print
     7=Rename

   Opt  Address        Name                 Status  Description
    __
    __  40000A010111   TOKENRING1           Active  SYS01 -- Token Ring 1
    __  0002BA0200A6   D2BA0200A6           Active
    __  40000A020211   TOKENRING2           Active  SYS02 -- Token Ring 2
    __  50000E131311   GE13S02              Active  E/400 Gateway 13
    __  50000E010122   GE01S01              Active  E/400 Gateway 01
    __  0000F61B9EE0   D0F61B9EE0           Active
    __  50000E919111   GE91S01              Active  E/400 Gateway 91
```

Figure 11-10: WRKLANADPP command for adapter TOKENRING1.

Figure 11-10 shows the result of that command. From this screen, you can do several things. Put a 5 on the option line and you can get a description of the LAN adapter profile as shown in Figure 11-11.

```
                        Display Adapter Profile
                                                System:   SYS01
   Product ID . . . . . . . . . . . . :   000000000000000000000000000000000000
   Licensed internal code . . . . . . :   F0F0F0F8F4F4F0F4F940
   Group address  . . . . . . . . . . :   C00080000000
   Adapter address  . . . . . . . . . :   40000A010111
   Adapter name . . . . . . . . . . . :   TOKENRING1
   Adapter description  . . . . . . . :   SYS01 -- Token Ring 1

   NAUN address . . . . . . . . . . . :   0002BA0200A6
   NAUN name  . . . . . . . . . . . . :   D2BA0200A6
   NAUN description . . . . . . . . . :


                                                Functional
   Function                                     Address
   Ring Error Monitor                           C00000000008
   Configuration Report Server                  C00000000010
```

Figure 11-11: LAN adapter profile for TOKENRING1.

If you press the F10 key, you'll get the status of the adapter.

```
                        Display LAN Status
                                                System:   SYS01
   Line description . . . . . . . . . . . :   TOKENRING1
   Ring status  . . . . . . . . . . . . . :   Normal
```

Figure 11-12: Status of adapter TOKENRING1.

This displays the LAN adapter information as well as the next LAN adapter from it on the network (in the NAUN ADDRESS parameter). This can help you troubleshoot a token-ring problem by identifying the next adapter for you to check.

In Figure 11-12, the adapter status is NORMAL (meaning just that). Other possible statuses are TEMPORARY1 through TEMPORARY5 and PERMANENT. For a full description of status categories, see *AS/400 LAN and Frame Relay V3R2*, section 2.4.3.6, Display Token-Ring Network Status.

11.5 ETHERNET

An Ethernet LAN supports one of two standards: Ethernet Version 2 and the IEEE 802.3 standard. You're better off using the IEEE 802.3 standard on the AS/400 because it is acknowledged; Version 2 is unacknowledged.

Ethernet uses the Carrier Sense Multiple Access with Collision Detection (CSMA/CD) protocol. Basically, when a station has something to transmit, it checks to see if the line is busy. If the line is not busy, the station transmits and monitors the line while transmitting in case another station also transmits. If one station does transmit, that causes a collision and both stations first will stop transmitting, then wait some random amount of time, and then try again.

Ethernet networks can be tricky because they really don't have any traffic management capability. Therefore, a lot of transmissions on the line causes many collisions to occur and performance can rapidly decay. Part of setting up and maintaining an efficient Ethernet network is knowing exactly what transmission level is acceptable and what the level will be on your line. NOTE: transmission activity level is independent of the number of workstations on the line.

The original Ethernet transmits data at 10 Mbps. A newer, fast Ethernet transmits data at 100 Mbps. An Ethernet network uses a coaxial cable. To connect your AS/400 to an Ethernet network, you need an Ethernet controller card on the AS/400, a *transceiver* that is attached to or built into the network coaxial cable, and a cable to connect the controller card and transceiver. The controller must come from IBM, but the plug, cable, transceiver, and coaxial cable can come from any vendor.

11.5.1 Ethernet Adapter Addressing

The Ethernet adapter address is a 6-byte or 48-bit address. Read the bytes in the same order they are transmitted—from bit0/byte0 to bit7/byte5. Figure 11-13 is a sample address. Note that two bits are reserved.

Byte 0							
0	1	2	3	4	5	6	7
						UL	IG

Byte 1							
0	1	2	3	4	5	6	7

Byte 2							
0	1	2	3	4	5	6	7

Byte 5							
0	1	2	3	4	5	6	7

Figure 11-13: Ethernet adapter address.

❖ UL—Universal/local:

   ✓ The 0 means the address is universally administered.

   ✓ The 1 means the address is locally administered.

❖ IG—Individual/group:

   ✓ The 0 means the address is an individual address or one associated with a particular station on the network.

✓ The 1 means the address is a group address or that it is destined for more than one destination.

The range of valid adapter addresses are Hex 000000000000 through hex FFFFFFFFFFFF. However, the implications of these two bits on possible valid addresses are:

❖ If bit7/byte0 = 0, then Byte 0 must be an even number.

❖ If bit6/byte0 = 1, then Byte 0 must be in the range hex 020000000000 through hex FEFFFFFFFFFF and the second digit must be 2, 6, A, or E.

Heterogeneous LANs using bridges must pay particular attention to Ethernet addressing. If this description fits your shop, see *AS/400 LAN and Frame Relay V3R2,* section 4.8.2.1.

11.5.2 Ethernet Configuration

Ethernet controller descriptions and SSAPs have maximum frame sizes, but their line descriptions do not. The line description defaults to a value somewhere around 1500. When Ethernet connects, the frame size is the smallest of these frame sizes:

❖ Default line description maximum frame size (around 1500—you cannot specify this on the line description).

❖ SSAP MAXFRAME parameter value.

❖ Controller MAXFRAME parameter value.

If an Ethernet network passes its frames across a bridge, you must take that into consideration in your frame-size calculation. If you define a frame size too large for the bridge, that frame will be discarded when the network tries to send it through the bridge. Unfortunately, the network doesn't automatically incorporate the bridge frame size in its calculations. You must do the calculation. Make certain your bridge size is at least as large as the smallest of one of the three frame sizes listed earlier. To bring up an Ethernet connection on an AS/400, do the following as shown in Figure 11-14.

11.5.2.1 Create Line Description (Ethernet) (CRTLINETH)

```
               Create Line Desc (Ethernet) (CRTLINETH)

Type choices, press Enter.

Line description . . . . . . . . > ETHLINE1       Name
Resource name  . . . . . . . . > LIN121          Name, *NWID, *NWSD
Online at IPL  . . . . . . . . .   *YES           *YES, *NO
Vary on wait . . . . . . . . . .   *NOWAIT        *NOWAIT, 15-180 (1 second)
Local adapter address  . . . . > 020055010111    020000000000-7EFFFFFFFFFF...
Exchange identifier  . . . . . .   *SYSGEN        05600000-056FFFFF, *SYSGEN
Ethernet standard  . . . . . . .   *ALL           *ETHV2, *IEEE8023, *ALL
SSAP list:                        _
  Source service access point  . > 04            02-FE, *SYSGEN
  SSAP maximum frame . . . . . . > *MAXFRAME      *MAXFRAME, 265-1496, 265...
  SSAP type  . . . . . . . . . . > *CALC          *CALC, *NONSNA, *SNA, *HPR

  Source service access point  . > 08            02-FE
  SSAP maximum frame . . . . . .   *MAXFRAME      *MAXFRAME, 265-1496, 265...
  SSAP type  . . . . . . . . . .   *CALC          *CALC, *NONSNA, *SNA, *HPR
                   + for more values _
```

```
               Create Line Desc (Ethernet) (CRTLINETH)

Type choices, press Enter.

Text 'description' . . . . . . .   Ethernet Line 1 description
```

Figure 11-14: CREATE LINE DESCRIPTION for AS/400 Ethernet network (part 1 and 2).

Note the local adapter address because any remote nodes will have to use this address to communicate to this node. In this case, I made up an address. I could have used the adapter's preset address.

The ETHERNET STANDARD (ETHSTD) parameter is important to determine ahead of time because this value will determine the maximum frame size. The ETHSTD parameter cannot be changed after the line description has been created. Possible values are:

❖   *ALL (the default).

❖   *IEEE8023.

❖   *ETHV2.

If AUTOCREATE CONTROLLER(*YES) is specified on the last screen, any controllers the system needs but doesn't have will be created for you by the system when a communication event starts. That saves you the next step. When it does, the system will specify that the controller may also automatically create any device descriptions it needs, saving you the step after that as well.

11.5.2.2 Create Controller Description (APPC) (CRTCTLAPPC) (Optional)

```
                    Create Ctl Desc (APPC) (CRTCTLAPPC)

Type choices, press Enter.

Controller description . . . . . >  APPCETH1      Name
Link type  . . . . . . . . . . . >  *LAN          *ANYNW, *FAX, *FR, *IDLC...
Online at IPL  . . . . . . . . .    *YES          *YES, *NO
APPN-capable . . . . . . . . . . >  *NO           *YES, *NO
Controller type  . . . . . . . .    *BLANK        *BLANK, *FBSS, 3174, 3274...
Switched line list . . . . . . . >  ETHLINE1      Name
                + for more values
Maximum frame size . . . . . . .    *LINKTYPE     265-16393, 256, 265, 512...
Remote network identifier  . . .    *NETATR       Name, *NETATR, *NONE, *ANY
Remote control point . . . . . .                  Name, *ANY
Exchange identifier  . . . . . .                  00000000-FFFFFFFF
Initial connection . . . . . . .    *DIAL         *DIAL, *ANS
Dial initiation  . . . . . . . .    *LINKTYPE     *LINKTYPE, *IMMED, *DELAY
LAN remote adapter address . . . >  020055010222  000000000001-FFFFFFFFFFFF
LAN DSAP . . . . . . . . . . . .    04            04, 08, 0C, 10, 14, 18, 1C...
LAN SSAP . . . . . . . . . . . . >  08            04, 08, 0C, 10, 14, 18, 1C...
```

```
                    Create Ctl Desc (APPC) (CRTCTLAPPC)

Type choices, press Enter.

Autocreate device  . . . . . . .    *ALL          *ALL, *NONE
Text 'description' . . . . . . .    Ethernet controller APPCETH1-line ETHLINE1
```

Figure 11-15: CREATE CONTROLLER DESCRIPTION for AS/400 Ethernet network (part 1 and 2).

Note that the switched-line list is the name of the line you created in Figure 11-14. The line must exist before it is used on the CRTCTLAPPC command. The remote address must be the address of the remote line (not the local).

The AUTOCREATE DEVICE (*ALL) parameter and value on the second screen tells the AS/400 to go ahead and create a device description for you when one doesn't exist when a communications event starts. If the controller is set up this way, you can skip the next step.

11.5.2.3 Create Device Description (APPC) (CRTDEVAPPC) (Optional).

```
                    Create Device Desc (APPC) (CRTDEVAPPC)

Type choices, press Enter.

Device description . . . . . . . > APPCETH1       Name
Remote location  . . . . . . . . > APPCETH2       Name
Online at IPL  . . . . . . . . .   *YES           *YES, *NO
Local location . . . . . . . . .   *NETATR        Name, *NETATR
Remote network identifier  . . .   *NETATR        Name, *NETATR, *NONE
Attached controller  . . . . . . > APPCETH1       Name
Mode . . . . . . . . . . . . . .   *NETATR        Name, *NETATR
              + for more values
Message queue  . . . . . . . . .   QSYSOPR        Name, QSYSOPR
   Library . . . . . . . . . . .   *LIBL          Name, *LIBL, *CURLIB
APPN-capable . . . . . . . . . . > *NO            *YES, *NO
Single session:
   Single session capable . . . .  *NO            *NO, *YES
   Number of conversations  . . .  _____         1-512
```

Figure 11-16: CREATE DEVICE DESCRIPTION for Ethernet connection.

If the controller description (Figure 11-15) specifies *ALL on the AUTOCREATE DEVICE parameter, devices are created automatically for you when a communications session starts (if a device description is not found.)

11.6 DISTRIBUTED DATA INTERFACE

Distributed data interface (DDI) is a LAN that supports the ANSI X3T9.5 standard. DDI devices are attached on two counter-rotating rings that run at 100 Mps. One ring is designated the primary ring and is active most of the time. The other, the secondary ring, can maintain the network if a device becomes inactive. Each FDDI ring consists of two fibers: one for transmitting and one for receiving.

On the AS/400, you'll usually see DDI referred to as FDDI (fiber optic DDI) or CDDI (Copper DDI). FDDI is optical cable. CDDI is shielded twisted pair. It is very common to use DDI to connect multiple AS/400s for superior file-transfer speeds. DDI networks consider all devices as members of one of two classes.

❖ Class A. Devices attached to both rings.

❖ Class B. Devices attached to only one ring or attached to the ring through a concentrator.

DDI is normally used to connect two or more AS/400s over a high-speed network. As such, all you need are the ring media (the cables) and the appropriate adapters in the AS/400s. Unless you're connecting LAN devices to your DDI ring, you don't need other hardware like the other protocols.

You also can connect personal computers to your DDI ring, but you have to use a concentrator (IBM's is the 8240 FDDI Concentrator). One side of this concentrator attaches to the DDI rings. The concentrator contains one or more (up to a maximum of six) *device attachment* (DA) *cards*. These cards connect to the personal computers. You purchase DA cards for fiber or copper connections. Each DA card can support up to four devices.

The DDI adapter uses the same 48-bit adapter address as the token-ring adapters. Frame size considerations are the same as those for token-ring frame sizes. On a DDI network, valid frame sizes range from 265 through 4444 (with the default being 4105).

Sometimes DDI networking people refer to frame sizes in *symbols* (with two symbols representing one byte). Therefore, a DDI network supporting a frame size of 8210 symbols is, in other words, the same way as saying it supports a 4105-byte frame size.

11.6.1 DDI Configuration

To configure a DDI network over two AS/400s, create these objects in the following sequence. See Figures 11-17 and 11-18.

11.6.1.1 CREATE LINE DESCRIPTION (DDI) (CRTLINDDI)

```
                  Create Line Desc (DDI) (CRTLINDDI)

Type choices, press Enter.

Line description . . . . . . . . > DDILIN1      Name
Resource name  . . . . . . . . > LIN441        Name, *NWID
Online at IPL  . . . . . . . . .   *YES         *YES, *NO
Vary on wait . . . . . . . . . .   *NOWAIT      *NOWAIT, 15-180 (1 second)
Maximum controllers  . . . . . .   40           1-256
Maximum frame size . . . . . . .   4105         265-4444
Logging level  . . . . . . . . .   *OFF         *OFF, *ERRORS, *ALL
Local manager mode . . . . . . .   *OBSERVING   *OBSERVING, *NONE
Local adapter address  . . . . > 400050010111 400000000000-7FFFFFFFFFFF...
Exchange identifier  . . . . . .   *SYSGEN      05600000-056FFFFF, *SYSGEN
SSAP list:
  Source service access point  .  *SYSGEN      02-FE, *SYSGEN
  SSAP maximum frame . . . . . .                265-4444, *MAXFRAME
  SSAP type  . . . . . . . . . .                *CALC, *NONSNA, *SNA
              + for more values _
```

```
                  Create Line Desc (DDI) (CRTLINDDI)

Type choices, press Enter.

Text 'description' . . . . . . .   DDI line on system 1


                        Additional Parameters

Network controller . . . . . . .                Name
Group address  . . . . . . . . .   *NONE        800000000000-FFFFFFFFFFFE...
              + for more values
Token rotation time  . . . . . .   *CALC        4-167, *CALC
Link speed . . . . . . . . . . .   *MAX         *MIN, 1200, 2400, 4800...
Cost/connect time  . . . . . . .   0            0-255
Cost/byte  . . . . . . . . . . .   0            0-255
Security for line  . . . . . . .   *NONSECURE   *NONSECURE, *PKTSWTNET...
Propagation delay  . . . . . . .   *LAN         *PKTSWTNET, *LAN, *MIN...
User-defined 1 . . . . . . . . .   128          0-255
User-defined 2 . . . . . . . . .   128          0-255
```

Figure 11-17: CREATE LINE DESCRIPTION for DDI network (part 1 and 2).

11.6.1.2 CREATE CONTROLLER DESCRIPTION (CRTCTLAPPC)

```
                    Create Ctl Desc (APPC) (CRTCTLAPPC)

Type choices, press Enter.

Controller description . . . . . > SYS01        Name
Link type  . . . . . . . . . . . > *LAN         *ANYNW, *FAX, *FR, *IDLC...
Online at IPL  . . . . . . . . .   *YES         *YES, *NO
APPN-capable . . . . . . . . . .   *YES         *YES, *NO
Switched line list . . . . . . . > DDILIN1      Name
             + for more values
Maximum frame size . . . . . . .   *LINKTYPE    265-16393, 256, 265, 512...
Remote network identifier  . . .   *NETATR      Name, *NETATR, *NONE, *ANY
Remote control point . . . . . . > SYS02        Name, *ANY
Exchange identifier  . . . . . .                00000000-FFFFFFFF
Initial connection . . . . . . .   *DIAL        *DIAL, *ANS
Dial initiation  . . . . . . . .   *LINKTYPE    *LINKTYPE, *IMMED, *DELAY
LAN remote adapter address . . . > 400050010222 000000000001-FFFFFFFFFFFF
LAN DSAP . . . . . . . . . . . .   04           04, 08, 0C, 10, 14, 18, 1C...
LAN SSAP . . . . . . . . . . . .   04           04, 08, 0C, 10, 14, 18, 1C...
APPN CP session support  . . . .   *YES         *YES, *NO
```

Figure 11-18: CREATE CONTROLLER DESCRIPTION for DDI network.

Create these two objects on each AS/400 you wish to connect.

11.7 FRAME RELAY

Frame relay is a packet-switching protocol that is similar to X.25, but much faster (up to 2 Mbps). Frame relay uses established data-communications networks. You connect to such networks by becoming a subscriber. Built-in reliability is such an accepted part of established data-communications networks that frame relay doesn't provide as much error handling as the other protocols.

Frame relay is very expensive for in-house LANs or even across the same city. It is generally used to connect two LANs (or two AS/400s) across very large distances. It is the protocol of choice for wide-area network (WAN) support.

A frame-relay LAN can be configured as direct or bridged. A *direct-frame relay* is typically two or more AS/400s connected over a frame-relay network and running APPC or APPN.

A *bridged frame-relay* network is similar except that the remote device is a remote bridge (such as the IBM 6611 Network Processor) to a LAN. Another AS/400 can be on the remote LAN, but it is not necessary. Through a bridged frame-relay network, an AS/400 can communicate with workstations on a remote LAN as efficiently as if they were locally attached.

The frame relay physical pieces are more complex than those used by the other protocols. The AS/400 is referred to as *terminal equipment* (TE) on a frame relay network. A network node on a frame-relay network (much like an intermediate node in APPN) is referred to as a *frame handler* (FH). TEs are connected to FHs through a device that is really two bundled devices. The bundled devices are a *data service unit* (DSU) and a *channel service unit* (CSU). Together they are referred to as a *DSU/CSU*.

All together, you'll have an AS/400 (the TE) connected by some physical wiring into a DSU/CSU. The DSU/CSU connects to an FH and the FH then connects to the frame-relay network. At other points on the frame-relay network, other FHs come off and connect to other TEs through DSU/CSUs.

Although you need at least the cabling and FH on both ends of the frame-relay network, each end also can be an *SNA-direct connection* or bridged. An SNA-direct connection allows SNA systems to connect directly to the FH. Otherwise, token ring, Ethernet, and DDI all connect to an FH by a bridge.

You can connect two AS/400s using frame relay without going through a frame-relay network. The result is much like connecting two PC communication ports by directly using a modem eliminator rather than a modem. In this case, you can use the high-speed benefits of a frame relay without the expense of joining the network. Just configure one AS/400's network interface description as LMIMODE(*FH) and the others as LMIMODE(*TE).

Let's drill down into this physical stuff a little more. The AS/400 requires a 2666 High Speed Communications Input/Output Processor (IOP). This IOP only has one adapter (IOA) and will support any of four *physical interfaces* (or cable connectors). The possible physical interfaces, their cable connectors, and parameter values (see the following section on CRTNWIFR) are:

Physical Interface	Cable Connector parameter value	Interface
EIA RS-449	ISO4902 (37-pin)	*RS449V36
CCITT V.36	ISO4902 (37-pin)	*RS449V36
CCITT X.21	ISO4903 (15-pin)	*X21
CCITT V.35	ISO2593	*V35

Except the last one, CCITT V.35, which can only communicate up to 64,000 bps, all physical interfaces can communicate at up to 2,048,000 bps.

11.7.1 Frame-Relay Addressing

A single physical cable between nodes can support up to 256 virtual circuits. A virtual circuit between two nodes is referred to as a *permanent virtual circuit* (PVC) and is identified by a *data link connection identifier* (DLCI). The DLCI number can be between 1 and 1018 (although you can only have 256 of them on one physical cable). Numbers are assigned by the frame-relay network provider at subscription time.

You must have the DLCI number when you configure either the line or network interface description. If you specify it on the line, you'll put it in on the NWIDLCI parameter. If you specify the DLCI number on the network interface description, you'll have to specify both the DLCI number and the line description name.

Unlike the other protocols in this chapter, frame-relay communications adapters do not come with preset addresses. This address is not required for SNA direct connections. But for token-ring, Ethernet, and DDI-bridged connections, you must specify the local adapter address on the line description.

The REMOTE ADAPTER ADDRESS (ADPTADR) parameter on the controller description must match the adapter address of the remote system.

11.7.2 Frame-Relay Configuration

To set up a frame-relay connection, you must create the following objects in sequence. In the example that follows, I've include samples of setting up a two-AS/400, frame-relay network. With my example, one AS/400 is in Phoenix and one is in New York. You are in Phoenix and the remote system is in New York.

11.7.2.1 *Network Interface Description*

Use the CREATE NETWORK INTERFACE DESCRIPTION (FRAME RELAY) (CRTNWIFR) command as shown in Figure 11-19.

❖ Key items to specify:

  ✓ Physical interface used.

  ✓ Line speed.

  ✓ LMI mode.

  ✓ LMI timer and retry.

  ✓ DLCI numbers assigned to the virtual connections.

```
                Create Network Interface (FR) (CRTNWIFR)

Type choices, press Enter.

Network interface description  . > FRPHX         Name
Resource name  . . . . . . . . > LIN211         Name
Online at IPL  . . . . . . . .   *YES           *YES, *NO
Vary on wait . . . . . . . . .   *NOWAIT        *NOWAIT, 15-180 (1 second)
Data link connection ID:         _
  DLCI number  . . . . . . . .   *NONE          1-1018, *NONE
  Line description . . . . . .   _____     Name
            + for more values _
NRZI data encoding . . . . . .   *NO            *NO, *YES
Physical interface . . . . . .   *RS449V36      *RS449V36, *V35, *X21
Clocking . . . . . . . . . . .   *MODEM         *MODEM, *LOOP
Line speed . . . . . . . . . .   1536000        56000-2048000, 56000...
LMI mode . . . . . . . . . . .   *TE            *TE, *FH, *NONE, *ANNEXA
Polling interval . . . . . . .   10             5-30
Full inquiry interval  . . . .   6              1-255
```

Figure 11-19: CREATE NETWORK INTERFACE DESCRIPTION for the frame relay AS/400 located in Phoenix. The remote AS/400 is in New York.

Note that the PHYSICAL INTERFACE and LINE SPEED parameters are supplied by the frame-relay network provider. Although I could have, also note that I did not specify the DLCI here.

11.7.2.2 *Line Description*

You can use any of the following commands. See Figure 11-20 for an example.

❖ Frame Relay. CREATE LINE DESCRIPTION (FRAME RELAY) (CRTLINFR). For SNA direct connections, you must connect to a controller created with the LINKTYPE(*FR) parameter.

❖ Token Ring. CREATE LINE DESCRIPTION (TOKEN RING) (CRTLINTRN). For a bridged token-ring connection, you must connect to a controller created with the LINKTYPE(*LAN) parameter.

❖ Ethernet. CREATE LINE DESCRIPTION (ETHERNET) (CRTLINETH). For a bridged Ethernet connection, you must connect to a controller created with the LINKTYPE(*LAN) parameter.

❖ DDI. CREATE LINE DESCRIPTION (DDI) (CRTLINDDI). For a bridged DDI connection, you must connect to a controller created with the LINKTYPE(*LAN) parameter.

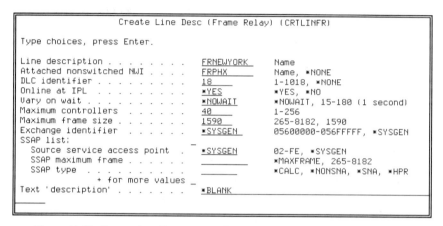

Figure 11-20: CREATE LINE DESCRIPTION for frame relay AS/400 located in Phoenix. The remote AS/400 is in New York.

Remember that the DLCI parameter comes from the frame-relay network provider. Also, refer to the following section on calculating the maximum frame size (MAXFRAME).

11.7.2.3 Controller Description

See Figure 11-21 for an example. You can use either of these commands:

❖ CREATE CONTROLLER DESCRIPTION (APPC) (CRTCTLAPPC). Most common, controller supports communication between AS/400s and personal computers. Use APPN(*YES).

❖ CREATE CONTROLLER DESCRIPTION (HOST) (CRTCTLHOST). For
connections that support SNA, such as a System 390 or a 3745
Controller running NCP. Use APPN(*YES).

```
                  Create Ctl Desc (APPC) (CRTCTLAPPC)

Type choices, press Enter.

Controller description . . . . . > FRNEWYORK     Name
Link type  . . . . . . . . . . . > *FR           *ANYNW, *FAX, *FR, *IDLC...
Online at IPL  . . . . . . . . .   *YES          *YES, *NO
APPN-capable . . . . . . . . . .   *YES          *YES, *NO
Switched line list . . . . . . . > FRPHX         Name
             + for more values
Maximum frame size . . . . . . .   *LINKTYPE     265-16393, 256, 265, 512...
Remote network identifier  . . .   *NETATR       Name, *NETATR, *NONE, *ANY
Remote control point . . . . . . > NEWYORK       Name, *ANY
Exchange identifier  . . . . . .                 00000000-FFFFFFFF
Initial connection . . . . . . .   *DIAL         *DIAL, *ANS
Dial initiation  . . . . . . . .   *LINKTYPE     *LINKTYPE, *IMMED, *DELAY
LAN DSAP . . . . . . . . . . . .   04            04, 08, 0C, 10, 14, 18, 1C...
LAN SSAP . . . . . . . . . . . .   04            04, 08, 0C, 10, 14, 18, 1C...
APPN CP session support  . . . .   *YES          *YES, *NO
APPN node type . . . . . . . . .   *ENDNODE      *ENDNODE, *LENNODE...
```

*Figure 11-21: CREATE CONTROLLER DESCRIPTION for frame relay AS/400 located in
Phoenix. The remote AS/400 is in New York.*

The LINKTYPE parameter is set at *FR (frame relay). If this frame relay connects
via a bridge to a token-ring, Ethernet or DDI network, you must specify
LINKTYPE(*LAN).

11.7.2.4 *Device Description.*

Use the CREATE DEVICE DESCRIPTION (CRTDEVAPPC) command. See Figure 11-22.

```
                    Create Device Desc (APPC) (CRTDEVAPPC)

Type choices, press Enter.

Device description . . . . . . . > FRNEWYORK    Name
Remote location  . . . . . . . . > NEWYORK      Name
Online at IPL  . . . . . . . .     *YES         *YES, *NO
Local location . . . . . . . . .   *NETATR      Name, *NETATR
Remote network identifier  . . .   *NETATR      Name, *NETATR, *NONE
Attached controller  . . . . . . > FRNEWYORK    Name
Mode . . . . . . . . . . . . . .   *NETATR      Name, *NETATR
            + for more values
Message queue  . . . . . . . . .   QSYSOPR      Name, QSYSOPR
  Library  . . . . . . . . . .     *LIBL        Name, *LIBL, *CURLIB
APPN-capable . . . . . . . . . .   *YES         *YES, *NO
Single session:
  Single session capable . . . .   *NO          *NO, *YES
  Number of conversations  . . .                1-512
Text 'description' . . . . . . . > 'FR connection in Phoenix for remote in New
York'
```

Figure 11-22: CREATE DEVICE DESCRIPTION for frame relay AS/400 located in Phoenix. The remote AS/400 is in New York.

The device description parameter is the name of the remote system (in this example, FRNEWYORK), the remote location name is the name of the remote system, and the attached controller is the name of the remote system's controller.

When you configure objects for frame relay, you must be concerned with the maximum frame size. The frame relay network provider provides a "frame size" referred to as the "N203" number. The number can be between 262 and 8192 bytes for everything except bridged DDI and Ethernet. Most commonly, the number is 1600 bytes. Bridged DDI can be between 262 and 4488 and bridged Ethernet can be between 262 and 1522. When you configure your network, you need to subtract routing information from this number to come up with a good number for the maximum frame size. The number you subtract is dependent on the connection type and protocol.

Here's a guideline (presuming you take the maximum frame size for each protocol):

	Size of Routing Data	Maximum Frame Size
Direct:		
SNA	10	8182
IP	2	8190
IPX	2	8190
Bridged:		
Token Ring	44	8148
DDI	44	4444
Ethernet	26	1496

You can specify the maximum frame size in three places during your configuration:

❖ Line description MAXFRAME parameter.

❖ Line description SSAP has a maximum frame-size parameter.

❖ Controller description MAXFRAME parameter.

11.8 TCP/IP

TCP/IP stands for Transmission Control Protocol/Internet Protocol. Actually two protocols used together, TCP/IP allows sharing resources and information exchange between nodes on a network.

TCP/IP is almost always thought of as the Internet. The Internet is the vast assortment of networks and gateways that use TCP/IP protocols to connect universities, research institutions, corporations, and individual PCs.

11.8.1 TCP/IP Addressing

One theme you should be getting used to in this chapter is that each node on a network requires its own unique adapter address. This is true whether you use the manufacturer's preset address or make up your own local address. TCP/IP is no exception and its international use as the Internet protocol can make addressing administration an unusual experience.

First, consider that each TCP/IP address is a 32-bit integer expressed in terms of four three-digit numbers. Here's how it works. A typical Internet address might be 204.145.193.104:

```
Bit positions'
       values:  128  64  32  16 |  8   4   2   1
      Byte 0:    1   1   0   0  |  1   1   0   0  =  204 (Hex=X'CC')
      Byte 1:    1   0   0   1  |  0   0   0   1  =  145 (Hex=X'91')
      Byte 2:    1   1   0   0  |  0   0   0   1  =  193 (Hex=X'C1')
      Byte 3:    0   1   1   0  |  1   0   0   0  =  104 (Hex=X'68')
```

From the chart, you can see that you may also refer to Internet address 204.145.193.104 in hexadecimal terms as X'CC91C168'.

You can bring up a TCP/IP network between your AS/400(s) and other nodes and, if it is entirely local (never joining the actual Internet), you are free to make up your own TCP/IP addresses.

However, if you will ever be part of the Internet, you must get unique addresses for all your nodes. There is a central organization that issues the addresses and ensures that no two identical addresses ever exist. That organization is the In-terNIC Registration Services at the following address:

Network Solutions
InterNIC Registration Services
505 Huntmar Park Drive
Herndon, VA 22070
Phone: 1-703-742-4777   Fax: 1-703-742-4811
Internet: internic.net

Access to the Internet is obtained from one of many *service providers*. There are plenty in every metropolitan area. If you aren't aware of any service providers in your area, InterNIC Information Services can get you a list. Contact them at:

InterNIC Information Services
General Atomics
PO Box 85608
San Diego, CA 92186-9784
Phone: 1-619-455-4600   Fax: 1-619-455-4640

For accessing the Internet, you'll also need a *domain name*. Use your company name followed by .com (for example, mycompany.com). Like addresses, domain names must be unique and are administered by the same organization, InterNIC. If you are planning to bring up an Internet site in the future, you can reserve a domain name now through InterNIC.

Subnet masks are a way of expanding the number of interface program (IP) addresses you can use for networked hosts without requesting special IP addresses from InterNIC. Your overall network is "known" to the remote network by the special IP address, but it can apply the mask to communicate between local hosts. Note that subnet masks are not final addresses; they merely set the stage for legitimate addresses later.

Before getting into a discussion of subnet mask construction, you need to know that there are two forms of *special IP addressing*:

❖ Any 4-bit element of the address containing all zeros means "this" host. It's useful when a host is trying to determine its address from a remote server.

❖ Any 4-bit element of the address containing all ones means "any" host. You'll see a lot of these in subnet masks.

Because 4-bit values of 0 and 15 have special meaning, they are not advisable in IP addressing.

Remember that a byte is composed of two 4-bit sections. The numeric value for all 1s in the left 4-bits is 240. For all 1s in the right 4-bites, the numeric value is 15. The numeric value for all 1s in both sides is 255. You'll see a lot of subnet mask addresses with the form 255.255.255 (meaning "any" station for the first three significant bytes of the address).

It is common to set byte 4 of the subnet mask to either 128 (10000000) or 240 (11110000). But the mask is only a mask; it is not an address. When you calculate host addresses on such a line, you won't use addresses 0 or 15 (because they're special). Therefore, a subnet mask of 255.255.255.128 on a host with an IP address of 29.4.72.113 will allow local host addresses of 29.4.72.129 through 29.4.72.142. A mask of 255.255.255.240 on a host with an IP address of 8.3.133.29 will allow local host addresses of 8.3.133.241 through 8.3.133.254.

11.8.2 TCP/IP Configuration

Just like other protocols, you'll need to configure a line, controller, and device to bring up TCP/IP. The lines, controllers, and devices you configure don't concern themselves with the IP address and are suspiciously similar to any line, controller, or device configuration previously discussed. The unusual TCP/IP matters such as addresses are a factor when you add the TCP/IP interface and host table names after you've configured the line.

11.8.2.1 Configure a Line

If a physical line for an IOP is already configured, one thing to keep in mind is that you can use it for TCP/IP. This is true even if the IOP already is configured for token ring, Ethernet, DDI, frame relay, or any of the other OSI or SNA protocols. All you have to do is an SSAP. Use one of the CREATE LINE DESCRIPTIONS discussed in previous sections, but pay particular attention to the SSAP:

❖ If the line is token-ring, Ethernet IEEE802.3, DDI, or wireless, X'AA' must be specified as an SSAP. You can add it to the SSAP on an existing line. If you leave the SSAP parameter default at *SYSGEN, X'AA' will be included for you.

❖ If the line is Ethernet V2 or *ALL, no special SSAPs needs to be configured.

❖ Configure the TCP/IP interface using the ADD TCP/IP INTERFACE (ADDTCPIFC) command or option 1 from the Configure TCP/IP (CFGTCP) command. Figure 11-23 shows a prompted version of that command.

```
                    Add TCP/IP Interface (ADDTCPIFC)

Type choices, press Enter.

Internet address . . . . . . . . >  '204.145.193.104'
Line description . . . . . . . . >  TCP_IP01      Name, *LOOPBACK
Subnet mask  . . . . . . . . . >  '255.255.255.0'
Type of service  . . . . . . . .   *NORMAL       *MINDELAY, *MAXTHRPUT...
Maximum transmission unit  . . .   *LIND         576-16388, *LIND
Autostart  . . . . . . . . . . .   *YES          *YES, *NO
PVC logical channel identifier                   001-FFF
               + for more values   ___
X.25 idle circuit timeout  . . .   60            1-600
X.25 maximum virtual circuits  .   64            0-64
X.25 DDN interface . . . . . . .   *NO           *YES, *NO
TRLAN bit sequencing . . . . . .   *MSB          *MSB, *LSB
```

Figure 11-23: Prompted version of command ADDTCPIFC.

Later, if you want to review the TCP/IP part of the line, use the WORK WITH
TCP/IP STATUS (WRKTCPSTS) command:

```
                    Work with TCP/IP Interface Status
                                                System:    SYS02
Type options, press Enter.
  5=Display details   8=Display associated routes   9=Start    10=End
  12=Work with configuration status

        Internet        Network            Line      Interface
Opt    Address         Address         Description   Status
__     127.0.0.1       127.0.0.0       *LOOPBACK     Active
__     204.145.193.104 204.145.193.0   TCP_IP01      Active

                                                               Bottom
F3=Exit   F4=Prompt   F5=Refresh   F11=Display line information   F12=Cancel
```

Figure 11-24: Results of command WRKTCPSTS.

You can press F11 to get more information. Figure 11-25 shows what you get
when you do press F11.

```
                       Work with TCP/IP Interface Status
                                                    System:    SYS02
   Type options, press Enter.
     5=Display details    8=Display associated routes    9=Start    10=End
    12=Work with configuration status

          Internet          Subnet            Type of                  Line
   Opt    Address           Mask              Service        MTU       Type
    __    127.0.0.1         255.0.0.0         *NORMAL        576       *NONE
    __    204.145.193.104   255.255.255.0     *NORMAL        4091      *TRLAN
```

Figure 11-25: WRKTCPSTS—*line information.*

11.8.2.2 *Work with Host Table Entries*

You must know the IP address and the system name. Add new entries with the
ADD TCP/IP HOST TABLE ENTRY (ADDTCPHTE) command or option 10 from the
CONFIGURE TCP/IP (CFGTCP) command. See Figure 11-26.

```
                    Add TCP/IP Host Table Entry (ADDTCPHTE)

   Type choices, press Enter.

   Internet address . . . . . . . . > '204.145.193.104'
   Host names:                       _
     Name . . . . . . . . . . . . . > 'SYS02.TCP'


                   + for more values _
   Text 'description' . . . . . . . > 'SYS02 VIA TCP/IP'
```

Figure 11-26: Add TCP/IP HOST TABLE ENTRY (ADDTCPHTE).

❖ Change entries with the CHANGE TCP/IP HOST TABLE ENTRIES
  (CHGTCPHTE) command.

❖ Remove entries with the REMOVE TCP/IP HOST TABLE ENTRIES
  (RMVTCPHTE) command.

11.8.2.3 *Configure the Domain and Host Names*

To associate the domain name with the host AS/400 name, use option 12 from the CONFIGURE TCP/IP (CFGTCP) menu. See Figure 11-27.

```
                    Change Local Domain and Host Names
                                                System:     SYS02
Type choices, press Enter.

   Local domain name . . .    MYCOMPANY.com


   Local host name . . . .    SYS02_TCPIP
```

Figure 11-27: Associate local domain name to local host name

11.8.3 TCP/IP CL Commands

To see if TCP/IP is even running on your system, enter on a command line:

WRKACTJOB SBS(QSYSWRK) JOB(QT*). You'll be looking for job QTCPIP.

To start TCP/IP, you can either take option 3 from the TCP/IP administration menu (GO TCPADM) or issue the command STRTCP. Either way, you have to start TCP/IP before you can do anything with it.

To end TCP/IP, you can either take option 4 from the TCP/IP administration menu (GO TCPADM) or issue the command ENDTCP.

Messages from a TCP/IP session go to two queues: the operator's (QSYSOPR) and its own (QTCP). To display messages, use either the DSPMSG QSYSOPR command or the DSPMSG QTCP command.

If you have problems and find no messages or you find nondescriptive messages, look for the TCP/IP job log with the command WRKSPLF QTCP.

One function you'll find in all TCP/IP sites is the PING function. It is used to verify that a connection exists between two TCP/IP nodes. You can PING a remote system by name or IP address PING RMTSYS(SYS01) or PING '204.145.193.104'.

You can see if the ping was successful by checking message in the job log. If you're currently online and did the PING from the command line, use the DISPLAY JOB LOG (DSPJOBLOG) command.

The PING function is one of those open things for which the AS/400 prides itself. If you prefer, you can use the more typical AS/400 command: VERIFY TCP/IP CONNECTION (VFYTCPCNN).

To perform many TCP/IP network functions, use the WORK WITH TCP/IP STATUS (WRKTCPSTS) command and follow the menu.

11.9 AS/400 LAN CL COMMANDS

After you've configured your LAN, you'll need to use CL commands common to all protocols. Use the WORK WITH CONFIGURATION STATUS (WRKCFGSTS) command to work with adapters, lines, controllers, or devices. You can display their attributes, vary them on and off, display the mode or connection status, and hold or release a device. Figure 11-28 shows a sample of that command set up to work with the line, controller, and devices for all token-ring LANs.

```
                  Work with Configuration Status (WRKCFGSTS)

 Type choices, press Enter.

 Type . . . . . . . . . . . . . . . > *LIN        *NWS, *NWI, *LIN, *CTL, *DEV
 Configuration description . . . > *TRLAN        Name, generic*, *ALL, *CMN...
 Output . . . . . . . . . . . . .   *             *, *PRINT
 Range  . . . . . . . . . . . . .   *NET          *NET, *OBJ
 Status . . . . . . . . . . . . .   *ALL          *ALL, *ACTIVE, *FAILED...
```

Figure 11-28: Prompted screen for WRKCFGSTS command.

```
                    Work with Configuration Status              SYS02
                                                 12/05/96   07:34:18
Position to  . . . . .    _____    Starting characters

Type options, press Enter.
  1=Vary on   2=Vary off   5=Work with job   8=Work with description
  9=Display mode status ...

Opt  Description       Status           ------------Job-------------
■_   TCP_IP01          ACTIVE
_      TCP_INET        ACTIVE
_        TCP_ITCP      ACTIVE           QTCPIP      QTCP        036772
_    TOKENRING1        ACTIVE
_      GE11S02         ACTIVE
_      WDRSE           ACTIVE
_        QPCSUPP       ACTIVE/TARGET    WDRSE       PCS         046630
_      WSHSE           ACTIVE
_        QPCSUPP       ACTIVE/TARGET    WSHSE       PCS         046749
                                                               More...
Parameters or command
===> _____
F3=Exit   F4=Prompt   F12=Cancel   F23=More options   F24=More keys
```

Figure 11-29: Token ring lines, controllers, and devices from the WRKCFGSTS command.

Figure 11-29 shows the screen after you press Enter. Notice from this screen that you can do a lot of work with the lines, controllers. and devices. For more information, see *OS/400 Communications Management V3R2*.

Another CL command is the WORK WITH HARDWARE RESOURCE (WRKHDWRSC) command. Figure 11-30 shows its basic formatted form. The example requests information about communication (*CMN) resources.

```
                  Work with Hardware Resources (WRKHDWRSC)

Type choices, press Enter.

Type . . . . . . . . . . . . . . >  ■CMN          *CMN, *CSA, *LAN, *LWS...
```

Figure 11-30: Formatted version of the WRKHDWRSC command.

Communications: LANs, Frame Relay, and TCP/IP ❖ *279*

Figure 11-31 shows the next screen after you press Enter key.

```
                         Work with Communication Resources
                                                        System:    SYS02
     Type options, press Enter.
       5=Work with configuration descriptions   7=Display resource detail

     Opt   Resource       Type   Status               Text
      ▮    CMB01          9162   Operational          Combined function IOP
      _      LIN01        2612   Operational          Comm Adapter
      _        CMN01      2612   Operational          V.24 Port Enhanced
      _      LIN02        2612   Operational          Comm Adapter
      _        CMN02      2612   Operational          V.24 Port Enhanced
      _    CC02           2618   Operational          Comm Processor
      _      LIN04        2618   Operational          LAN Adapter
      _        CMN03      2618   Operational          FDDI Port
      _    CC01           2619   Operational          Combined function IOP
      _      LIN03        2619   Operational          LAN Adapter
      _        CMN04      2619   Operational          Token-Ring Port
      _      LIN10        605A   Operational          Virtual Controller
      _    CC03           2623   Operational          Comm Processor
      _      LIN07        2609   Operational          Comm Adapter
      _        CMN05      2609   Operational          V.24 Port Enhanced
                                                                    More...
     F3=Exit    F5=Refresh    F6=Print    F12=Cancel
```

Figure 11-31: IOPs, adapters, and lines displayed by the WRKHDWRSC command.

11.10 SUMMARY

This chapter covers lots of technical ground. When you're getting started, remember to use the AS/400 as much as you can. Refer often to section 11.2.2 General Notes on Configuring LANs, and especially whenever you are supporting a small LAN.

With your configuration in place, when you vary on the line, controller, and devices, you're basically in business. The AS/400 should start communicating through the LAN.

11.11 BIBLIOGRAPHY

AS/400 LAN and Frame Relay Support V3R2

AS/400 Token-Ring Network Architecture Reference

OS/400 Communications Configuration V3R2

OS/400 Communications Management V3R2

OS/400 TCP/IP Configuration and Reference V3

Appendix A

SYSTEM VALUES (ALPHABETICAL ORDER)

System value	Description	Parameters: values
QABNORMSW	Previous end of system indicator	0=Normal
		1=Abnormal
QACGLVL	Accounting level	*JOB Job resource use is written to a journal.
		*NONE No accounting information is written to a journal.
		*PRINT Spooled and printer file resource use is written to a journal.
QACTJOB	Initial number of active jobs	1-32767
QADLACTJ	Additional number of active jobs	1-32767
QADLSPLA	Spooling control block additional storage	1024-32767
QADLTOTJ	Additional number of total jobs	1-32767
QALWOBJRST	Allow object restore option	*ALL All objects are restored regardless of security sensitive attributes.
		*NONE No objects with security sensitive attributes are restored.
		*ALWYSSTT - Programs with the system state attribute are restored.
		*ALWPGMADP - Programs with the adopt authority attribute are restored.
QALWUSRDMN	Allow user domain objects in libraries	Name of libraries that can contain user domain user objects
QASTLVL	User assistance level	*BASIC
		*INTERMED
		*ADVANCED

System value	Description	Parameters: values
QATNPGM	Attention program	*NONE
		*ASSIST
		Library/program name
QAUDCTL	Auditing control	*AUDLVL
		*OBJAUD
QAUDENDACN	Auditing end action	*NOTIFY
		*PWRDWNSYS
QAUDFRCLVL	Force auditing data	*SYS
		1-100
QAUDLVL	Security auditing level	*SECURITY
		*AUTFAIL
		*DELETE
		*OBJMGT
		*CREATE
		*SAVRST
		*SPLFDTA
		*SYSMGT
		*SERVICE
		*PGMADP
		*JOBDTA
QAUTOCFG	Autoconfigure devices	0=Off
		1=On
QAUTORMT	Autoconfigure of remote controllers	0=Off
		1=On
QAUTOSPRPT	Automatic system disabled reporting	0=Off
		1=On
QAUTOVRT	Autoconfigure virtual devices	0-9999
QBASACTLVL	Base storage pool activity level	1-32767
QBASPOOL	Base storage pool minimum size (sizes in kilo-bytes)	256-2147483647
QBOOKPATH	Book and bookshelf search path for books. Default: /QDLS/QBKBOOKS/BOOKS	Directories to be searched
QCCSID	Coded character set identifier	1-65535

System value	Description	Parameters: values
QCHRID	Graphic character set and code page	Character ID: 1-32767 Code page: 1-32767
QCMNRCYLMT	Communications recovery limits	Recovery limit attempts: 0-99 Time interval in minutes: 0-120
QCNTRYID	Country identifier	Country abbreviation
QCONSOLE	Console name	Device description
QCRTAUT	Create default public authority	*CHANGE
		*ALL
		*USE
		*EXCLUDE
QCRTOBJAUD	Create object auditing	*NONE
		*USRPRF
		*CHANGE
		*ALL
QCTLSBSD	Controlling subsystem	Library/Subsystem name
QCURSYM	Currency symbol	Character
QDATE	System date	Date (refer to QDATFMT, next, for format)
QDATFMT	Date format	YMD
		MDY
		DMY
		JUL
QDATSEP	Date separator	Numeric code:
		1=/
		2=-
		3=.
		4=,
		5=blank
QDAY	Day	1-31
QDBRCVYWT	Database recovery wait indicator	0=Do not wait
		1=Wait

System value	Description	Parameters: values
QDECFMT	Decimal format	1=blank(Period for decimal, zero suppression)
		2=J(Comma for decimal, one leading zero)
		3=I(Comma for decimal, zero suppression)
QDEVNAMING	Device naming conventions	*NORMAL
		*S36
		*DEVADR
QDEVRCYACN	Device I/O error action	*MSG
		*DSCMSG
		*DSCENDRQS
		*ENDJOB
		*ENDJOBNOLIST
QDSCJOBITV	Time interval in minutes before disconnected jobs end	*NONE
		5-1440
QDSPSGNINF	Sign-on display information control	0=Do not display
		1=Display
QDYNPTYSCD	Dynamic priority scheduler	0=Off
		1=On
QFRCCVNRST	Force conversion on restore	0=Off
		1=On
QHOUR	Current hour of the day	Hour (0-23)
QHSTLOGSIZ	Maximum history log records	1-32767
QIGC	DBCS version installed indicator	0=Not installed
		1=Installed
QIGCCDEFNT	Double byte code font	Library/font name
QINACTITV	Inactive job time-out (minutes)	*NONE
		5-300
QINACTMSGQ	Inactive job message queue	*ENDJOB
		*DSCJOB
		Library/message queue name

System value	Description	Parameters: values
QIPLDATTIM	Date and time to automatically IPL	*NONE or
		IPL date: MM/DD/YY
		IPL time: HH:MM:SS
QIPLSTS	IPL status indicator	0=Operator panel IPL
		1=Auto-IPL after power is restored
		2=Restart IPL
		3=Time of day IPL
		4=Remote IPL
QIPLTYPE	Type of IPL to perform	0=Unattended IPL
		1=Attended IPL with dedicated service tools
		2=Attended IPL, console in debug mode
QJOBMSGQFL	Job message queue full action	*NOWRAP
		*WRAP
		*PRTWRAP
QJOBMSGQMX	Maximum size in megabytes of job message queue	8-64
QJOBMSGQSZ	Job message queue initial size (in kilobytes)	1-16384
QJOBMSGQTL	Job message queue maximum initial size (in kilobytes)	1-16384
QJOBSPLA	Spooling control block initial size(in bytes)	3516-32767
QKBDBUF	Type ahead and/or attention key option	*TYPEAHEAD
		*YES
		*NO
QKBDTYPE	Keyboard language character set	Language/Country abbreviation
QLANGID	Language identifier	Language abbreviation
QLEAPADJ	Leap year adjustment	0-3
QLMTDEVSSN	Limit device sessions	0=Do not limit
		1=Limit

System value	Description	Parameters: values
QLMTSECOFR	Limit security officer device access	0=Do not limit
		1=Limit
QLOCALE	Locale path name	*NONE
		Locale path name
QMAXACTLVL	Maximum activity level of system	*NOMAX
		2-32767
QMAXSGNACN	Action to take for failed signon attempts	Numeric code:
		1=Disable device
		2=Disable profile
		3=Disable device and profile
QMAXSIGN	Maximum sign-on attempts allowed	*NOMAX
		1-25
QMCHPOOL	Machine storage pool size(in kilobytes)	256-2147483647
QMINUTE	Current minute of the hour	Minute (00-59)
QMODEL	Current system model number	System model number
QMONTH	Current month of the year	Month (1-12)
QPFRADJ	Automatic performance adjustment	0=No adjustment
		1=Adjustment at IPL
		2=Adjustment at IPL and automatic adjustment
		3=Automatic adjustment
QPRBFTR	Problem log filter	Library/name of problem log filter
QPRBHLDITV	Problem log hold interval	0-999
QPRTDEV	Printer device description	Name
QPRTKEYFMT	Print header and/or border information	*PRTHDR
		*PRTBDR
		*PRTALL
		*NONE
QPRTTXT	Print text	text

System value	Description	Parameters: values
QPWDEXPITV	Password expiration interval in days	*NOMAX (passwords don't expire)
		1-366
QPWDLMTAJC	Limit adjacent digits in password	0=adjacent digits OK
		1=adjacent digits not OK
QPWDLMTCHR	Limit characters in password	*NONE
		characters not allowed
QPWDLMTREP	Limit repeating characters in password	0=Can be repeated
		1=Cannot be repeated
		2=Cannot be repeated consecutively
QPWDMAXLEN	Maximum password length	1-10
QPWDMINLEN	Minimum password length	1-10
QPWDPOSDIF	Limit password character positions	0=Can be the same
		1=Cannot be the same
QPWDRQDDGT	Require digit in password	0=Not required
		1=Required
QPWDRQDDIF	Duplicate password control	Numeric code:
		0=Duplicates allowed - or - Cannot be the same as any in the last
		1=32 passwords
		2=24 passwords
		3=18 passwords
		4=12 passwords
		5=10 passwords
		6=8 passwords
		7=6 passwords
		8=4 passwords
QPWDVLDPGM	Password validation program	*NONE
		Library/program name
QPWRDWNLMT	Maximum time in seconds for PWRDWNSYS *IMMED	0-32767

System value	Description	Parameters: values
QPWRRSTIPL	Automatic IPL after power restored	0=Not allowed
QRCLSPLSTG	Days to reclaim spool storage	*NONE
		*NOMAX
		1-366
QRMTIPL	Remote power on and IPL	0=Not allowed
		1=Allowed
QRMTSIGN	Remote sign-on control	*FRCSIGNON
		*SAMEPRF
		*REJECT
		*VERIFY - or -Library/Remote session sign-on program
QRMTSRVATR	Remote service attribute	0=Off
		1=On
QSCPFCONS	IPL action with console problem	0=End IPL
		1=Unattended IPL
QSECOND	Current second of the minute	Second (0-59)
QSECURITY	System security level	10=Physical security only
		20=Password security only
		30=Password and object security
		40=Password, object, and operating system integrity
		50=Password, object, and enhanced operating system integrity (C2)
QSETJOBATR	Set job attributes from locale	*NONE - or - Job attributes option
QSFWERRLOG	Software error logging	*LOG
		*NOLOG
QSPCENV	Special environment	*NONE
		*S36
QSRLNBR	System serial number	System serial number

System value	Description	Parameters: values
QSRTSEQ	Sort sequence	Library/name
		*HEX
		*LANGIDUNQ
		*LANGIDSHR
QSRVDMP	Service dump control	*DMPUSRJOB
		*DMPSYSJOB
		*DMPALLJOB
		*NONE
QSTRPRTWTR	Start print writers at IPL	0=Do not start
		1=Start
QSTRUPPGM	Start-up program	*NONE
		Library/name
QSTSMSG	Display status messages	*NONE
		*NORMAL
QSVRAUTITV	Server authentication interval in minutes	1-108000
QSYSLIBL	System part of the library list (can be many entries)	Sequence/library name
QTIME	Current time of day	Time in HH:MM:SS format
QTIMSEP	Time separator	Numeric code:
		1=:
		2=.
		3=,
		4=blank
QTOTJOB	Initial total number of jobs	1-32767
QTSEPOOL	Time slice end pool	*NONE
		*BASE
QUPSDLYTIM	Uninterruptible power supply delay time in seconds	*CALC
		*BASIC
		*NOMAX
		0-99999
QUPSMSGQ	Uninterruptible power supply message queue	Library/message queue name
QUSRLIBL	Default user part of the library list	Sequence/library (may be many)

System value	Description	Parameters: values
QUTCOFFSET	Coordinated universal time offset	-24:00 to +24:00
QYEAR	Current year	Year (0-99)

Appendix B

SYSTEM VALUES (BY FUNCTION)

B1: Character Sets/Languages

System Value	Description	Parameters
QCCSID	Coded character set identifier	1-65535
QCHRID	Graphic character set and	Character ID: 1-32767
	code page	Code page: 1-32767
QCURSYM	Currency symbol	Character
QDECFMT	Decimal format	1=blank(Period for decimal, zero suppression)
		2=J(Comma for decimal, one leading zero)
		3=I(Comma for decimal, zero suppression)
QIGC	DBCS version installed	0=Not installed
	indicator	1=Installed
QIGCCDEFNT	Double byte code font	Library/font name
QKBDTYPE	Keyboard language character set abbreviation	Language/Country
QLANGID	Language identifier	Language abbreviation

B.2 DATE/TIME

System Value	Description	Parameters
QDATE	System date	Date (refer to QDATFMT, next, for format)
QDATFMT	Date format	YMD
		MDY
		DMY
		JUL
QDATSEP	Date separator	Numeric code:
		1=/
		2=-
		3=.
		4=,
		5=blank
QDAY	Day	1-31
QHOUR	Current hour of the day	Hour (0-23)
QLEAPADJ	Leap year adjustment	0-3
QMINUTE	Current minute of the hour	Minute (00-59)
QMONTH	Current month of the year	Month (1-12)
QSECOND	Current second of the minute	Second (0-59)
QTIME	Current time of day	Time in HH:MM:SS format
QTIMSEP	Time separator	Numeric code:
		1=:
		2=.
		3=,
		4=blank
QUTCOFFSET	Coordinated universal time offset	-24:00 to +24:00
QYEAR	Current year	Year (0-99)

B.3 DISASTER

System Value	Description	Parameters
QABNORMSW	Previous end of system indicator	0=Normal
		1=Abnormal
QAUTOSPRPT	Automatic system disabled reporting	0=Off
		1=On
QCMNRCYLMT	Communications recovery limits	Recovery limit attempts: 0-99
		Time interval in minutes:
		0-120
QDBRCVYWT	Database recovery wait indicator	0=Do not wait
		1=Wait
QDEVRCYACN	Device I/O error action	*MSG
		*DSCMSG
		*DSCENDRQS
		*ENDJOB
		*ENDJOBNOLIST

B.4 IPL

System Value	Description	Parameters
QIPLDATTIM	Date and time to automatically IPL	*NONE or IPL date: MM/DD/YY
		IPL time: HH:MM:SS
QIPLSTS	IPL status indicator	0=Operator panel IPL
		1=Auto-IPL after power is restored
		2=Restart IPL
		3=Time of day IPL
		4=Remote IPL
QIPLTYPE	Type of IPL to perform	0=Unattended IPL
		1=Attended IPL with dedicated service tools
		2=Attended IPL, console in debug mode
QPWRDWNLMT	Maximum time in seconds for	0-32767
		PWRDWNSYS *IMMED
QPWRRSTIPL	Automatic IPL after power restored	0=Not allowed
QRMTIPL	Remote power on and IPL	0=Not allowed
		1=Allowed
QSCPFCONS	IPL action with console problem	0=End IPL
		1=Unattended IPL
QSTRPRTWTR	Start print writers at IPL	0=Do not start
		1=Start
QSTRUPPGM	Start-up program	*NONE
		Library/name

B.5 MISCELLENEOUS

System Value	Description	Parameters
QACGLVL	Accounting level	*JOB Job resource use is written to a journal
		*NONE No accounting information is written to a journal
		*PRINT Spooled and printer file resource use is written to a journal
QBOOKPATH	Book and bookshelf search path	Directories to be searched for books. Default: /QDLS/QBKBOOKS/BOOKS
QCNTRYID	Country identifier	Country abbreviation
QKBDBUF	Type ahead and/or attention key option	*TYPEAHEAD
		*YES
		*NO
QLOCALE	Locale path name	*NONE
		Locale path name
QMODEL	Current system model number	System model number
QRMTSRVATR	Remote service attribute	0=Off
		1=On
QSETJOBATR	Set job attributes from locale	*NONE - or - Job attributes option
QSPCENV	Special environment	*NONE
		*S36
QSRLNBR	System serial number	System serial number
QSRTSEQ	Sort sequence	Library/name
		*HEX
		*LANGIDUNQ
		*LANGIDSHR
QSRVDMP	Service dump control	*DMPUSRJOB
		*DMPSYSJOB
		*DMPALLJOB
		*NONE
QSTSMSG	Display status messages	*NONE
		*NORMAL

B.5 MISCELLENEOUS

System Value	Description	Parameters
QUPSDLYTIM	Uninterruptible power supply delay time in seconds	*CALC
		*BASIC
		*NOMAX
		0-99999
QUPSMSGQ	Uninterruptible power supply message queue	Library/message queue name

B.6 PROBLEM REPORTING

System Value	Description	Parameters
QPRBFTR	Problem log filter	Library/name of problem log filter
QPRBHLDITV	Problem log hold interval	0-999
QSFWERRLOG	Software error logging	*LOG

B.7 SECURITY		
System Value	*Description*	*Parameters*
QALWOBJRST	Allow object restore option	*ALL All objects are restored regardless of security sensitive attributes
		*NONE No objects withsecurity sensitive attributes are restored
		*ALWYSSTT Programs with the system state attribute are restored
		*ALWPGMADP - Programs with the adopt authority attribute are restored
QAUDCTL	Auditing control	*AUDLVL
		*OBJAUD
QAUDENDACN	Auditing end action	*NOTIFY
		*PWRDWNSYS
QAUDFRCLVL	Force auditing data	*SYS
		1-100
QAUDLVL	Security auditing level	*SECURITY
		*AUTFAIL
		*DELETE
		*OBJMGT
		*CREATE
		*SAVRST
		*SPLFDTA
		*SYSMGT
		*SERVICE
		*PGMADP
		*JOBDTA
QCRTAUT	Create default public authority	*CHANGE
		*ALL
		*USE
		*EXCLUDE

B.7 SECURITY

System Value	Description	Parameters
QCRTOBJAUD	Create object auditing	*NONE
		*USRPRF
		*CHANGE
		*ALL
QDSCJOBITV	Time interval in minutes before disconnected jobs end	*NONE
		5-1440
QDSPSGNINF	Sign-on display information control	0=Do not display
		1=Display
QFRCCVNRST	Force conversion on restore	0=Off
		1=On
QINACTITV	Inactive job time-out (minutes)	*NONE
		5-300
QINACTMSGQ	Inactive job message queue	*ENDJOB
		*DSCJOB
		Library/message queue name
QLMTDEVSSN	Limit device sessions	0=Do not limit
		1=Limit
QLMTSECOFR	Limit security officer device access	0=Do not limit
		1=Limit
QMAXSGNACN	Action to take for failed signon attempts	Numeric code:
		1=Disable device
		2=Disable profile
		3=Disable device and profile
QMAXSIGN	Maximum sign-on attempts allowed	*NOMAX
		1-25
QPWDEXPITV	Password expiration interval in days	*NOMAX (passwords don't expire)
		1-366
QPWDLMTAJC	Limit adjacent digits in password	0=adjacent digits OK
		1=adjacent digits not OK
QPWDLMTCHR	Limit characters in password	*NONE
		characters not allowed

B.7 SECURITY

System Value	Description	Parameters
QPWDLMTREP	Limit repeating characters in password	0=Can be repeated
		1=Cannot be repeated
		2=Cannot be repeated consecutively
QPWDMAXLEN	Maximum password length	1-10
QPWDMINLEN	Minimum password length	1-10
QPWDPOSDIF	Limit password character positions	0=Can be the same
		1=Cannot be the same
QPWDRQDDGT	Require digit in password	0=Not required
		1=Required
QPWDRQDDIF	Duplicate password control	Numeric code:
		0=Duplicates allowed - or - Cannot be the same as any in the last 1=32 passwords
		2=24 passwords
		3=18 passwords
		4=12 passwords
		5=10 passwords
		6=8 passwords
		7=6 passwords
		8=4 passwords
QPWDVLDPGM	Password validation program	*NONE
		Library/program name
QRMTSIGN	Remote sign-on control	*FRCSIGNON
		*SAMEPRF
		*REJECT
		*VERIFY - or -Library/Remote session
		sign-on program

B.7 SECURITY

System Value	Description	Parameters
QSECURITY	System security level	10=Physical security only
		20=Password security only
		30=Password and object security
		40=Password, object, and operating system integrity
		50=Password, object, and enhanced operating system integrity (C2)
QSVRAUTITV	Server authentication interval in minutes	1-108000

B.8 SPOOL FILE CONTROL

System Value	Description	Parameters
QADLSPLA	Spooling control block additional storage	1024-32767
QJOBSPLA	Spooling control block initial size(in bytes)	3516-32767
QRCLSPLSTG	Days to reclaim spool storage	*NONE
		*NOMAX
		1-366

B.9 SYSTEM CONFIGURATION

System Value	Description	Parameters
QALWUSRDMN	Allow user domain objects in libraries	Name of libraries that can contain user domain user objects
QASTLVL	User assistance level	*BASIC
		*INTERMED
		*ADVANCED
QATNPGM	Attention program	*NONE
		*ASSIST
		Library/program name
QAUTOCFG	Autoconfigure devices	0=Off
		1=On
QAUTORMT	Autoconfigure of remote controllers	0=Off
		1=On
QAUTOVRT	Autoconfigure virtual devices	0-9999
QCONSOLE	Console name	Device description
QCTLSBSD	Controlling subsystem	Library/Subsystem name
QDEVNAMING	Device naming conventions	*NORMAL
		*S36
		*DEVADR
QDYNPTYSCD	Dynamic priority scheduler	0=Off
		1=On
QHSTLOGSIZ	Maximum history log records	1-32767
QJOBMSGQFL	Job message queue full action	*NOWRAP
		*WRAP
		*PRTWRAP
QJOBMSGQMX	Maximum size in megabytes of job message queue	8-64
QJOBMSGQSZ	Job message queue initial size (in kilobytes)	1-16384
QJOBMSGQTL	Job message queue maximum initial size (in kilobytes)	1-16384

B.9 SYSTEM CONFIGURATION

System Value	Description	Parameters
QPFRADJ	Automatic performance adjustment	0=No adjustment
		1=Adjustment at IPL
		2=Adjustment at IPL and automatic adjustment
		3=Automatic adjustment
QPRTDEV	Printer device description	Name
QPRTKEYFMT	Print header and/or border information	*PRTHDR
		*PRTBDR
		*PRTALL
		*NONE
QPRTTXT	Print text	text
QSYSLIBL	System part of the library list (can be many entries)	Sequence/library name
QUSRLIBL	Default user part of the library list	Sequence/library (may be many)

B.10 WORK MANAGEMENT

System Value	Description	Parameters
QAC TJOB	Initial number of active jobs	1-32767
QADLACTJ	Additional number of active jobs	1-32767
QADLTOTJ	Additional number of total jobs	1-32767
QBASACTLVL	Base storage pool activity level	1-32767
QBASPOOL	Base storage pool minimum size (sizes in kilobytes)	256-2147483647
QMAXACTLVL	Maximum activity level of system	*NOMAX 2-32767
QMCHPOOL	Machine storage pool size (in kilobytes)	256-2147483647
QTOTJOB	Initial total number of jobs	1-32767
QTSEPOOL	Time slice end pool	*NONE *BASE *NOLOG

Glossary

activity level The number of jobs in a subsystem that the system will allow to be active at one time.

adopted authority A security feature where a running program takes on the authority of the program creator instead of the program user.

advanced peer-to-peer communications (APPC) The protocol for communicating between two AS/400s.

advanced peer-to-peer networking (APPN) The protocol for most AS/400 network computing. LAN communication runs under APPN.

automatic mode When an AS/400 is IPLed, it will come up automatically, without operator intervention (unless there is a problem.)

authorities In security, authorities are "permissions" for a person to access an AS/400 object.

authorization lists A list of authorized users and their authorization level. This is a fast method of granting the same authorities to many objects.

base memory pool Special shared memory pool that contains all unallocated memory available to all subsystems.

batch job A program or set of commands that runs in the background in intervals and segments. It does not tie up a workstation while it runs. *See* interactive job; *see* job.

bridged frame relay A frame-relay network where the remote attachment is a bridge into a LAN.

broken chain Journal receivers are sequentially numbered and should be accessed that way. A broken chain occurs when one or more receivers are missing.

Carrier Sense Multiple Access with Collision Detection (CSMA/CD) The protocol used by Ethernet networks. Transmissions are made when the network thinks the line is not busy. If it detects another transmission made at the same time (a collision occurs), it will attempt to resend both after waiting a random amount of time.

channel service unit (CSU) Half of the attachment device into a frame-relay network. *See* data service unit (DSU); *see* CSU/DSU.

class-of-service User-defined preferences for each link and node on a network. The AS/400 will take these preferences into consideration when routing network transmissions. The result should be transmission routing that the user prefers.

concentrator A communication device that allows multiple devices to be used where one would normally be used. For example, a single wire may support one workstation. If a concentrator is attached to that wire, it may support up to seven workstations.

control points Information kept on network node servers about the adjacent links and nodes. Used to calculate optimum routing of transmissions.

controller A device to control sending and receiving information to DASD or workstations. Controllers are connected to IOPs.

data link connection identifier(DLCI) A unique number to identify each permanent virtual circuit (PVC) on a frame relay physical connection.

data service unit Half of the attachment hardware into a frame-relay network. *See* data service unit (DSU); *see* CSU/DSU.

data striping AS/400's method of writing data to disk.

DDI network Direct Data Interchange network protocol. Uses two counter-rotating rings.

destination service access points (DSAP) The SAP of the remote (the receiving) computer. *See* service access points (SAP*); see* source service access points (SSAP).

device Any apparatus connected to an AS/400 (printer, workstation, tape drive, etc.)

device attachment (DA) card Used to connect remote workstations to a DDI network.

device configuration The description and simple operating characteristics of a device.

direct frame relay Frame relay consisting of two or more AS/400s running APPC/APPN.

domain name In Internet addressing, the easy way of addressing a node.

DSU/CSU The device used to attach into a frame-relay network. Think of the DSU/CSU as a modem.

end nodes Nodes on a network that do not participate in routing transmissions beyond themselves. They can only send and receive their own transmissions.

Ethernet A LAN that supports one of two standards: Ethernet Version 2 or the IEEE 802.3 standard. *See* Carrier Sense Multiple Access with Collision Detection CSMA/CD).

faulting When the AS/400 is running a job and it unexpectedly finds a page missing from memory. It finds the page on disk and restores it. Usually a symptom of an out-of-capacity AS/400 or a poorly tuned one.

file A collection of records. *See* physical file; *see* logical file.

frame handler (FH) A intermediate (not end) node on a frame-relay network.

frame relay A packet-switching protocol that is similar to X.25 that uses established data communications networks.

frame size In frame relay, the size of each frame or packet that the network can handle.

general shared pools A memory pool sharable among subsystems.

initial program load (IPL) The AS/400 way of referring to bootstrapping the system.

Internet A collection of networks for the public to use for business, recreation, reference and other purposes.

interactive AS/400 terminology for online.

interoperable An IBM term referring to how sharable data between operating system releases are. If two releases are interoperable, saved data from one can be restored on another.

IOP (input-output processor) The last piece of AS/400 communications equipment before the controller. Disk data being written goes through an IOP and then a DASD controller. Out-going screen data goes through an IOP then a workstation controller.

job On an AS/400, a job is a program or set of programs run as a unit. When a user signs onto the system, he or she starts an interactive job that doesn't end until her or she signs off. *See* interactive jobs; *see* batch jobs.

job queue A queue—like a bank teller line—where jobs wait their turn to run.

journaling A feature you turn on that records every operation against one or more files and many system operations. Great security and disaster-recovery tool.

journal identifier A label put on a file that it is currently being journaled.

journal receiver The repository for data being journaled (record before images and afterimages, file open and close, etc.).

list management rights The capability to create, change, and delete authorization lists.

logical file A file with no data; just a key index.

low-entry nodes *See* end nodes.

machine pool The memory pool reserved for machine tasks.

manual mode When an AS/400 is IPLed, it will stop to give the operator a chance to do something before it is fully operational.

members An AS/400 file can consist of one or more members, each one of which can be processed as a complete file. All AS/400 files contain at least one member.

memory pools An amount of memory set aside for use by one or more subsystems.

native support An indication that IBM supports something used by the AS/400, such as a communications protocol, without using emulation.

network nodes Intelligent nodes on a network that not only send and receive their own transmissions, they can receive and reroute transmissions for other nodes. Network nodes build control-point information about the links and nodes attached to them.

network node server A network node capable of administering its own traffic, other traffic on the network, and transmissions to and from end nodes or low-entry nodes. Network nodes become network node server through the CHANGE NETWORK ATTRIBUTES (CHGNETA) command. Up to five network node servers are allowed per APPN application.

network topology database The aggregate knowledge about the network accumulated by all network nodes' control-point information. If a link or node goes down, adjacent network nodes will reconfigure this network topology database.

nodes Devices that can send and receive into the network.

normal mode *See* automatic mode.

object Everything on the AS/400 is an object. The object type determines what the object really is (for example, a file or a device).

object type *See* object.

OS/400 The name of the AS/400 operating system.

outfile Many informational commands can send their output to physical files referred to as outfiles.

output queue Output scheduled for a printer will wait in an output queue until it has a chance to be printed.

paging Efficient use of memory by keeping little-used sections, or pages, on a disk until they are needed.

permanent virtual circuit (PVC) In frame relay, a single physical cable can support up to 256 virtual circuits, each one of which is referred to as a permanent virtual circuit (PVC) and is identified by a data-link connection identifier (DLCI).

physical file A file that actually contains records. *See* file; *see* logical file.

physical interfaces The connector used on network cabling.

pool *See* memory pools.

pool identifier In a subsystem, the relative number of the memory pools it will use.

preset address The unique address assigned by the manufacturer to LAN adapter cards.

private pool A memory pool dedicated to one subsystem that cannot be shared by other subsystems.

Program Temporary Fix (PTF) An added feature or a solution to an operating-system problem. PTFs are released sporadically.

public authority Permission for any user without specific authorization to access an object.

resource name Used in the AS/400 for all LAN connections merely as an addressing method. A concatenation of the adapter and port of that adapter the object will use.

restricted state An AS/400 with only the controlling subsystem (QCTL) active.

route addition resistance A user can indicate a preference that the network should or should not use a particular route for transmissions.

route congestion A way of indicating user preference of transmission routing. When APPN determines that a route is congested, it will start to route transmissions away from the congestion. APPN concludes that congestion happens when the link is 90 percent full. Users can lower the percentage-full number and can start routing away from the link sooner.

save file A special file that contains the output from a save operation. You cannot use this file directly like others, but you can copy it to tape or restore it.

save-while-active A special AS/400 feature that allows files to be saved while users are accessing them.

server node *See* network server node.

service access points (SAP) Simple, two-digit addressing used at the adapter level on an AS/400. These addresses can be assigned by the user or the user can allow the AS/400 to assign them. *See* source service access points (SSAP); *see* destination service access points (DSAP).

service providers For Internet and frame-relay networks, companies provide access into the public-use networks. You will be a subscriber to them.

session When an interactive user signs onto the system, he or she has created a session. Many terminals allow multiple sessions where the user can acquire another sign display and sign on again, creating a second session.

shared pool Memory pools are sharable among subsystems.

SNA-direct connection In frame relay, the SNA systems can connect directly to the frame handler.

Source Service Access Points (SSAP) The SAP of the source (the sending) computer. *See* service access points (SAP); *see* destination service access points (DSAP).

special authorities Associated with a user profile to allow users such as system operators—who don't have any access to some objects—to work with objects and do routine system functions such as save and restore.

special IP addressing In TCP/IP, some addresses (all bit 1s or all bit 0s) take on special meaning.

special shared pools Machine pools and base pools are set up by IBM. Customers have limited control over the pools.

specific authorities The user profiles grant some authority to each object. Specific authorities reside with the objects.

spooled output file Printed output from jobs or programs do not usually go directly to a printer on the AS/400. They are held as spooled output files until directed to an output queue to which a printer is attached.

storage pool *See* memory pool.

subsystem A run-time environment for specific types of jobs. All interactive jobs run in an interactive subsystem. All batch jobs run in a batch subsystem.

switched Theoretically a line is switched if devices attach by dialing up. However, with the AS/400's automatic configuration, any line or device unknown to the AS/400 can be configured as soon as its presence is detected. These lines/devices are referred to as switched.

symbols In DDI networks, frame sizes are often referred to in double-byte or symbols.

TCP/IP *See* transmission control protocol/Internet protocol.

terminal equipment (TE) On frame-relay networks, the end AS/400s.

thrashing The point where an AS/400 spends more time faulting and paging than it does working on jobs or programs. Usually, only a symptom of a very out-of-capacity AS/400 or one that is very poorly adjusted.

token ring A LAN protocol that supports the IEEE 802.5 standard. A token— an object or message—passes data over a ring topology.

transceiver On an Ethernet network, a device that connects any nodes into the cable.

transmission control protocol/Internet protocol (TCP/IP) The standards allowing computers to exchange information. AS/400s and workstations can be connected with the TCP/IP protocol.

user Generally, the person working on a workstation attached to the AS/400 or receiving reports from the AS/400. However, in the AS/400, some tasks have their own pseudo user. For example, ODBC jobs typically are represented by their own user (who is not the person making the ODBC request).

user profile A user is made known to the AS/400 through an object, called a user profile, that contains basic information about who the person is and what they are authorized to do on the system.

vary on/vary off Essentially, you can turn devices on and off from any workstation attached to an AS/400. This is a soft turn on or off that is similar to, but not really the same as, switching mechanical switches on and off.

workstation AS/400 terminology for a display station.

writer AS/400 terminology for a printer.

Index

Symbols

#BATCH, 213, 215
#BATCHSC, 213, 215
#CONNECT, 215
#INTER, 213, 215
#INTERSC, 213, 215

*ADVANCED, 105, 117
*ALL, 107, 145, 146, 168, 222, 253, 259, 261, 274
*ALLOBJ, 110, 151
*ALLUSR, 138, 139
*ANY, 221, 232
*ANYNW, 209
*APPC, 208
*APPN, 244
*APPNLCL, 222
*APPNRMT, 222
*ASYNC, 208
*AUTL, 124
*BASE, 39, 40, 41, 42, 47, 48, 66, 188
*BASIC, 9, 105, 117
*BREAK, 108
*BSC, 208
*CALC, 9
*CHANGE, 88, 89, 107
*CMN command, 242, 279
*CNN, 205
*CNTRLD, 12, 68
*CONT, 163
*CURRENT, 171
*DELAY, 244
*DEVADR, 7
*DFT, 108
*DIAL, 244
*ENCRYPTED, 206
*EXCLUDE, 107, 124, 125
*FAX, 209
*FIRST, 171
*FNC, 208
*FR, 209
*FREE, 145, 164
*GEN, 163
*GRPPRF, 107
*GUARDCND, 206
*HIGH, 218

*HOLD, 108
*HOST, 208
*IBM, 138
*ILAN, 209
*IMMED, 12, 68, 244
*INTERACT, 41, 44
*INTERFACE, 205
*INTERMED, 105
*INTERMEDIATE, 117
*JOB, 84
*JOBCTL, 64, 111
*JRN, 153
*JRNRCV, 89, 153
*LAN, 206, 209
*LAST, 171
*LASTSAV, 171
*LCLNETID, 221
*LIB, 144
*LINKONLY, 31
*LINKTYPE, 244
*LOC, 227
*LOCAL, 209
*LOW, 218
*LWS, 208
*MACHINE, 39, 40, 41, 43, 47
*MATCH, 146
*MAX, 206
*MED, 218
*MIN, 206
*MSG, 81
*NEG, 244
*NET, 208
*NETATR, 212, 221
*NETNODE, 220
*NEW, 145, 146
*NO, 109, 118, 119, 143
*NOLIST, 81
*NOMAX, 9, 106
*NONE, 87, 107, 124
*NONSECURE, 205
*NONSTD, 227
*NONSYS, 138
*NORMAL, 7
*NOTIFY, 87, 108
*OBJAUD, 88, 89
*OLD, 145, 146
*ONLY, 34

*OUTFILE, 22
*PARTIAL, 109
*PGMR, 105
*PKTSWTNET, 205, 206, 213
*PKTSWTNWK, 215
*PRINT, 84
*PRV, 22
*PUBLIC, 118, 119, 123, 125
*PWRDWNSYS, 87, 89
*RTL, 208
*RWS, 208
*SAME, 219
*SATELLITE, 206
*SAVF, 32, 51, 133, 143, 146
*SAVSYS, 110, 151
*SBSD, 54, 71
*SDLC, 209
*SECADM, 105, 111
*SECLVL, 81
*SECOFR, 105
*SECURECND, 206
*SERVICE, 32, 111
*SHRPOOL1, 41
*SHRPOOL5, 44
*SHRPOOL6, 50
*SPLCTL, 111
*SPOOL, 41
*SYNCLIB, 144
*SYSDFN, 143
*SYSOPR, 105
*SYSVAL, 106, 108, 117
*TAP, 208
*TDLC, 209
*TELEPHONE, 206
*UNDGRDCBL, 206
*USE, 107
*USER, 105
*USRPRF, 54, 71, 106, 107
*VWS, 208
*WRKSTN, 108
*X25, 209
*YES, 109, 223, 251, 260

A

activity level, 42
abnormal
  end, 3
  IPL, 11, 36
access path information,
  file, 155
access paths, 155
accounting code, 107
ACCPTH(*YES), 151
ACGCDE, 107
active job, 42
active-to-ineligible jobs,
  185
active-to-wait, 185, 186
activity level, 39, 42, 43,44,
  45, 66, 189, 190
adapter address, 249
Add Job Queue Entry, 57,
  64
Add TCP/IP Host Table
  Entry, 276
ADDAJE, 56
ADDDSTQ, 230
ADDDSTRTE, 229
ADDJOBQE, 57, 64
ADDPJE, 56
address percentages,
  temporary and
  permanent, 4
address,
  adapter, 249
  functional, 247
  group, 247
  present, 243
  sources, 247
addresses used, 3
  destination, 247
  subnet mask, 273
ADDRTGE command, 68
adopted authorities, 130
ADPTADR, 266
advanced peer-to-peer
  communications, 196
advanced peer-to-peer
  networking, 199
advanced program-to-
  program
  communications, 208
afterimage, 154, 169
ALLONCMS, 128

Allow automatic cleanup,
  98
Allow object differences,
  118, 119
APPC, 195, 196, 198, 199,
  205, 206, 210, 211, 224,
  227, 228, 231, 234, 264
  controllers created automatically, 244
  device configuration,
  229
  functions, 196
  interfaces, 197
  programming for, 197
APPC/APPN
  configuration, 203
  controller, 220
  controller descriptions,
  207
  device descriptions, 211
  network, 225
  session routes, 215
  system supports, 221
application and program
  measurements, 173
applying PTFs, 35
APPN, 195, 196, 198, 202,
  205, 210, 211, 219, 220,
  222, 224, 225, 231, 234,
  264
  configuration, 233
  controller, 207
  network, 199, 212, 225
  node, 211, 220
  using, 225
APPN(*NO), 225
APPN(*YES), 225, 268
APYJRNCHG command,
  167, 168
APYPTF command, 33, 34
architecture, systems
  network, 196
AS/400
  automatically powering
  an, 12
  capacity planning for
  the, 173
  communications, 196
  LAN CL commands,
  278
  performance, 173
  performance com-
  ponents, 173

powering down an, 11
remote start for an, 11
starting an, 3, 10
ASP, 23, 51, 156, 158, 166,
  174
  considerations, 52
  number, 160
assistance level, 105
asynchronous
  communications, 208
asynchronous database IO,
  193
attended IPL, 5, 8
  audit control, 87
  end action, 87
  force level, 87
  level, 88
auditing, security, 111
AUDLVL, 88
AUT(*EXCLUDE), 89
authorities, 101, 121
  adopted, 130
  private, 137
  special, 110, 129
  that can be granted to
  *PUBLIC, 125
authority,
  group, 107
  public, 124
authorization lists, 124, 137
autoconfiguration, 70
Autocreate Controller, 251,
  260
Autocreate
  Controller(*YES), 253
Autocreate Device, 253,
  261
Autocreate Device(*ALL),
  253, 260
Autocreate Device(*YES),
  251
AUTOCRTCTL, 206
AUTOCRTCTL(*YES),
  244
AUTOCRTDEV(*YES),
  244
AUTODLTCTL, 206
automatic
  configuration, 58, 235
  installation, 23
  IPL, 8
  mode IPL, 5
autostart job, 56

SDLC, 205, 224
SDLC (synchronous data
   link), 198
SECADMIN, 13
SECOFR, 13, 118, 119,
   123, 125
security, 110, 117, 205, 216
   audit journal, 86
   audit journal receivers,
      viewing, 90
   audit journaling, 90
   audit log, 75
   audit, keeping a, 121
   audit, setting up for a,
      86-88
   auditing, 111
security, 101, 118
   level 10, 118
   level 20, 118
   level 30, 118
   level 40, 119
   level 50, 119
   objects, 117, 134
   officer, 114
   restores, 144
sender jobs, 230
service access points, 243
session, 55
set major system options, 6,
   58
setup menu, 112
SEV, 108
severities, 81
severity, 108
shared memory pools, 47
signoff command, 81, 109
sign-on attempts,
   maximum, 119
single session location, 212
SNA, 195, 196, 242, 267
   direct connection, 265
   distribution services,
      196, 228
   host, 208
   pass-through, 197, 203
SNADS, 196, 226, 228,
   229, 230, 231
   configuration, 231
   miscellaneous, 232
   setting up, 231
SNDDSTQ, 230
SNDMSG, 109
SNDNETF, 32

SNDPTFORD command,
   27, 30
SNGSSNLOC, 212
source addresses, 247
SPCAUT, 106
special authorities, 129
special authority, 106
speed, 249
SQLs, 177
SSAP, 243, 248, 258, 274
SSAP address, 243
start a service tool, 149
start journal access path,
   160, 161
start journal physical file,
   160
start mode, 225
start pass-through, 233
starting journal receiver,
   171
starting sequence number,
   169
STATUS, 105
STATUS(*DISABLED),
   105
STATUS(*ENABLED),
   105
STG(*FREE), 164
storage areas, IPL, 10
storage pool, 39, 42, 189
   memory, 39, 57
   pools, user auxiliary, 51
storage size field, 44
stress tests, 173
STRJRNAP command,
   160-162
STRJRNPF command, 160,
   161
STRJRNPF options, 161
STRMOD command, 225
STRPASTHR command,
   233
STRPCO, 109
STRSBS, 44
STRSST, 149
submit job, 228
submit remote command,
   228
subnet mask addresses, 273
subsystems, 22, 65, 68, 73
superseded PTFs, 33
synchronous DASD IO,
   193

synchronous data link, 198
SYS, 180
SYS task, 181
system
   administrator, 114
   audit, managing, 89
   auxiliary storage, 3
   cleanup, 98
   configuration, 39, 134,
      136
   configuration, testing, 9
   disk data recovery, 10
   distribution directory,
      228, 229
   distribution queue, 229,
      230
   distribution routing
      table., 229
   information, 155
   journals, 99
   logs, 99
   network architecture,
      196
   name/group, 229
   names in APPC/APPN,
      198
   operator, 114
   options menu, set major,
      7
   options, set major, 7
   power hardware ready,
      9
   processor loading, 9
   processor testing, 9
   reply list, 93
   reply list table, 94, 97
   resource management
      objects, 134
   planning for multiple,
      21
   service tools, 149
   space, 18
   tasks, 180
   upgrade, 21
   values, 117
   values, setting, 87

T

tape device, 20
tape drive, 20

tapes, 149
  status of, 149
tasks, monitoring, 184
TCP/IP (transmission
  control protocol/internet
  protocol), 241, 271
  addressing, 271
  administration menu,
  277
  CL commands, 277
  configuration, 274
  interface, 274
  network functions, 278
TDLC, 224
terminal equipment, 265
testing system main
  storage, 9
tests, stress, 173
text
  parameter, 106
  message, 81
time cleanup starts each
  day, 98
token ring, 195, 198, 205,
  241, 245, 265, 268
  adapter data., 136
  adapter addressing, 245
  adapter cards, 248
  addresses, 247
  considerations, 248
  destination address, 246,
  257
  LAN, 245
  LAN adapters, 253
  LAN CL commands,
  253
  network, 224, 248, 250
  network, configuring a,
  249
  source address, 246
transfer pass-through, 234
traps in planning, 22
TRFPASTHR
  command,, 234
TRFPASTHR command,
  234
TSD, 126
tuning
  AS/400 performance,
  173
  performance, 183, 190,
  194

U

UL (universal/local), 246,
  247, 257
unattended IPL, 8
unattended remote IPL, 8
use APPN function, 212
use PTF numbers to
  select(*ALL), 33
user, 101
  group, 107
  ID, 128
  ID/address, 228
  identification, valid, 54
  libraries, 135
  profile, 101, 108, 110,
  121, 126
  profile commands, 103
  profile name, 104
  profile, group, 107
  profile, more than one,
  111
  profile, parameter
  considerations for a, 108
  profiles, 106, 114, 137
  profiles, deleting, 112
  profiles, managing, 103
  profiles, restoring, 144
  roles, 114
users
  forgetful, 109
  new, 109
USRCLS, 105
USRPRF, 104

V

VAR (value-added
  reseller), 17
vary on, automatic, 200

W

wait-to-ineligible, 186
wait-to-ineligible
  jobs, 185
  ratio, 184
work active jobs command,
  179
work object, 127, 148
work system status, 3
work system value, 117
  work with active jobs,

work with active jobs
  command, 175
work with configuration
  list, 234
work with configuration
  status, 252, 278
work with controller
  description, 207
work with directory, 231
work with distribution lists,
  231
work with distribution
  queues, 230
work with hardware
  resource, 279
work with PTFs, 35
work with subsystems
  command, 47
work with system status,
  186
work with system values, 8
work with TCP/IP status,
  275, 278
workstation
  entries, 55, 57, 70
  entry, 106
  messages, 99
WRKACTJOB command,
  12, 82, 112, 180
WRKACTJOB
  SBS(QSYSWRK)
  JOB(QT*), 277
WRKCFGSTS command,
  252, 278
WRKCNNL, 203
WRKCTLD command, 207
WRKDDMF, 226
WRKDIR command, 229,
  231, 232
WRKDSTQ command, 230
WRKHDWRSC command,
  253, 279, 280
WRKJOB, 82
WRKJOBD command, 61,
  80
WRKJRNA, 89
WRKLIND, 204, 238
WRKMSGD command, 92
WRKNWID, 204
WRKOBJ command, 123,
  127 148
WRKOUTQ, 82
WRKSBS command, 47